Neil Young

AND THE POETICS OF ENERGY

Musical Meaning and Interpretation
Robert S. Hatten, editor

Profiles in Popular Music
Glenn Gass and Jeffrey Magee, editors

Neil Young

AND THE POETICS OF ENERGY

William Echard

INDIANA UNIVERSITY PRESS

Bloomington and Indianapolis

This book is a publication of

Indiana University Press
601 North Morton Street
Bloomington, IN 47404-3797 USA

http://iupress.indiana.edu

Telephone orders   800-842-6796
Fax orders   812-855-7931
Orders by e-mail   iuporder@indiana.edu

The paper used in this publication meets the minimum requirements of American National Standard for Information Sciences—Permanence of Paper for Printed Library Materials, ANSI Z39.48-1984.

Manufactured in the United States of America

Library of Congress Cataloging-in-Publication Data

Echard, William, date-
Neil Young and the poetics of energy / William Echard.
p. cm. — (Profiles in popular music) (Musical meaning and interpretation)
Includes bibliographical references and index.
ISBN 0-253-21768-7 (pbk. : alk. paper) — ISBN 0-253-34581-2 (cloth : alk. paper)
1. Young, Neil—Criticism and interpretation. I. Title. II. Series. III. Series: Musical meaning and interpretation
ML420.Y75E34 2005
782.42166′092—dc22

2004022314

1 2 3 4 5   10 09 08 07 06 05

Contents

Acknowledgments

First, apologies to those I am about to forget. Hopefully I can make it up to you later. Thanks to Lillian for holding down the fort during long writing binges, and also to my parents and everyone else in my family for constant support over the years. Early stages of the research were assisted through a doctoral fellowship from the Social Sciences and Humanities Research Council of Canada, and also through the collegial and stimulating atmosphere provided by the Graduate Programme in Musicology and Ethnomusicology at York University, Toronto. Thanks to the many people who were at York with me, who have shaped my view of the world and provided material and moral support. They include (but are not limited to) Jonathon Bakan, Sterling Beckwith, Jody Berland, Rob Bowman, Annette Chretien, Genevieve Cimon, Austin Clarkson, Jeff Cupchik, Mike Daley, Beverley Diamond, Annemarie Gallaugher, Doug Gifford, Barbara Godard, Anna Hoefnagels, David Lidov, Charity Marsh, Andra McCartney, Chris McDonald, David Mott, Marcia Ostaschewski, Karen Pegley, Lilian Radovac, Jay Rahn, Trichy Sankaran, Richard Stewardson, Jim Tenney, Matt Vander Woude, Jacqueline Warwick, Melissa West, and Robert Witmer. Thanks also to Paul Bouissac for crucial early intellectual support. After that, the School for Studies in Art and Culture and the faculty of Arts and Social Sciences at Carleton University, Ottawa, have been generous in allowing me extra time to write at crucial moments. Some people at or about Carleton who have had an impact on the shape of this book include Virginia Caputo, Murray Dineen, Chris Faulkner, Geraldine Finn, Mitchell Frank, Barbara Gabriel, Bryan Gillingham, Alan Gillmor, Elaine Keillor, Laura Marks, Charles O'Brien, Allan Ryan, John Shepherd, and Paul Théberge. Thanks also to Keir Keightley and Serge Lacasse for occasional but crucial conversations. Finally, thanks to Gayle Sherwood, Donna Wilson, and Robert Hatten at Indiana University Press for taking an interest in my work and for making the process of publication so smooth.

Neil Young

AND THE POETICS OF ENERGY

Introduction

Every one of my records, to me, is like an ongoing autobiography. I can't write the same book every time.[1]

A text just has whatever coherence it happened to acquire during the last roll of the hermeneutic wheel. . . . What we say [as interpreters] must have some reasonably systematic inferential connections with what we or others have previously said, [but] there is no point at which we can draw a line between what we are talking about and what we are saying about it.[2]

In this quotation, and in many other places, Neil Young speaks of change. Yet he does so from a singular perspective, seemingly as a meta-Neil who at different times writes these different selves. Similarly, Rorty does away with absolute truth as a value but immediately replaces it with a concept of community. In other words, as they try to say something about the way new meanings come into existence, both Young and Rorty enact a similar balance between continuity and disjunction. Also, both are a little (and exquisitely) disingenuous. I believe Rorty knows that textual coherence doesn't "just" happen, and he is acutely aware of the many stories that need to be told about the social dynamics of meaning. Similarly, I would guess that Neil Young knows his impossible-to-pin stance is itself a well-established feature of rock auteurship. His changeability, since it has been a constant and since it is of a kind frequently valorized in the rock culture of the 1960s and 1970s, does much to stabilize his identity.

The construction of selfhood and persona, not only despite but *by means of* change and contradiction, will be one theme of this book because it has been a continuous theme in Neil Young reception. What does it mean to be an artist who is expected to surprise? What does the existence of such an artist tell us about the stylistic profile of rock music and the identities that may be negotiated there? Another central concern of the book is to fine-tune existing methods of describing the energetic and affective dimensions of musical meaning, again because notions of emotional commitment and intensity are key themes in Neil Young reception. This is an academic book, so a "reasonably systematic" spirit will sometimes get the upper hand. However, this is less a book *about* Neil Young and more a book which tries to respond to him. When Young speaks of autobiography, I do not think he is inviting us to decode a hidden story. He has, throughout his career, frequently said he wants to avoid being pinned down by interpreters. So I do not intend to try and pin him down, even though I do intend to explore issues raised by his work, to talk about why he has been read in certain ways more frequently than others, to pursue some of the ideological dimensions of his reception history, and to map the key landmarks in his sonic world. However, I hope that by the end of this exercise the terrain appears wider, not more narrow. This is one of many different books that could be written about Neil Young.

Shortly after giving a paper in Seattle that eventually developed into chapter 2, I discovered a report about the conference on the Internet. *Rusties* is the self-chosen name for members of the Rust list, the largest and most active online Neil Young discussion forum (more details about the Rust list will be given later). Evidently, a rustie was in the audience for my talk and had this to say:

> My two cents: Echard did not reveal any startling conclusions about
> Neil Young that any one or three rusties couldn't come to over a pint or
> a campfire—the difference is that he used a lot of "high brow" language
> and cited references as one must in order to receive a Ph.D. Still and all, I
> admire the guy—it's pretty hip (and it was probably a lot of fun) to write
> your doctoral thesis about Neil.[3]

I cite this response to agree with it, and not just the part about having fun with my dissertation. I don't want to end up saying things that would seem completely alien to the larger world of people listening to and talking about Neil Young. If anything, I see my work as a kind of response and contribution to the dialogues already entered into by journalists and various other kinds of listeners, academic and otherwise. Of course this *is* an academic project, and I would defend the highbrow language and references as a tool for putting my work in dialogue with that of other academics. However, I am deeply influenced by the lead of those theorists for whom scholarly work is part of a continuum of music discussion and appreciation that includes fans, music makers, and many others.[4] I try to cite at least as many rock critics as academics, and while I don't cite as many rusties directly, their ongoing discussion has been a major influence on my work. Although technical in parts, I hope that the spirit of this book is not too far removed from the enthusiasm and desire for dialogue that underlie the discussions taking place daily between fans about music they love. I am both a fan of Neil Young and a critical scholar. I see this work both as a contribution to scholarship and also as an attempt to explicate and expand my intuitions as a native listener. As a result, it is inevitable that parts of the work will be too academic for some fans and other parts too casual for some academics. Rather than attempt a forced reduction to one side or the other, I have decided to leave myself in this intermediate space. I tend to agree with Middleton when he suggests that the *scholar-fan* is in a unique position to bridge discourses. This is especially true when the study is concerned with questions of perceived expressive intensity and affective response. To discuss such topics, we need to engage with the body, with personal feeling, and with metaphorical styles of interpretation, in which case "the analyst is no more privileged than any other participant because he or she is totally reliant on implicit theory."[5] Many of the theoretical discussions to follow are attempts to make at least a small part of that implicit theory more explicit, but not to altogether abandon the position of the practically engaged fan.

Middleton's position has hermeneutic overtones in that he is not only interested in perspectivally specific dimensions of experience, but especially in how these can be read through formal analysis of musical texts. The scholar-fan is trying to find something out about how the music works, but in an intellectual frame where the distinctions between text and interpretation, knowledge and action, are necessarily blurred. Philosophical hermeneutics in general tends to undercut such distinctions since it emphasizes the way in which we are always already thrown into a world of meanings so that the resulting understanding is "finite, changeable, multidimensional, forced to compete with other understandings, and limited by the expandable horizons of the individual."[6] Middleton's scholar-fan is responding to this intellectual current in at least two ways. First, the scholar-fan couples formal analysis to the exploration of lived experience and meaning. And second, the image of understandings competing and negotiating with one another mirrors the process of a researcher participating in other kinds of listening communities, internalizing the sometimes competing, sometimes resonant understandings found in these various listening worlds. I began this introduction with a quotation from Rorty because I am aiming, in the most general way, for a *neo-pragmatic* style of interpretation, one which always conceives the researcher as embedded in social practice and the research process as a form of dialogue.

Sources and Scope

I will base my discussion throughout the book on four main sources: (i) the academic literature on popular music studies, and the literature on musical meaning more generally; (ii) major writings about Neil Young in the UK and North American music press from the 1960s to the present; (iii) discussions on the Neil Young Internet discussion group, the Rust list;[7] and (iv) my own analysis of Neil Young's studio recordings. When general analytic points are made, unless otherwise indicated the corpus includes all studio recordings released by Reprise records and Geffen records as Neil Young solo albums: from *Neil Young* (1968) to *Greendale* (2003). None of these sources are treated as objects of study, but rather as discursive spheres to be evoked and juxtaposed to build up a multi-faceted picture of Neil Young's work. They provide reports of listener experience which help identify the main themes and trends in Neil Young reception that in turn become the main themes of this book. For example, themes of surprise, unpredictability, and stylistic diversity are prevalent among both rusties and rock critics, and so I develop a detailed analysis of these. Similarly, many listeners over the years have remarked on Young's ability to construct intensely expressive and distinctive guitar solos from a limited repertoire of playing techniques, and so that too becomes a central theme in parts of the book. In some cases, I have chosen to highlight themes which are relatively absent from the critical literature and fan discussion but which are of central concern to current academic study of popular music. My discussion of gender is one example of such a topic. And in some cases I have chosen to present detailed explanations of my own idiosyncratic reactions to the music, as is the case with the *drifting* metaphor incorporated into the melodic analysis of chapter 5.

So rather than standing as objects for study, the discursive traces left by rusties and rock critics serve as a background of interpretation to which my own work stands as a detailed response and addition. The disadvantage of this approach is that a great deal needs to be taken at face value, and in many cases I raise issues which would ideally require a fuller social contextualization than I have space to provide. The advantage, I hope, is that readers will gain a sense of the lively and complex discussion that has taken place around Neil Young's work, and that my own analysis can gain in mobility what it might sometimes lose in sociological depth. My goal in using these materials is not to study or theorize the nature of fan communities or rock criticism, but rather to ensure that my own reading of Neil Young takes into account a wide range of what has already been said. The topics I choose to discuss in depth are those which are both central to Neil Young reception and about which I have something substantial to contribute. They are not necessarily always the most important topics which could have been discussed. Some crucial areas—for example questions of class, ethnicity, and industrial organization—are touched upon quite lightly, not because they could not have become major themes, but simply out of limitations in space.

Poetics of Energy

Much of my analysis is based on conceptualizations of *energy* (and *space*), understood as a family of metaphors. These very general concepts will arise in a number of guises. For example, the forceful and sometimes oppositional nature of Young's relationship to rock traditions will be interpreted in terms of energies which both enable and constrain identity formation. Other energy-related conceptualizations include the particular expressive intensity often attributed to Young (the emotional energy of musical sound), a general theory of musical meaning and gesture (energy as a basic category in theories of virtual space and iconicity), and the many metaphors found in Neil Young reception which suggest energy as a central concept (for example, mobility and restlessness, chaos and noise, the contrast between aggressive and introspective moods). The use of a single word to cover such a wide range of themes is not an established practice in music theory, and I do not intend to develop a single coherent theory of energetics. However, one key task in the book is to suggest that many of the metaphors in current social theory (for example Bourdieu's model of social fields as a network of positions and forces) and those in current music theory (for example persona and actoriality, or harmony and melody treated as fields of compulsion and tendencies of movement) can be productively juxtaposed under the single idea of energetics, and that this invites a series of metaphorical interpretations which link diverse strands of musical practice.

My use of the term *poetics* is slightly more orthodox. As Zak has noted, the word can refer to a wide range of topics, but the core of the concept is aesthetic, signaling an interest in the interface between compositional choices (understood mostly with respect to their structural traces) and broader value systems.[8] My use of the term is closest to that suggested by Krims, for whom poetics represents the attempt to say how particular compositional choices are motivated by and participate in the broader social work of music, with special attention to questions of affect and aesthetic value.[9] For such authors, an interest in poetics signals three things at once: first, that analytic specificity about sonic detail is a valid and necessary element of discussion; second, that such analysis needs to be framed and guided by the actual social history of the music in question; and third and perhaps most importantly, that formal analysis can be a means to look for mechanisms which enable and constrain the affective energies and aesthetic priorities invested in the music. As Burnham has put it, we need to make evident "the implicitly poetic basis of explicitly formalist analysis [and also] the implicit positivist basis of explicitly poetic criticism."[10]

By putting the phrase *poetics of energy* in my title, I want to indicate that various literal and metaphorical senses of energy will be key to my discussion of Neil Young's work, and that my purpose is to highlight feelings and aesthetic responses which listeners have reported, both in order to illuminate particular textual details and to view these details as specific fragments of more general cultural practices. My own interest in poetics as a paradigm is that it allows the juxtaposition of minute textual particularity with abstract reflection, suggesting a hybrid space which is neither readerly nor writerly, neither text-based nor audience-based nor analyst-based. The space of poetics thus conceived is like the philosophical space described by Deleuze as an Erewhon, "signifying at once the originary 'nowhere' and the displaced, disguised, modified and always re-created 'here-and-now'."[11] Such a space is productive and suggestive rather than explanatory, and forms an attractive model for the study of an artist who, like Neil Young, is still very active. It is too early for final statements on the nature and significance of Young's work, and so the present book is offered as a provocation more than a summation.

The chapters fall into three main types. Some establish basic historical detail and theoretical frameworks. Chapter 1, for example, presents an overview of Young's career and suggests some of the most important features of his work with respect to general issues in cultural theory. Readers not familiar with Young's work should look at chapter 1 first, since it provides background information assumed in other chapters. Similarly, chapter 4 develops in detail the theoretical perspective on musical signification which underlies the rest of the book. Readers with a special interest in musical meaning, or who are curious about theories of space and persona, or who want to see the most systematic material first, should consult chapter 4. Secondly, some of the chapters are designed to treat single themes in depth. These include chapter 2, which develops a dialogic theory of genre in order to address Young's stylistic diversity, and chapter 3, which is concerned with noise, oppositionality, and improvisation. Readers who are interested in seeing synthetic discussions of single topics might want to start with these chapters. Finally, chapters 5 and 6 focus on particular details of musical text, attempting to be more specific about the sonic devices which generate the effects discussed in a more general way in other chapters. Readers with a special interest in detailed discussion of Young's musical style may want to start with these.

1 | Words

A NEIL YOUNG RECEPTION PRIMER

There are two things often said about Neil Young that form central threads in this study. First, there is the idea that Young is one of the most unpredictable songwriters and performers of the 1960s rock generation, working within an exceptionally wide range of styles and at times defying expectations so forcefully as to endanger his career. Second, there is the fact that many listeners attribute unique expressive intensity to much of Young's work. In both cases, a broad perspective on Young's career is required to assess the claims, first because we need to establish that these themes have indeed been central to Neil Young reception, and second because the claims themselves imply a long frame of reference (the first obviously so, but also the second insofar as the unique intensity of periods such as the mid-1970s or the early 1990s comes into sharp relief when situated within the overall profile of Young's work). In order to set up such a context, this chapter presents an overview of Neil Young reception history, juxtaposing a summary of writings in the rock press against a survey of the major aspects of Young's work at these various times. For readers not familiar with Young's career, the chapter can serve as an introduction both to the details of his history and also to the main themes in the critical commentary. Since there are already several existing biographies of Neil Young but no detailed studies of reception history as such, I have placed more emphasis on critical reaction than on establishing basic facts.[1]

In addition to summarizing the reception history, I will at times enter into lengthy theoretical discussions, placing certain aspects of Young's work in a broad culture theoretic perspective. Like the historical summary itself, these theoretical capsules are not meant to present complete arguments, but rather to sketch out the principal issues associated with Young's work. In many cases, they provide the opportunity to comment upon topics which are of crucial importance to popular music studies in general but do not arise elsewhere in the book (where discussions more specific to musical signification take precedence). These mini-studies are connected to moments in the historical narrative which seem to invite them. For example, a discussion of gender is given in conjunction with *Harvest,* since Young has frequently spoken of his more pop-oriented material as being "feminine," and a discussion of camp and irony is attached to the 1980s, a period which saw Young's most mannered stylistic experimentation. But I do not want to imply that the issues raised in conjunction with a particular career phase are *only* relevant to that phase. Indeed, a whole book could be written about Neil Young and gender, or irony, or industry, and so the discussions presented in this chapter are only meant to provide general background for the more detailed arguments developed in other chapters.[2]

Early Solo Years

Neil Young's involvement in Buffalo Springfield, beginning in 1966, was his entry point into the Southern California folk-rock scene. In both image and songwriting, Young appeared ambivalent and introverted, in contrast to the more extroverted Stephen Stills. He left and rejoined the band several times, seemingly caught between a desire for stardom and deep reservations, and his lyrics at the time tended to explore feelings of loss and alienation in an abstract, oblique style. The image of Young as a brooding, poetic loner, established during his time with Buffalo Springfield, would carry over into his solo career. There was also a sharp dualism in Young's contributions to the band's musical output, as he was responsible for some of their most elaborate production numbers ("Nowadays Clancy Can't Even Sing," "Broken Arrow") and also some of their most direct rock songs ("Mr. Soul"). This tendency to move between different styles and working methods would also remain in place, and be amplified, throughout Young's subsequent solo career. A final feature to note about the Springfield years is that it was during this time that Young became associated with First Nations themes, albeit in a mostly theatrical manner (dressing in a seemingly random assortment of Native clothes in contrast to Stills' cowboy image). This detail is important both for what it may say about Young's politics (discussed later), and also since the costumes of this time represent the first of many personas deployed by Young throughout his career.

Neil Young's first solo album, released in 1968, built upon both sides of his Springfield persona. Some of the material was quiet and reflective and some was in a loud rock vein. The album was carefully arranged and recorded in a painstaking manner, making use of many overdubs. What reviewers tended to notice was the overall mood of contemplation and poetic reflection. However, despite the generally introspective and often psychedelic quality of the record, the album also contributed in an indirect way to Young's slowly growing reputation as a proactive and controlling businessperson. This was the result of a new technique tried on the mastering of the record, which produced a poor-sounding final product. Young was unwilling to accept the result and negotiated with Reprise for a new version of the album to be quickly released.[3] This incident, along with the album's complex production values, began to build for Young a reputation as a perfectionist who controlled and attended to details of arrangement and was an active player in his business relationships.

In 1969, Young picked up a Los Angeles rock band, The Rockets, renamed them Crazy Horse, and made them his backing band. At about the same time, he also joined the new supergroup Crosby, Stills, Nash & Young. CSNY played folk-rock music with intricate arrangements and specialized in lush vocal harmonies. Their lyrics were explicitly countercultural, but the music was highly accessible, and CSNY quickly became one of the largest moneymakers in the rock industry of the early 1970s. Through his involvement with the group, Young would at last be exposed to a truly mass audience, and he would also deepen his association with commercially oriented folk rock. However, Young's work with Crazy Horse, unfolding in parallel with CSNY, was markedly different. Young characterized Crazy Horse as "funkier, simpler, more down to roots [than CSNY]," and pointed out that the bands had almost completely exclusive repertoires, with CSNY playing the more technically advanced material.[4] Young wrote many of the Crazy Horse songs quickly, later saying that three had been composed in one afternoon while he had been ill.[5] The band was given only minimal rehearsal before making an album, which was recorded mostly live with as few overdubs as possible. In interviews of the time, Young explicitly contrasted this working method with the elaborate overdubs of his first solo record[6] and noted further that he was trying to capture the sound of a band which had just recently been drawn together "because that never gets recorded . . . just the bare beginnings."[7] The seemingly live, unpolished sound of Crazy Horse would eventually prove one of Young's most characteristic and widely praised devices. At the time, however, critical reaction was mixed. For some reviewers, immediacy and roughness were less an exciting new development in their own right than a step down from Young's more carefully polished productions.[8]

It was also around 1969 that the distinctive timbre of Young's voice began to be the subject of extended comment in the press. The following description includes most of the interpretive moves common among critics of the time:

> Neil Young does not have the kind of "good" voice that would bring praise from a high school music teacher. . . . [But] rock & roll does not flourish because of "good" voices. . . . While Neil Young is a fine songwriter and an excellent guitarist, his greatest strength is in his voice. Its arid tone is perpetually mournful, without being maudlin or pathetic. It hints at a world in which sorrow underlies everything.[9]

By the beginning of 1970, then, many of the major features of Neil Young's persona were in place. His work had divided into distinct streams, one of them in a quieter singer-songwriter style with elaborate production values, the other in a studiously minimalist garage-rock vein. This stylistic split was paralleled by divergent group memberships. Two of the main critical value judgments associated with his work had appeared: Crazy Horse had been characterized as technically limited but energetic enough to make up for it, and Young's voice had been characterized as unusual, even bad by conservative standards, but uniquely expressive. In the middle of all this, another characteristic trait would emerge: Young refused to resolve or explain the contradictions, and instead openly expressed feelings of restlessness and a willingness to frequently change bands and styles when he felt the need.[10]

Young's third solo LP, *After the Gold Rush*, combined all these tendencies into one package. The album was attuned to the more cynical, disillusioned tone of early 1970s rock culture, and it was during this period that Young first began to be described as a kind of sensor or prophet of his generation, although of a very different kind than other 1960s figures like Bob Dylan or the Beatles. Neil Young had been skeptical and apprehensive about large movements and proclamations since his time with Buffalo Springfield. His new status as generational spokesperson in the early 1970s was based largely on an increasing malaise within rock culture, which caused Young's loner stance to seem more relevant, rather than being the result of a shift in Young's own work toward a more prophetic or politicized stance. At the same time, some of Young's idiosyncrasies were drawing increasingly hostile responses. On the one hand, he was being described as a "genius, [a] broken voice now finding the true path,"[11] who "with his plaintive voice and subtle but brilliantly incisive guitar . . . has an unmatched ability to create a mood."[12] However, some also found the music to be inadequately prepared for recording,[13] Young's voice to be uncontrolled and childlike in an unappealing way,[14] and the overall tone at times to be one of "irritating bathos."[15] Some critics attempted to acknowledge both aspects of the work at once, in the process reaching for ideas that would be key to Neil Young reception thereafter. Perhaps most influential among these strategies was the argument that the music was not best approached from an intellectual stance and that the technical flaws were revelations of a deep emotional statement.[16]

Early Years, Auteurship, and Lyrics

Neil Young was clearly one key figure in the development of a critical discourse of rock auteurship. More will be said about auteurship in chapter 2, but a few exploratory comments can be made here. Several theorists have discussed the manner in which the community of rock critics, a new phenomenon in the late 1960s, created a set of values emphasizing individuality, oppositionality to the mainstream, and creative agency strongly mirroring modernist notions of auteurship already established in areas such as film and European concert music.[17] It would be an oversimplification to imply that there was just one ideological framework shared by all rock critics. Nonetheless, there was a general tendency for rock critics at the time to celebrate values which artists like Neil Young seemed to embody: self-assuredness, distinctiveness verging on iconoclasm, disruptively intense seriousness, and formal experimentation. As a model of cultural production, auteur theory has been rightly criticized and in popular music studies largely superseded by less naive viewpoints concerning the constraints on individual agency. Nonetheless, ideologies of authenticity and the figure of the auteur continue to loom large in popular culture. The case of Neil Young is especially interesting since his work and persona were a topic of intense debate at the very time these ideologies were coalescing into a practice of rock criticism.

Differences of opinion evident among early critics regarding Neil Young help to show how the very terms of auteurship and achievement were topics of intense negotiation. Some critics seemed intent to base rock's cultural capital in its ability to approach a level of complexity and virtuosity comparable to that seen in Western classical music. For such critics, Young's work presented a problem since it could in certain respects be aligned with these values (for example the elaborately constructed suites such as "Broken Arrow" or "The Old Laughing Lady"), but in other respects seemed to defy such an aesthetic (especially with Young's idiosyncratic voice and rudimentary guitar technique). On the opposite side, critics such as Lester Bangs, who based their model of auteurship precisely on the *rejection* of such values, could point to Young's work with Crazy Horse as an achievement worth celebrating and construct him as an auteur of another kind. One area in which there seemed to be unanimity was on the question of emotional engagement and honesty (a model of authenticity common among those invested in the singer-songwriter tradition). Although, interestingly, on this count there was critical disagreement as to whether Young's clearly high level of expressivity was perhaps *too* intense, representing a lamentable lack of control. Another point of general agreement was that Young had developed a truly distinctive style of singing and playing guitar. As Gracyk has noted, rock musicians often spend as much time creating their distinctive sound as they do on songwriting or other aspects of performance practice, and artists like Neil Young and Bob Dylan are often valued by critics as much for this achievement as for anything else.[18] Although not all critics valued Young's uniqueness in the same way, none questioned that he *was* in fact unique and that this made him a figure to whom critics were obliged to respond in some manner.

There is an inherent paradox in auteurship. Auteurs are celebrated for their supposed individualism and control, yet they only become auteurs when validated as such by a critical community. Similarly, they are celebrated for originality, but such distinctiveness is premised upon deep involvement with a network of pregiven generic and stylistic norms. Who is the author of the auteur? As we will shortly see, Neil Young himself certainly became aware that the individuality accorded him by critics and other listeners was not entirely of his own making, and could serve as a constraint. It would be an oversimplification, though, to say that there was *one* Neil Young persona in play at this time and that auteurship was one of its properties. Every critic created a different Neil Young (and some, as we will see, constructed strikingly different Neils at different times). One thing that put these diverse constructions in resonance with one another was the generally accepted idea that auteurship was an important issue; but auteurship did not represent in each case exactly the same set of values. This kind of multiplicity is to be found in the persona of any public figure, but it was especially striking in the case of Neil Young since his multi-faceted work and his own personal ambivalence toward participation in public life highlight the manner in which personas develop as diverse, partly overlapping instances rather than as single coherent entities. Which is not to say that there was not, in fact, some kind of a core or average "Neil Young" who would be familiar to most critics and listeners of the time and about whom various people could agree on many points. Or rather, any particular person would have such a naturalized Neil in mind, based on the way that person had personally weighted and blended the various specific Neil instances he or she had encountered at various times. This brings us close to a general theoretical issue—identity as an emergent synthetic property—that will be central to many other arguments in this book.

A good deal of Young's early persona and critical reputation was linked to his lyrics. The central lyrical themes and poetic devices tended to remain fairly consistent through Young's early stylistic changes, and so helped to establish a sense of coherent authorial identity. However, the themes and devices in themselves exhibited certain instabilities and tensions resonant with Young's overall changeability. Indeed, one thing which made Young's artistic vision distinctive was the degree to which he took his own changeability and ambiguity as central themes, and this reflexive impulse, along with the generally poetic register of his language, placed Young firmly in the singer-songwriter tradition, although his tendency toward obliqueness and abstraction generally prevented his work from seeming frankly confessional. Similarly, while it seemed clear that Young's work was somehow vitally concerned with American identities and histories, the exact nature of that connection is vague. Some songs evoked particular times and places ("Southern Man"), but others pointed to American history and contexts more obliquely, sometimes simply by evoking images in the song titles themselves ("After the Gold Rush," "Cowgirl in the Sand"). This constant yet often subtle remobilization of Americana was one factor placing Young among artists like The Band and Bob Dylan, who made American histories and identities a key part of their work. By contrast, despite his early years as a Canadian and occasional passing reference to Canadian places, Canadian identity has never been a central theme in Young's work. Nonetheless, some have suggested that Young's distinctive attitude toward American themes— a mixture of attraction and pessimism, fellow-feeling and alterity— mirrors that of other late 1960s musicians of Canadian background and is partly attributable to that background.[19]

Some of Young's earliest songs were concerned with childhood and adolescent insecurity. In some cases this tone is simply implied in the imagery ("Helpless," "I Am a Child"), but in others the lyrics explicitly evoke a growing responsibility and loss of innocence ("Sugar Mountain," "Tell Me Why"). This particular feeling tone—description of a moment at once hopeful and desperate, promising and stifling—was also picked up in mood pieces not specific to childhood, sometimes in the form of a general ennui ("Everybody Knows This Is Nowhere") and sometimes as a full-blown sense of dread or disorientation ("The Loner," "Mr. Soul"). In these cases, Young frequently struck a balance between realism and a more symbolist tone. For example, there is only a fine line distinguishing songs that seem to be about his own feelings and those which seem to treat moods and ideas in themselves, as a series of poetic abstractions ("Broken Arrow," "Don't Let It Bring You Down," "The Old Laughing Lady"). Young would also sometimes use an implied narrative mostly as an opportunity to develop symbolism ("Last Trip to Tulsa"), and actual historical events as metaphors (the best example of this, "Cortez the Killer," came mid-career). His lyrics about romantic relationships were similarly ambiguous, seeming to be biographical but avoiding clear details, dwelling more on imagery and overall mood. There was also a striking dualism in the apparent affective state of their protagonists. Some songs were idyllic to the point of abstraction ("Cinnamon Girl," "I've Loved Her So Long"), where others explored stances of bitterness, paranoia, and violence ("Down by the River" and to a lesser degree "Cowgirl in the Sand"). These swings of narrative mood will be discussed further when we consider gender in detail, but for now it should be noted that Young's tendency to juxtapose themes of innocence and hopelessness, need and paranoia, did much to establish his early image as a sensitive, unpredictable loner, or at least, for critics less inclined to read lyrics in biographical terms, to stake out these themes as Young's signature territory.

Since Young's early lyrics were centrally concerned with mood and emotional ambiguity, a few comments on particular imagery are in order. One thing which immediately stands out is Young's emphasis on visual imagery, and more specifically, upon striking visual events juxtaposed with themes of paralysis or immobility. There are many early songs in which an immobile protagonist—the reasons vary: burnt out, afraid, defeated, paralyzed with uncertainty—witnesses extraordinary visual displays. A few examples of this common device are "Cowgirl in the Sand," "Helpless," "The Loner," "Broken Arrow," and "Don't Let It Bring You Down." In contrast to the frequent images of immobility, when movement does occur it is sometimes positive and emancipatory ("Cinnamon Girl," "When You Dance I Can Really Love"), but just as often it is out of control, seemingly compulsive or self-destructive (running down the hall in "Broken Arrow," the blind man running at night in "Don't Let It Bring You Down," and the frightened rider in "Tell Me Why"). One type of image which also frequently occurs, and which combines these tendencies of stasis/entrapment and movement/emancipation, is that of a flying thing witnessed from below, with the viewer in a despondent or otherwise depressed frame of mind (UFOs in "After the Gold Rush," airplanes in "Helpless," feathers falling in "Birds"). As with movement in general, however, not all flight is portrayed in negative terms. There are also the nostalgically described balloons of "I Am a Child" and, later, the free flight of "Danger Bird."

The connection between these specific images and the general themes of doubt and ambiguity, discussed above, should be clear. Also striking is the way they all seem to imply a dimension of transcendence and a dream-like focus on fleeting details (often visual). This dream-like, portentous tone is thrown into even sharper relief by the large number of archetypal characters inhabiting Young's lyrics, many of them magical or mythic. In connection with ideas of transcendence, most noteworthy are the guide figures who constantly appear. Some are humans in guiding roles (the parent in "I Am a Child," the ex-lover in "Birds"), but some seem more dream-like or supernatural, and while some of these can be supportive (the native of "Broken Arrow" and the "Cinnamon Girl"), others seem more threatening or ambiguous ("Mr. Soul," "The Old Laughing Lady").

This discussion of early lyrics has been highly selective, but it outlines some of the factors which made Neil Young a distinctive lyrical voice in the late 1960s and how those lyrical themes and devices resonated with larger aspects of his authorial persona. In terms of stylistic associations, they put him within the singer-songwriter tradition, but they also distanced him from it. In terms of persona, they established themes of sensitivity and vulnerability, but also violence. Archetypes and even clichés were prevalent, but juxtaposed in an idiosyncratic and striking manner. The stories, often only implicit, emphasized moments of high drama, but frequently from a perspective marked by entropic fatalism.

Harvest and the Gendering of Style

By 1972, Neil Young was becoming a major star in North America and the UK, due largely to the sales of *Harvest.* The album was on the *Billboard* LP chart for forty-one weeks (two weeks at number 1), placed two singles in the *Billboard* singles chart ("Heart of Gold," number 1, and "Old Man," number 31), and was responsible, along with his involvement in CSNY, for establishing Neil Young as one of the major stars in 1970s rock music. Some of the critical response was favorable, but much was not. Complaints included the length of time it took to make the record ("a painfully long year-plus"),[20] its similarities to Young's earlier work, and the relative passivity of the material compared to his work with Crazy Horse ("comfortable but uninspiring").[21] Perhaps the most distinctive feature of *Harvest,* aside from its commercial success, was the presence throughout of pedal steel guitar, played by Ben Keith in a unique style which highlighted the instrument without relying on many identifiable country music clichés. Similarly, it was noteworthy that the album was recorded in Nashville, yet was not a country rock album in any narrow sense. These details will be discussed further in chapter 2.

Among Young's early solo records, *Harvest* stands as the prime example of his involvement with commercially oriented country rock, even though the album contains other stylistic elements in addition to these. There are many ways the contrast (and continuity) between this record and the rest of his output could be described, but one of the most striking is to consider the gender coding of Young's various styles. In the early 1990s, while promoting *Harvest Moon,* Young himself suggested a gendered division within his work, stating that the quieter pop material was in his view feminine and, by implication, that the louder and more experimental material was masculine.[22] Although Young did not elaborate, we could surmise that this binary division encompasses many different elements: musical features, lyrical themes, selection of performing forces, marketing, style of staging in live performance, and others. Since the conception appears quite encompassing, I would like to consider Young's construction of masculinities and femininities in a very general way, with respect to the conventional gender coding of stylistic categories, and also with respect to personas developed in his lyrics.

There are many respects in which Young's gender assumptions mirror those of the 1960s rock counterculture in general (insofar as generalizations are possible in such a complicated area). Whiteley mobilizes a common interpretation of the era when she states that "it is a salutary fact that the counter culture, despite its challenging stance against inequality and its recognition of music as part of its revolutionary strategy, was largely reactionary in its attitude towards women."[23] One feature of such reactionary views on gender is their resistance to change, and it can be noted that Young's portrayal of gender in his work, as we will see, has shifted only very slightly over the years. Similarly, the entourage surrounding at least some of his projects (especially the Crazy Horse tours) remains strongly and homosocially male. Kim Gordon, speaking about Sonic Youth's stint as an opening act for Crazy Horse in 1991, has commented that "the Neil Young tour was actually the first time I encountered so-called sexism."[24] However, even the entrenched and traditional masculinities of 1960s rock music are not monolithic, and "men do not constitute one homogeneous group experiencing the same type of masculinity."[25] We have already identified self-doubt, alienation, and vulnerability as key themes in early Neil Young lyrics, and we have contrasted these against other key themes of violence and self-determination. These traits have strong conventional gender associations, and so the same complexities already identified in Young's work can be given a gendered reading.

Early on, critics took note of Young's sometimes strikingly ambiguous rearticulation of masculine clichés. Perhaps the song most widely discussed was "A Man Needs a Maid," which simultaneously portrays a deep personal inadequacy and seems to endorse a traditional attitude of male entitlement. Also noted was the violence of "Down by the River," in which Young enacts a well-established male archetype: the paranoid and psychotic girlfriend killer found in folk ballads such as "The Banks of the Ohio." In both cases, Young perched between traditional masculine-coded properties (violence, entitlement) and more ambiguous or feminine-coded properties (confusion, dependence). Similar ambivalence can be found on the stylistic level. In one sense, his own feelings about the masculine and feminine characteristics of styles and genres mirror those entrenched in popular music cultures more generally. As Coates has noted, "in this schema, rock is metonymic with 'authenticity' while 'pop' is metonymic with 'artifice.' Sliding even further down the metonymic slope, 'authentic' becomes 'masculine' while 'artificial' becomes 'feminine.'"[26] Not only do Young's explicitly gendered comments bear out this stylistic code, but his own reservations about the success of *Harvest* and his willful detour into non-commerciality in subsequent years suggest that the feminine, pop material is somehow a threat to be contained.[27]

Although the degree of fit between this line of critique and Young's gendering of styles is striking, there are important nuances to take into account. First, it is difficult to disentangle *Harvest*'s commerciality from its gendering in such a way that just one could be seen as the principal threat. Young's comments suggest that he saw the album as in some respects feminine, and also that he was worried that the success of the record would oblige him to play in a similar style indefinitely. His apprehension could to a degree represent reactionary gender attitudes, since it is the feminine-coded style that is represented as a threat to freedom. However, Young had on many previous occasions indicated his discomfort with being pigeonholed in *any* style, and he had taken steps (such as working with CSNY) which equally precluded remaining exclusively in the more masculine-coded Crazy Horse style. In other words, it was not only feminine-coded styles which Young found threatening, but all styles which could in any way limit his subsequent mobility, although in the case of *Harvest* the confluence of feminine coding, commerciality, and threat is striking. And although I am arguing against simple excription or misogyny in Young's work, there is still a powerful set of masculine features to be described. A compulsion toward mobility and the avoidance of binding attachments are themselves character traits conventionally coded as masculine, and so while they complicate the exclusivity of Young's masculinity on one level, they reinforce it on another.

In order to get further into the issues, we need to consider specific gendered personas common in Young's lyrics. In terms of masculine characters, the emphasis is on figures in crisis with respect to their own traditional power positions, positions which are presented as problematic but also assumed to be fundamental. Sometimes this negotiation is presented in the form of father figures, who in some songs (especially later ones) are positive and nostalgic ("Old Man," "Daddy Went Walkin'") and in earlier songs can be ambiguous ("Ambulance Blues"). The emphasis here is on defiance, self-reliance, and benevolent patriarchy, most forcefully embodied by the character of Grandpa in *Greendale.* These figures are not always in crisis, but they do frequently speak of futility, compromise, and dignity in the face of a confusing world. They will loom large in my discussion of Young's politics. On the other extreme are the many fanatics, drifters, loners, and petty criminals, representing the sociopathic extremes of self-reliance. Young's lyrics frequently explore the slippage between these archetypes. This slippage is often developed in terms of male figures placed in ethically ambiguous crisis situations, forced to make life-defining decisions. Sometimes these are adolescents ("Powderfinger," "Captain Kennedy") and sometimes they are middle-aged anti-heroes ("Mideast Vacation," "Crime in the City"). Often, Young seems to be questioning his own motives and weaknesses, developing his own persona as one poised on the edge of asocial destructiveness ("Tired Eyes," "Violent Side," "Fuckin' Up"). What emerges from all this is a complex engagement with masculinities in process, at once traditional in its basic terms of reference and its implied ideals and untraditional in its open reflexivity.

These masculinities are all staunchly heterosexual and so are frequently developed through their relationship with equally archetypal female figures. One striking thing about Young's early lyrics is the one-dimensionality of the female characters. In general, they closely follow the female archetypes of 1960s rock lyrics described by Whiteley.[28] There are the fantasy figures—"etherealized and inscribed within a dreamlike and unreal world . . . defined by the male as a fantasy escape"—which in songs such as "Cinnamon Girl" are presented as entirely benign and in others such as "Like a Hurricane" appear more frighteningly supernatural. Related to the supernatural women, because they also represent a threatening ambiguity, are the castrating or unmanageable women, met with rejection, insult, and sometimes explicit violence ("Cowgirl in the Sand," "Stupid Girl," "Down by the River"). At the opposite extreme, and closely related in Young's world to the dream women, are the earth mothers ("Change Your Mind," "Hangin' on a Limb," "Mother Earth"). Another type of imagery described by Whiteley but much less common in Young's work is the "hardcore" approach to sex: explicit and domineering. There are occasional songs in which Young develops moderately explicit sexual references, most playful ("Welfare Mothers," "Saddle Up the Palomino"), and in just one case slightly violent ("Bite the Bullet"), but this is rare. Much more common is a kind of figure not described by Whiteley but central to Young's lyrics, which I will call the *placeholder woman*. This is a female character who has no developed characteristics at all other than being the recipient of the singer's devotion or the object of his desire. Young's lyrics are full of such figures, in early years more often as objects of desire ("I've Loved Her So Long") and in later years associated with affirmations of long-term commitment ("Already One," "Such a Woman").

In many cases, these songs are clearly about or for particular women, and so the lack of character detail in the lyrics is partly offset by context. If the song is for someone in particular, then the lyrics just need to convey a sentiment, not to develop a character. However, when listened to without thinking about context, it is striking how many of these lyrics treat the female characters in an entirely superficial manner, as tokens for Young's ruminations on his own feelings and actions. Although that is a typical attitude for a male rock musician of the 1960s and so could be read as more evidence of a reactionary attitude, we should remember that Young tended, especially in his early work, to treat *all* subjects in this manner, not just women or heterosexual relationships. Also, these ubiquitous one-dimensional female characters are offset by another figure, who appears in songs such as "Unknown Legend" and "Razor Love." In these lyrics, the tone is strikingly different. They discuss the lives and experiences of the female character, describe her motives and feelings, and, in the case of "Razor Love," develop a compelling parallel between the experiences of the female character and Young's own early life. Most strikingly, these women are portrayed as drifters, at least in spirit, and so are active participants in the mobility that is one of Young's principal themes. This character is almost entirely absent from Young's earlier work, but becomes more common by the 1990s. And on *Greendale*, there is another kind of developed female actor in the teenage artist/activist Sun Green.

In summary, the traditional and perhaps even reactionary nature of gendering in Young's work seems impossible to miss, yet difficult to assess. The sites at which he troubles these assumptions and explores alternatives are not numerous, but they are often striking. In addition, we should be wary of always accepting established codes at face value. As Fast notes, if we rush to immediately read rock clichés as masculine and phallic, we run the risk of invalidating alternative readings.[29] Specifically, we may miss instances in which the normative gender roles implied in the text do not map smoothly onto the roles inhabited by listeners or even by the artists themselves.[30] In her own work, Fast has noted that many female Led Zeppelin listeners gravitate toward the most putatively "masculine" characteristics of the music, and the same is true of some rusties. An instance in which this became explicit was a discussion on the Rust list of the song "Such a Woman," which is perhaps the most extremely one-dimensional of Young's feminine-coded songs. Janet and Randy saw it as a good and moving song. Janet asked rhetorically, "What woman wouldn't want their man singing this to them?" Randy commented, "My wife loves his quiet songs. Neil certainly seems to have a fine grasp of the female psyche." In this case, the association of stylistic markers with gender is upheld in statements about listening preferences: these are stories about women having a special affinity for the feminine material. Other rusties, including two women, found the song to be insipid, cloying, and facile. At other times, many women on the list have expressed a preference for the hard rock material, and some of the men prefer the quieter songs. I have never seen a rustie using "masculine" or "feminine" (or a direct synonym) as a stylistic descriptor, although categories like "romantic," which clearly do presume assumptions about gender, are not uncommon.

Neil Young himself also seems aware that feminine and masculine codes do not necessarily align with female and male subjects in a simple manner. One of the most interesting instances to consider are his comments about the Madison Square Garden tribute concert to Bob Dylan on October 16, 1992. Sinead O'Connor was a guest performer along with Neil Young and others. O'Connor was booed by the audience, presumably because of her controversial political views (for example, two weeks before this event she had torn up a photograph of Pope John Paul II while appearing on NBC's *Saturday Night Live* television show). Young felt that O'Connor, who cut her set short and expressed anger that subsequent performances went on as scheduled, did not handle the situation well, commenting:

> She got a good reaction. . . . It was a New York reaction, okay? It was a strong reaction. They were booing her, but at least they were reacting. . . . [Interviewer: She seemed pretty distraught] I'm surprised by that. . . . [Would you have taken that kind of hostility in your stride] Absolutely. Shit, I've been booed for my music . . . but they never made me run. . . . Look at it this way. If Sinead had gone out there and done what she went out there to do, it would have been one of the most beautiful and moving moments of her musical career, of the entire show. . . . She's supposed to be in control. . . . I'm sure she has plenty of good reasons for the things she does. More power to her. You want to protest, go ahead. . . . But there's a time when it's gonna come back on you. You have to be strong.[31]

There is a complicated dynamic at play here. Young is certainly displaying what one critic calls "damn redneck machismo,"[32] but he is inviting O'Connor to do the same. Under a generous reading, this could be seen as a decoupling, in Young's view, of certain desirable character traits from their traditional gendered associations. What Young misses, of course, is the more basic question of why acts of protest must necessarily unfold in a conflictual, hostile manner. By opposing certain social values, why must O'Connor be seen as inviting hostility? Can there not be a wide spectrum of options with regard to disruptive strategies and their reception? I would suggest that there is a parallel here with descriptions given by many women and girls of their experience in music stores, where interactions with staff members, usually male, frequently become a game of one-upmanship, with conspicuous hierarchies based on knowledge of equipment.[33] Just as there are girls and women who become the kind of tough, confrontational artist admired by Young, there are those who learn to succeed in the existing culture of music stores. However, the deeper question is, why is the standard of success in these cases assimilationist? Why, to borrow a phrase from Manners, must the behavior of female artists always be "fixed" to fit prevailing patterns, rather than the other way around?[34]

Dark Period, Abjection, the Blues

Despite *Harvest*'s enormous success, and partly because of it, this was not a happy or rewarding time for Neil Young. The first public signs of Young's distress were evident with the *Time Fades Away* tour of early 1973. Young's voice was in poor condition, he was becoming increasingly discontented with the stadium concert format, and there were serious tensions within the touring band. The live album which came out of this tour, *Time Fades Away,* did nothing to hide these flaws and tensions. In fact, it highlighted them. Many critics felt the LP was simply of poor quality, interpreting its rough edges as sloppiness. Some, however, viewed its roughness as a powerful artistic decision. The one song on the LP which drew the most favorable comment was "Don't Be Denied," which Landau characterized as "one of the few attacks on the star system that a rock musician has made creditable."[35] More critics would shortly take Landau's side and come to celebrate *Time Fades Away* as a bold rejection of commerciality, but not right away, and not until after the confusion was first made more acute with Young's next tour.

The album and tour which are now taken to encapsulate the spirit of Young's mid-1970s work are *Tonight's the Night.* The album was largely completed in 1973 but was not released in that year because both Young and Reprise records felt it was too unpolished and unrelentingly pessimistic. However, Young did tour the material, and in a manner that baffled and angered many who were not expecting such a bleak, disjointed show. In time these performances would be among the most lauded in Young's career and would be an important model for subsequent rock musicians choosing to challenge or even confront audiences. Given the central importance of these performances, it is worth quoting a description at length.

> It took everyone by surprise. . . . It was the kind of "you had to be there" rock 'n' roll experience that comes along only once in a lifetime. . . . It's unlikely that many in the audience had heard about the *Tonight's the Night* sessions when Neil Young finally arrived in Manchester on November 3, 1973. They did know, however, that Crazy Horse was going to play with Nils Lofgren on lead, so were prepared for a good-humoured rock 'n' roll-

ing time. . . . On the musky stage was a decrepit old piano, with what appeared to be battered boots hanging from it; a wooden Indian figure and, way downstage, a full-size fake palm tree. When Young stumbled out of the darkness and into the gloom, he looked wrecked—greasy hair hanging lank and heavy over his shoulders, unkempt beard, a soiled white jacket, dark sunglasses. Then came the first brooding notes of "Tonight's the Night". . . . "I picked up the telephone," Neil hollered, "and heard that he died out on the mainline . . . " The effect was shocking. When the song ended, the tentative applause very quickly subsided, and the theater was suddenly deathly silent. Young spoke: "Welcome to Miami Beach, ladies and gentlemen," Young said, turning again to face the audience, who laughed nervously, pleased to be offered some light relief. Then in a tortured, strangled voice, he began to scream out another unheard song, "Mellow My Mind." By the time he'd croaked through [a few more unfamiliar songs] those who had come to hear pleasant and folky melodies such as "Heart of Gold" were growing restless. The heckling began . . . but the show went on, 50 minutes of raucous, disturbing, totally unfamiliar material. It was a crazy, provocative thing for any performer to do to any audience, and Young knew it. . . . "If you can get back to where you were two years ago," he yelled at the barrackers, "I'll get back to where I was."[36]

By this point it seemed clear that Neil Young was either doing something powerfully new, or that he had lost his grip. Although many reviewers took the latter position, more began to come around to the former point of view, and this caused some to reassess *Time Fades Away* as well. Again, an extended quotation is instructive:

Mistakes and fluffs dot [*Time Fades Away*], and Young has made no attempt to correct them. For whatever reason, he's made a startlingly unorthodox album. . . . There are no hits, no familiar tunes; for that matter, there's hardly any audience response—it's quickly faded out at each song's end. . . . If Young appears foolish and arrogant at various points on the album, he seems to be allowing us a glimpse of these flaws. . . . *Time Fades Away* is an idiosyncrasy from one of rock's most idiosyncratic artists.[37]

When Young released his next studio album, *On the Beach,* some critics were willing to read it closely as a potentially important statement from an artist who was proving increasingly oppositional to the usual practices of the music business, and even to view the album as a diagnosis of "the collective paranoia and guilt of an insane society."[38] But many still expressed doubts. Christgau, for example, harshly criticizes Young's self-repetition and insularity. An important nuance of this review is that it describes Young's methodology as *instinctive* ("with an artist as instinctive as Young, talk of intentions is useless").[39] From this point forward, assertions of Young's instinctiveness are commonly deployed any time his work needs to be explained in relation to social issues.

It was in 1975 that Neil Young finally explained publicly what had happened to push him into the darker, oppositional period immediately following *Harvest*. This was the same year that *Tonight's the Night* was finally released. In sharp contrast to preceding years, Young gave several interviews during this period, allowing him to contextualize his mid-1970s work.[40] As early as during the recording of *Harvest*, Young was plagued by back problems and marital difficulties. Young was further troubled by the overdose death of guitarist Danny Whitten, an original Crazy Horse member, and of the roadie Bruce Berry. The core songs of *Tonight's the Night* were all recorded in one night, at a session marked by extreme alcohol and drug use which Young and others described as a wake for Whitten and Berry. The result was sloppy, dark, cathartic, and considered unsuitable for commercial release. Aside from a lack of technical polish, the recordings displayed a level of emotional distress foreign to most rock music. In the Scoppa interviews Young says that the band felt "spooked," and characterizes the album as "the first horror record." Young also notes that for much of the material he was consciously playing a role, adopting an extreme persona as a way of dealing with his grief. One result was the bizarre stage behavior during the *Tonight's the Night* concert tour. With Young's eventual explanation, and the release of *Tonight's the Night*, listeners could finally rationalize the post-*Harvest* material. Perhaps most forceful was Marsh's review in *Rolling Stone*,[41] which cast Young as a courageous auteur. However, some reviewers still did not respond well to the material. Bangs, for example, despite his favorable view of Young's late-1960s work, complained of "professional patheticness so ostentatious it became its own brand of creepy narcissism."[42] Bangs's position is interesting because although he was in general a champion of unpolished, expressive music, he felt that Young undermined the themes of the record by dwelling too much on his own personal feelings—essentially the same criticism made by Christgau concerning the political aspects of *On the Beach*.

Young had felt conflicted about rock culture and stardom from as early as the Buffalo Springfield era, so these mid-1970s projects, while unprecedented in their extremity, were not thematically isolated. Indeed, some have suggested that self-critique was a core feature of 1960s rock music in general and that "the dark side of the breakthrough experience, with the corruption of love and the presence of evil within us" is a theme to be found in many of the era's songwriters.[43] In this sense, Young's mid-1970s work responds to a general contradiction in the cultural logic of rock as a social formation, a formation which in Grossberg's words was both "utopian and disintegrative."[44] The apocalyptic tone of Young's work derives in part from the fact that this disintegration occurs within the medium he uses to express it. Since the mid-1970s, Young had been positioned as one of the harshest reporters of rock's self-destructive features, yet he never abandoned the form, and his resulting insider/ outsider status tends to intensify the sense of confusion and despair in some of his work. As Burns has noted, one is more likely to speak in apocalyptic terms, to fear the collapse of all values, if it is one's own power and value systems which are coming into crisis.[45]

The *abject* is a concept from psychoanalysis, literary theory, and some schools of feminism.[46] Abject things—be they people, acts, or substances —are those which, in a given social group, are utterly rejected, deeply felt to be vile, infused with death and corruption. Whether described in terms of individual psyches or collective ideologies, the abject is pushed to the margins and deeply repressed. It is also necessary and inescapable, since that which is desired and endorsed requires a set of others in order to be distinct, and also because there is an attraction to the abject, a kind of desire marked as shameful yet constantly present and often quite powerful. In theory, the purely abject would be completely unrecuperable, could never be assimilated nor identified with. In practice, however, pure abjection is rare, and the barriers to acceptance exert their own attraction. Most frequently, engagement with the abject represents a mixed blessing, an opportunity for growth but one which entails many risks. Perhaps the quintessential example of that, and certainly the most relevant to our present discussion, is experimentation with powerful drugs and 1960s rock hedonism more generally.

The concept of abjection throws into relief some aspects of Young's mid-1970s work. He seems to identify with the stark beauty of those events and actions which he also fears and loathes. He suggests that rock myths of fun and potency cannot be disentangled from anti-myths of death and disempowerment. He not only expresses these ideas, but he embodies them in excessive, barely controlled aesthetic decisions which threaten his professional well-being. The dilemma placed front and center in *Tonight's the Night* and other works of that period seems to be the same one identified by Butler when she discusses the abject in performative identity in general: "How will we know the difference between the power we promote and the power we oppose? . . . [One is] in power even as one opposes it, formed by it as one reworks it, and it is this simultaneity that is at once the condition of our partiality . . . and also the condition of action itself."[47] When phrased in that manner, we can see how the specific dilemma of drug use and self-destruction in rock culture is just one aspect of a broader theme in Young's work: the confusion and fragmentation of subjects as they negotiate intense experience and struggle to articulate beliefs. The paranoid romantic violence of "Down by the River," or the schizoid politics of "Rockin' in the Free World," are in this sense closely related to the death-in-joy poignancy of a song like "Come On Baby Let's Go Downtown." Furthermore, just as we cannot always tell the difference between what we would endorse and what we would reject, Young's drug songs do not, taken as a group, present a unified opinion. Some explore the abject, while others suggest that the use of certain drugs in certain situations can be fun ("Homegrown," "Roll Another Number for the Road") and a spur to creativity ("Will to Love," not in its lyrics but in its genesis, see chapter 6 for details). Ultimately, the dilemma foregrounded during the *Tonight's the Night* era is a general one for Young, and it has to do with intensity in general rather than drugs in particular, which becomes clear when he says things like this: "Rock 'n' roll is like a drug. I don't take very much rock 'n' roll, but when I *do* rock 'n' roll, I fuckin' do it. But I don't want to do it all the time 'cause it'll kill me."[48]

Another theme linked to *Tonight's the Night* by at least one critic, and which might at first seem like non sequitur, is that of Young's relationship to African American musical forms. The comment I have in mind is brief and was made considerably after the fact, but it is nonetheless striking: "It is the kind of boozy out-of-tune party Jimmy Reed would've sat in for, with the best spoken recitations by a white man since Hank Williams."[49] This observation seems both jarring and apt since Young's relationship to traditions such as blues and soul was at the time far from obvious. In recent years it has become more clear, and Young himself has recently named Reed as an influence.[50] However, in earlier years Young's work seemed strikingly *unconnected* to the blues and to

African American musical traditions in general, to the point that some commentators identified this apparent disconnection as a distinguishing feature of his persona.[51] In support of this view, one could point to Young's extended guitar solos with Crazy Horse, which stood out in part precisely because, unlike almost all other heavy rock guitar improvisation of the late 1960s, they did not betray much obvious blues influence.

Yet there are important ways in which Young has been connected to the blues and to soul music throughout his career. Even within the Crazy Horse tradition, one could argue for an oblique kind of affective alliance between Young and the blues, as when Fricke speaks about "blues in the great Young tradition—songs of tortured self-examination and love gone all wrong emphasized by his poignant vocals and brilliant ice-pick guitar."[52] There are more literal connections as well, to soul even more than to the blues. One of Young's long-term collaborators, Tim Drummond, was a James Brown band member in the late 1960s, and Young has worked on many occasions with members of Booker T and the MGs, once in order to make an album explicitly inspired by Stax soul: *Are You Passionate?* During the 1960s, he worked briefly in a band with Rick James and frequently cited the Rolling Stones as a key influence. Perhaps most clearly and yet least frequently noted, Young's harmonica style bears a striking resemblance to that of Jimmy Reed and did so long before the *Tonight's the Night* era, which era's obsession with self-destructive partying musicians itself seems strongly evocative of Reed's life.

What makes all this interesting is that, despite these many connections, the blues does not immediately present itself as an integral feature of Young's idiolect. Part of the reason is formal. Although he does employ canonical twelve-bar blues forms in some instances ("Vampire Blues," "Get Back on It"), and while some of his more idiosyncratic formal structures are clearly transformations of a twelve-bar form ("On the Beach," "Revolution Blues"), his work for the most part makes little formal use of blues idioms, even though the *word* "blues" does crop up with some frequency in song titles, notably on several songs which are formally not the blues at all ("Ambulance Blues," "Barstool Blues"). Nonetheless, while the bulk of Young's work is distant from the blues in terms of formal textual features, there is an affective alliance at play. Perhaps the most sustained manifestation of this affective alliance was the mid-1970s dark period. On all of Young's solo albums there are only five songs with "blues" in the title, and three of them are from *On the Beach.* But the tendency has been suggested at various other points in Young's career as well, for example when a reviewer of *Harvest* suggested that the more repetitive elements of Young's country-rock style may be his own "equivalent of the 12-bar blues,"[53] or when Young himself noted that both Mike Bloomfield and Paul Butterfield told him that he would be a natural at playing and singing the blues.[54] Young's own view of *This Note's for You,* the album representing his 1980s work with The Bluenotes, may perhaps be taken as a summary: "I don't really think it's blues. It's blue. . . . Three of the songs have a late-night, torch song kind of thing. You know, the club's empty kind of feeling."[55]

In all these cases, the blues is being treated as a stylistic and affective category, with its racial connotations downplayed or left altogether unmentioned. While the blues and soul play a secondary but continuous role in Young's work, blackness and ethnicity in general are excluded from consideration (which, on closer examination, causes Young's own ethnicity to loom large through its sheer unmarkedness). I do not raise the issue in order to bolster an essentialist idea about musical identities, since I agree with Tagg that there are no formal features of any musical style that can be definitively identified as "black,"[56] and with Gilroy that both essentialism and anti-essentialism are unsatisfactory strategies for confronting the hybridity of categories such as "black music."[57] There is no necessary reason why an artist who draws from the blues tradition should be explicitly concerned with issues of race. And yet, for a 1960s artist like Young, who so frequently skirts the issue both thematically and in terms of his collaborations, the omission seems striking. Perhaps it is an example of the tendency, noted by Grossberg, for the relationship between rock musicians and the blues to be ambiguous and "highly selective."[58] Grossberg is perhaps overstating the case when he argues that rock music "[did not] offer, even implicitly, an ideological criticism of racism in the U.S."[59]—Young did, after all, write "Southern Man"—but the comments nonetheless show some resonance with Young's own relationship to the African American origins of the blues and soul traditions. I do not believe this is the result of any active choice on Young's part, but rather the opposite. I see it as evidence of a passive rock-centrism displayed not just by Young but by many rock musicians and listeners of his generation.

The Late 1970s Rally

Around the time *Tonight's the Night* was finally released, Crazy Horse found a permanent replacement for Danny Whitten in guitarist Frank Sampedro. The album which followed, *Zuma,* introduced a number of important innovations. The emphasis was on long instrumental passages, strongly recalling the era of *Everybody Knows This Is Nowhere,* and the music sounded strikingly spacious, even epic, compared to the more claustrophobic productions of the mid-1970s. The album cover was white and featured a cartoon, in contrast to the grainy, dark photography of *Tonight's the Night,* and the lyrics mostly avoided any form of pessimism. In interviews, Young spoke of being happy and having found a new sense of direction.

The 1976 Crazy Horse tour set a format that the band still follows. Although this incarnation of the group would gain wider exposure a few years later and would be resurrected in the early 1990s, it was as a rebound out of the dark period of 1973–1975 that their distinctive sound was first heard. Billy Talbot commented that "it was an idyllic time, man, Neil was just sparkling,"[60] and critics began to speak of the new Crazy Horse in tones approaching awe: "Here was rock & roll so primal and unexplainable that I simply wanted to let it wash over me. . . . I figured I'd at last found the perfect target for that most overused of adjectives: mythic."[61] Several critics commented on the striking textures and sense of space created by the two guitarists Young and Sampedro. In a description that would prove prophetic of the band's 1990s work, Carson argued that "Young made his breakthrough with rock & roll as pure sound on *Zuma* after learning how to use raw noise on *Tonight's The Night.*"[62] The concepts of noise and "pure sound" in Young's work will arise often in subsequent chapters. Another thing which made *Zuma* noteworthy is the song "Cortez the Killer," which not only provides one of the strongest examples of the new Crazy Horse sound, but also reintroduced Young's interest in First Nations themes. The song is only vaguely historical, since Young's presentation of pre-Columbian cultures is intensely romanticized and combined with themes of science-fiction and romance. Critical opinion diverged. Scoppa felt the song was "an extended narrative tale that packs equal wallop as a classic retelling of an American legend, a Lawrencian erotic dreamscape, and Young's ultimate personal meta-phor,"[63] whereas Bangs complained that the album "reveals once again that Neil has no insights to offer about women . . . about druggie alien-ation . . . and, perhaps most offensively, about white European immi-grants and the people of color they walked over."[64]

The period following *Zuma,* from 1977 to 1980, could be seen as one of retrenchment and consolidation. In the spring of 1977, Young re-leased *American Stars 'n Bars,* an album mostly assembled from leftovers from other projects, and one which did not generate much response, positive or negative (except that it contained "Like a Hurricane," perhaps the most celebrated vehicle for Crazy Horse guitar improvisations dur-ing this period). In the fall, Young released a three-LP career retrospec-tive, *Decade,* and the other LPs made during this time similarly revisited familiar territory, with *Comes a Time* returning to the quiet country-rock of *Harvest* and two new Crazy Horse projects in the 1976 mold: *Live Rust* and *Rust Never Sleeps.* Young did break new ground during this pe-riod to a degree with the elaborate staging and costumes of the *Rust Never Sleeps* tour and concert film, and perhaps more significantly by expressing an admiration for the spirit of punk rock, which tended to set him apart from his contemporaries. For the most part, though, the late 1970s saw Neil Young underlining and reiterating the major themes of his earlier work.

In the years 1977 through 1979, critics almost unanimously lauded Neil Young as one of the most vital rock artists of his generation. Reti-cence and mixed reaction disappeared for a while, replaced by a desire to celebrate quirks that had once seemed irksome. In this context, Marcus could note that "Young never has and never will make a record without glaring flaws," without it sounding like a dismissal.[65] Perhaps most in-fluential was a major *New York Times* profile arguing that "along with Bob Dylan, Neil Young is probably the most important rock composer and performer North America has produced," although going on to note that Young never achieved the kind of iconic status accorded Dylan, partly because "Mr. Young has always been a more introverted sort, and he began to flower just as society stopped looking for musical heroes."[66] Around 1978, then, Neil Young was being positioned not just as a major and interesting artist, but as a required inclusion in the emerging canon of rock criticism. By the late 1970s rock's dominance within popular culture was waning, and the original 1960s generation was increasingly fading into the background. In this climate, critics began to lace their praise of Neil Young with comments on his longevity. As Christgau phrased it, "the miracle is that Young doesn't sound much more grizzled now than he already did in 1969; he's wiser but not wearier, victor so far over the slow burnout his title warns of."[67] Although this theme would mostly drop out of critical parlance during the 1980s, for reasons that will shortly be described, it would become in the 1990s one of the most central topics in Neil Young reception.

Young borrowed the phrase "rust never sleeps" from the Akron punk/new wave band Devo, who had originally devised it as part of a commercial jingle,[68] but the phrase quickly became emblematic of Young's long struggle against artistic and personal inertia. The paired songs "My My Hey Hey (Out of the Blue)" and "Hey Hey My My (Into the Black)" developed a simple but for the time powerfully resonant argument. There was the lurking danger ("rust never sleeps"), the promise of transcendence ("rock and roll will never die"), and the sacrifice necessary to realize that promise ("it's better to burn out than to fade away"). There could probably be no clearer statement of faith in rock as a social technology of affective empowerment, and it was presented here without any apparent irony, which is all the more striking given the tone of Young's preceding mid-1970s work.

It is significant that these songs appear on the same album as "Thrasher," an extended meditation on Young's need to cut ties from old associates. Young had previously written many songs exploring nuances of his frustration with collaborators, developing in the process themes of ambiguity ("Mr. Soul"), entropy and inertia ("Ambulance Blues"), and the cruelty of gossip ("Walk On," "Human Highway"). In all cases, Young's solution to the complex of inhibiting forces was simple mobility. Similarly, in contrast to the painstaking description of rock culture abjection throughout his mid-1970s work, Young's late-1970s antidote seemed to be more and better rock. In this respect, Young is a prime example of the kind of artist described by Lipsitz: "within the countercultural community, escapist tendencies led 'hippies' to fashion a better picture of what they were running from than of what they were running to."[69] According to Lipsitz, such artists often lapsed back into dominant patterns of empty celebrity, doing "little to interrogate the aces of power in society—the systematic racism, class domination, sexism, and homophobia that constrained individual choices."[70] Some of these issues have already been raised, and I will leave it as an open question whether Young's late-1970s rediscovery of a simpler and more optimistic rock mythology should be seen as a progressive or regressive move in political terms. In terms of his personal image, the late 1970s represents a kind of watershed, because after this period he was rarely described as fragile or vulnerable, which had been key adjectives applied by rock critics up to that point. Instead, he increasingly came to be described as a survivor and a forceful individualist.

Many Masks in the 1980s

Young's first LP of the 1980s, *Hawks and Doves,* was in some ways a typical Neil Young record in that it featured a mix of singer-songwriter material and country music. In this case, though, the introspective songs seemed especially abstract and veiled, and the country was stylistically more similar to an orthodox Nashville sound than anything Young had previously produced. Even more striking for many commentators, the political opinions expressed through the country songs, especially "Hawks and Doves," were notably right-wing. Those reviewers not offended by this tended to assume that Young was portraying a persona other than his own, at least until Young made public his strong support for Ronald Reagan. This in itself would be a striking enough event in Neil Young's reception history, and Young's political pronouncements did generate quite a bit of commentary (discussed shortly). However, the political revelations of the 1980s were partly overshadowed by the extreme stylistic experimentation Young engaged in during that whole decade. As an early example, the album which followed *Hawks and Doves, Re*ac*tor,* could scarcely have been more different. It was an electric Crazy Horse album, but one which seemed to many critics somehow askew, emphasizing as it did a mechanical, highly repetitious sound bearing little resemblance to the freely improvisatory profile of late-1970s Crazy Horse.

Hawks and Doves and *Re*ac*tor* were both slightly quirky but still notably within the stylistic territory defined by Young throughout the 1970s. It was with *Trans* that Young's more extreme 1980s experimentation began. For much of the album, Young's voice is processed by a vocoder, and the instrumental accompaniments are often synthesizer-based. For Neil Young—one of the staunchest advocates of basic, guitar-oriented rock—

to make moves toward electronic pop was perceived as a radical, and to many an unwelcome, development. It should be noted, though, that the negative reaction was much stronger among fans than among critics. Young did make efforts to link his work with synthesizers to his earlier material ("it's stuff I used to do with my acoustic guitar, alone. Now it's me alone with the machines"),[71] as did some critics, who noted that aside from arrangement, the songs were still concerned with familiar Neil Young themes and contained much of his typical harmonic and melodic sensibility.

In a few years, Neil Young would explain the circumstances leading up to *Trans,* but for a while it stood as a mystery, especially because it did not prove to be the beginning of a coherent new direction. *Trans* was Young's first album for Geffen records (he had been with Reprise since 1968), and it did not take long for tensions to develop between Young and his new label. Geffen wanted a product in a recognizable Neil Young style, and Young was determined to explore new directions. For the next few years, Young's output grew even more erratic. It was during this period that the term "unpredictable," which had been applied to Young on occasion in the 1970s, became almost universal in commentaries on his work ("it's become a critical cliché to greet each new Neil Young album as yet another surprising twist").[72] Young's major project following *Trans* was to be an entire country album, *Old Ways,* which Geffen initially rejected. In fact, Geffen sued Young for producing uncharacteristic music. Young responded by producing a half-hour-long rockabilly album, *Everybody's Rockin',* and touring the country material that Geffen was refusing to release. When *Old Ways* finally saw release, critical response was mostly negative. I have only found one truly favorable review.[73] Some were outright hostile[74] or simply unsure as to whether the record was meant seriously.[75] The critical reaction to *Old Ways* set a tone which continued through the 1980s. *Landing On Water* (something like *Trans* in its use of synthesizers) and *Life* (more like a conventional Crazy Horse record) were widely, although not universally, panned. *This Note's for You* (Young's stage-band blues record) was received with a bit more enthusiasm, partly because the title track was a focused attack on corporate music sponsorship, featuring a video which was at first refused airtime by MTV and later named MTV Video of the Year for 1988. But for the most part, many critics and fans grew tired and confused by Young's frequent changes in persona.

The situation began to change in 1988 when, as he had in the mid-1970s, Neil Young decided to explain what had been happening to him. In 1979, Young and his wife Pegi discovered that their son, Ben, was afflicted with severe cerebral palsy. This news would have been difficult enough, but Young already had one child with a milder case of the disease, born to Carrie Snodgrass in 1972. Further, shortly after receiving the news about Ben, Pegi was diagnosed with a potentially life-threatening brain condition. In a series of unusually frank interviews, Young finally explained how all of these events affected his work and how they, in combination with his difficulties at Geffen records, drove him into the continuous character-shifting style experiments of the 1980s as a way to keep working at a time when most of his energy needed to be diverted to his home life. Most poignantly, it became clear that the vocoderized voices on *Trans,* along with its science-fiction imagery, were for Young an exploration of Ben's difficulties in communicating and of his reliance on prosthetic technologies. Just as in 1976, once Young explained himself, critical and fan response became more favorable. By the early 1990s, Young's 1980s work would be seen as a unified period, although not one which has enjoyed the kind of critical rejuvenation that was visited on his mid-1970s work. This is perhaps the most striking feature of the period: it remains stubbornly marginal. Young's mid-1970s work reflected on themes of abjection and represented at least in part an attempted escape from stardom, but it is the 1980s material which actually remains unassimilated in rock canons and offers the starkest challenges to the coherence of Young's authorial persona. Questions of coherence and canon formation in the 1980s are treated in chapter 2, so for the moment I would like to consider a different aspect of the decade: what it can say about the place of humor and irony in Young's work more generally.

Constant movement between styles and bands has always been a major element of Young's career. It is probably significant that rusties and critics, partly at Young's urging, generally interpret these changes as expressions of a restlessness or multi-vocality within Young's personality. This seems especially pertinent when we notice that the same reading is not usually given for other popular artists who indulge in such boundary crossing. Madonna, for example, is usually interpreted as having a distanced and ironic relationship to the various styles she inhabits, and in these cases the preferred explanation for the changeability of her persona is the opposite of that usually given for Neil Young. That is, in the case of Neil Young, changes are interpreted as a symptom of personality —indeed, the difficulty in tracing a simple or direct relationship between authorial personas in the songs and Young's own person is inverted and turned into evidence of such an underlying person—whereas for an artist like Madonna, such complications are often taken to indicate a gap between the person of the artist and the personas in the songs. In chapter 2, we will consider more fully how this interpretive move derives from strong ideologies of authenticity and authorship active in rock culture. For now, I would like to point out that, in the 1980s, this line of interpretation seemed somehow foreclosed, or at least was made more difficult, and to say a little about the implications of this change.

Strategic Anti-essentialism, Irony, Camp

Lipsitz uses the term *strategic anti-essentialism* to describe situations in which artists "[take] on disguises in order to express indirectly parts of their identity that might be too threatening to express directly."[76] This strategy "gives the appearance of celebrating the fluidity of identities," but may not do so on a deeper level, since it can be reinterpreted as the expressive strategy of a relatively stable subject. Such a strategy certainly seemed to be in play with Young's mid-1970s work, for example when he played the part of a dissolute Miami Beach MC in order to reflect fears about his own complicity in garish self-destruction. The model also appears to work for projects such as *Trans,* in which Young's feelings about family relationships are obliquely expressed through a stylistic decoupling of his voice and his normal persona by means of vocoder technology. Most rusties and critics now speak of *Trans* respectfully, although few embrace it fully, probably for stylistic reasons reflecting the still perceptible although greatly diminished rift between rock music and electronic dance music. Similarly, other 1980s projects such as *Everybody's Rockin', Old Ways,* and *This Note's for You*—usually interpreted respectively as a kind of joke, as a mixed joke and tribute, and as an experiment of intermediate success—can be assimilated to the strategic anti-essentialism model, although in all cases their acceptance by fans and critics remains provisional in ways that the mid-1970s work does not. What are the barriers to full assimilation in these cases? Some of them are stylistic, discussed more in chapter 2. Others have to do with the presumed relationship between Neil Young as an agent and the personas presented in these works. To advance our discussion of this difference, we can suggest two questions. Does it make sense to call the 1980s style experiments ironic? Does it make sense to call them campy?

Linda Hutcheon characterizes irony as a strategy marked by three features: (i) it is differential, in that concepts or elements marked as different from one another are brought together in the same textual or performative space; (ii) it is inclusive, in that final choices are not forced or even necessarily allowed between the differential elements; (iii) it is relational, in that attention is drawn to the relationships between meanings and between people.[77] In other words, irony involves a textual level on which some disruption or unusual combination of elements seems to call for an explanation, and an intersubjective level on which the explanation, and therefore the very relationship between the utterer and interpreter, appears uncertain or problematic. As Hutcheon describes this relationship: "[I]rony is a 'weighted' mode of discourse in the sense that it is asymmetrical, unbalanced in favor of the silent and the unsaid. The tipping of the balance occurs in part through what is implied about the attitude of either the ironist or the interpreter: irony involves the attribution of an evaluative, even judgmental attitude."[78] Evaluation and judgment are highlighted because the ironic gesture throws into question the openness or sincerity of the relationship between utterer and interpreter. Irony is sometimes characterized as a form of intellectual detachment, "[b]ut the degrees of unease irony provokes might suggest quite the opposite. . . . There is an affective 'charge' to irony that cannot be ignored."[79]

Seen from the perspective of the interpreter, strategic anti-essentialism is one possible resolution of the problem presented by irony. If we judge a compositional decision to have been strategically anti-essentialist, we restore and stabilize the perceived contract between composer and listener, as seemed to occur in the general reception of *Trans*. Other 1980s albums seem to have remained for the most part in a problematic space and may therefore continue to suggest irony more strongly as an interpretation. The best candidates here would be *Old Ways, Everybody's Rockin',* and *This Note's for You*, because in each of these cases there is a high level of atypical genre experimentation. These kinds of obvious role playing and pastiche are exactly the kinds of differential strategies which Hutcheon suggests may lead interpreters to suspect an ironic attitude. The continued tendency for critics to marginalize these albums suggests that they present formidable problems with respect to Neil Young's overall authorial persona. In one sense, some of Young's 1980s projects go *beyond* irony and realize directly the fear of authorial disengagement which irony only suggests. If irony represents in part the interpreter's suspicion that the utterer has stepped back from the communicative contract, then Young's interviews of the later 1980s, in which he described much of this work as a deliberate attempt to hide his feelings and experiences, confirm the suspicion and collapse the irony. It would of course be too sweeping a generalization to suggest that such an event has taken place for all listeners. My intention is only to characterize the complex relationship between authorial persona, stylistic convention, and the desires of interpreters as engendered by Young's work in the 1980s.

One problem with the line of interpretation suggested above is that it seems far too heavy-handed. Most importantly, it is humorless. Is there another interpretive lens, then, which could shed additional light on the exaggerated style experiments of the 1980s without seeming quite as dire as those we have already tried? Could we, for example, call projects like *Everybody's Rockin'* or *Old Ways* instances of camp? On one level the connection seems tenuous, since the theory of camp has been most extensively developed in queer studies, and the practice of camp is often aligned with cultural spheres marked as queer or feminine, whereas the world of Neil Young is relentlessly coded as masculine and heterosexual. However, in a project like *Everybody's Rockin'*, Young flagrantly exaggerates clichés and displays a fluid balance between seriousness and play which does seem in some way campy. These projects are over the top in their theatricality. They seem to be premised on an absurdist, yet affectionate, foregrounding of their own conventions. From a queer theory perspective, camp can be understood as a reaction to a semiotic crisis, in which one must construct a position and a self-representation using the tools of a (straight) semiosphere where just about everything is potentially absurd or alien. What distinguishes camp from other strategies, for example irony or existential despair, is its theatricality, playfulness, and open affection for devalued means of expression.

In the mid-1970s, Neil Young experienced a personal crisis in his relationship to the conventions and institutions of rock music, and he expressed this crisis through overt theatricality and role playing. In these projects, the effect of the theatrical strategy was to highlight the crisis and to destabilize an expressive framework. Since there was little overt sense of playfulness or reinvestment in the devalued expressive resources (that came later, as a distinct career phase beginning with *Zuma*), there was nothing that could be called campy. In the 1980s, the situation was similar in that Young was again responding to a crisis in his expressive resources, but this time the strategy could be glossed as campy since it was based upon a playful restoration of creative energy to relatively devalued semiotic resources. Although this work is not queer under a narrow reading of the word, it is perhaps suggestive, given the implicitly heteronormative tone of most Neil Young reception, that the campier projects remain relatively unassimilated and continue to present problems of interpretation for listeners in ways that the mid-1970s work does not.

One effect of Young's rapid persona and style shifts in the 1980s was the occasional foregrounding of features that had been present but more tightly constrained in his earlier work. One example is humor, discussed briefly above. Another example would be politics and social commentary. We have already seen that in terms of race and gender, where Young develops explicit views at all, his perspective seems conservative. This was never much of an issue in Neil Young reception because Young's political statements were few and far between. Some of the early ones seemed consonant with a vague 1960s liberalism ("Southern Man") or an unspecific countercultural impulse ("Ohio"). In the 1980s and later, Young began to refer to political views in his lyrics with much greater frequency, but with no more clarity. The decade opened with his support of Ronald Reagan, a move toward country music, and songs such as "Hawks and Doves" in which he seems to inhabit a right-wing persona. However, despite his support for Reagan, Young was and is a vocal proponent of certain causes antithetical to the Republican perspective, most notably his involvement with the Farm Aid benefit concerts. He has also been a vocal opponent of both Bush administrations, and although he is not an ecological activist, he has written several songs expressing conservationist beliefs. These sorts of contradictions come most forcefully to light in the *Greendale* album, where Young seems to endorse stereotypes and values from both conservative and leftist branches of American politics.

We have seen that as early as the mid-1970s some critics were impatient with these ideological ambiguities in Young's work. However, it could be suggested that Young is simply an extreme example of the generally ambiguous nature of the rock-politics relationship. Although some accounts of the 1960s and 1970s place great emphasis on the belief that rock culture represented a politicized, anti-establishment movement, Grossberg argues instead that rock was never clearly oppositional to "the dominant liberal consensus or the major ideological assumptions (sexism, racism and classism) of that consensus."[80] Rock culture did, on average, celebrate a kind of mobility, but one which unfolded within a capitalist logic and in which any political views were usually by-products of an individualist ethos, rather than vice versa. Young's work mirrors this profile in at least two respects: first in its political ambiguity and second insofar as that ambiguity is the result of an essentially personal and individual approach to social issues. The same tendencies are evident in his relationship to the music industry. Young has on occasion described himself as a capitalist, and although a great deal of his work has flirted with commercial disaster an almost equal portion has seemed carefully designed and marketed for commercial success. He has on occasion written harsh condemnations of specific industry practices and yet has made no sustained efforts to work outside of the mainstream music industry. Indeed, although Young often speaks and writes about his relationship to the industry, he almost always does so in terms of personal relationships or questions of personal freedom. For example, recall that his reservations about the success of *Harvest* did not concern commercialism per se so much as they concerned the artistic and personal dangers of trying to recreate past successes. Young's comments of the period did not touch on any ethical feature of the music industry as an institution, but simply included it as one more factor which could limit his creative agency, along with static friendships and troubled romances. Similarly, songs such as "Surfer Joe and Moe the Sleaze," which implicitly critique music industry cultures, tend to focus on the personal failings of individuals rather than on systematic features.

I would suggest that individualism is the core social value in Young's work. Celebration of the individual has both conservative and liberal overtones, although in one case the individual is defined mostly in terms of self-reliance, and in the other mostly with respect to civic responsibility. In Young's case, individualism is in turn linked to an ideology of creative agency in which the artist's most important responsibility is to develop a singular viewpoint and to pursue this project with unwavering intensity. Although individualism is clearly not the only consideration here, it serves as one model of how a singularly pursued artistic instinct can lead in contradictory political directions. More generally, if we recall the central lyrical themes which seem to inspire the bulk of Young's work, some of them reinforce conservative values (a combative attitude toward disagreement, a longing for traditional heterosexual romance), whereas others seem more liberal (a deep sympathy for the underdog, aversion to violence, a suspicion of the profit motive). The tendency is for Young to project these general artistic themes into political discussions rather than to allow a fully conceived political program to minutely direct the art, and the result is a body of work which is sometimes passionately political, but never politically coherent.

Consolidation in the 1990s

In 1989, Neil Young returned to Reprise records and began to make albums which sounded more like his 1970s work. His commercial comeback began with *Freedom,* an album which, like *Rust Never Sleeps,* was split fairly evenly between acoustic and electric performances, and which lacked any confusing stylistic experimentation. Especially helpful was a rousing and memorable single, "Rockin' in the Free World," deliberately crafted as a rock anthem. The song also began to shift Young's political position in a more moderate direction, maintaining the theme of American patriotism but combining it with a critique of the social policies of the first Bush administration. Critical response to *Freedom* was generally one of pleasure and even relief. Many critics could again be seen to celebrate and canonize Neil Young in the present tense, effectively restarting the critical trajectory which had been stalled throughout the 1980s.

In the 1990s, Neil Young capitalized upon his "return" with a number of projects that returned to his classic themes and styles. In general, critics felt that these new projects were as good as the originals, if not better, and albums like *Ragged Glory* and *Harvest Moon* were perceived not as nostalgia pieces, but as creative revisitings of familiar themes.[81] Young in the 1990s also began to talk to the press far more than at any time before, always placing emphasis on the importance of live performance, the special chemistry of Crazy Horse, the importance of working by instinct rather than calculation, and his own unwillingness to follow trends or to be told what to do. For the most part, critics and fans in the early 1990s were happy to follow Young's lead and accept his assertions, although there were a few dissenting voices, such as Sutherland's argument that *Ragged Glory* seemed like a cynical concession to market demands.[82] Perhaps most noteworthy was Marsh's scathing, retroactive assessment of Young's career, especially since he had been one of Young's most prominent mid-1970s backers.[83] Nonetheless, for the most part Young retained artistic currency during the 1990s. In 1995, he collaborated briefly with the popular grunge band Pearl Jam. It had already been noted that Neil Young was an important influence on grunge musicians, and in the mid-1990s it became common to see Neil Young described as "the godfather of grunge." The 1990s also saw some of his most frankly experimental work. *Sleeps With Angels* was inspired partly by the suicide of Kurt Cobain, and Young refused to promote or tour the album, which features some arrangement techniques that represent a considerable departure for Crazy Horse. Even further afield, *Arc* is more *musique-concrète* than rock. Indeed, Crazy Horse performances throughout the decade became known for lengthy instrumentals in which distortion and extended playing techniques would considerably elaborate upon the aspects of "rock as pure sound" already noted in the *Zuma* era. Young's use of such techniques—a style which on the Rust list has been dubbed *grunge-jazz feedback*—is discussed in depth in chapter 3.[84]

Stylistic Incarnations, An Overview

At the start of this chapter, I identified two key themes in Neil Young reception: expressive intensity and stylistic diversity. A crucial task in the rest of this book will be to demonstrate relationships between the two through a theory of musical personas and a dialogic theory of style and genre. To prepare for that argument and to wrap up our overview of Young's career, I would like to summarize the particular ways in which Neil Young has deployed signifiers of various musical traditions. This discussion will be informal, not drawing directly on the more elaborate theory developed in later chapters. However, a few initial comments about terminology may be useful. Specifically, what kind of terms are the stylistic and generic labels so common in discussions of rock and closely related musics, words like "blues," "country," "folk," and so forth? In casual speech and in much journalistic writing, they are usually called styles and genres interchangeably. Since the terms are unavoidable and their nature is not obvious, it is necessary to clarify the sense in which I intend to use them.

If we look at how these words are actually used, we find that they have both taxonomic applications (asserting that a given piece of music is a token of a particular type) and also what may be called adjectival or adverbial applications, identifying features of the music without necessarily stipulating the piece as a token of the type usually associated with those features (e.g., funky without being funk). Additionally, they sometimes seem to refer mostly to textual features, but at other times serve as shorthand for social and/or historical categories and events. In other words, they are categories of social and institutional organization as well as linguistic categories. This makes such terms discursive in the full sense: they mediate the interactions between thought and action, individuals and institutions, serving as a source of both constraint and enablement. At least three things follow from this. First, the sense given to words like *style* and *genre* will be context-dependent. To mention just one consideration: when theorists of Western art music discuss stylistic and generic categories, there is usually little or no mention made of music industries, whereas when such terms are discussed by scholars of popular music, the role of these words as marketing tools is almost always highlighted. This is not only due to a difference in methodology between the scholars, but also to the more obvious and thoroughgoing commercial application of such terms in the twentieth century. Indeed, words like "rock" and "country" coevolved with the contemporary music industries. Theories of either kind will of course need to deal with economic questions and issues of marketing, but in different ways. Second, we should not assume that these terms form a hierarchical and consistent system, even though they are frequently used in contexts where hierarchy and systematicity are implied. As with all discursive categories, style and genre words are used in specific instances as if they correspond to a binding logic, but in fact their application is flexible and varies from case to case. To this degree, they are ideological. Finally, I suggest it is best to view style and genre categories as schemata for the interpretation and production of texts rather than as properties of the texts themselves. The full sense of *schema* will be discussed later, but for now we can note that it encompasses ideas of competency (both productive and interpretive) and also modes of description or categorization in a more general sense.

In later chapters, I will distinguish between *style* and *genre* to show how words such as "blues" or "rock" can in fact be used in either way. For the purposes of this chapter, however, it is better to treat such words as indicating musical *traditions*. A tradition is a complex social and textual category which includes stylistic and generic norms correlated to particular times, places, communities, ideologies, and events. I am treating traditions as discursive categories, but it is crucial to their character that they are generally used in a manner which claims a correlation to actual social configurations (a correlation which is in part actual, in part imagined or invented). The concept of tradition conveys an image of involvement and social production. When we speak of Neil Young mobilizing signifiers of particular traditions, we may be speaking of stylistic or generic codes on a variety of levels—musical, lyrical, behavioral, ideological, etc.—and we emphasize that he not only signifies a tradition in this way, but he brings himself into some kind of active relationship with it. Middleton uses the term *idiolect* in reference to the level of code which individuates a particular artist.[85] An idiolect mobilizes a variety of other levels of code, with genre being more general than idiolect, and individual works more specific. The advantage of thinking in terms of idiolect is similar to that of tradition: it involves specifying the textual details which implicate Young, as a social actor, in particular histories and communities. It draws attention to the manner in which discursive categories are both semantic and pragmatic. The discussion which follows can now be given a slightly more precise description: it seeks to show how Young's idiolect relies on reference to several distinct musical traditions.

Not all features represent their associated tradition to the same degree or in the same way. I would like to propose one distinction as especially pertinent to the case of Neil Young, the distinction between features I call *clichés* and those I call *typical features* of a tradition. Clichés are strongly and exclusively correlated to their tradition in the sense that, even if the feature appears elsewhere, surrounded by elements coded as belonging to other traditions, it will still function as a reference to its own tradition. An example would include certain vocal patterns which instantly evoke doo-wop, or Chuck Berry guitar licks which instantly evoke 1950s-era rock and roll, no matter what they are combined with. Typical features, by contrast, are an integral part of a tradition but are not unique to that tradition. They are salient and connote a tradition, but not as strongly and not as exclusively. For example, a central emphasis on acoustic guitars is a feature of some kinds of blues, some kinds of country, and also 1960s folk revivalism. As a result, the acoustic guitar in rock music has a range of associations, all of which are related, but in flexible ways. It is often the case that clichés tend to be specific configurations—for example, a particular riff or chord sequence or a particular kind of clothing—and typical features tend to be linked to more general kinds of resources—for example, poetic versus colloquial register in lyrics or the use of a certain instrument. The kind of signification possible using clichés is strong but shallow in that the cliché stipulates an object precisely, but it is an object already largely fixed in its associations and significance, and therefore shallow in that it leaves less room for further distinctive elaborations, while the signification possible using typical features is deeper but less definite. Finally, clichés and typical features have different relationships to the persona of the artist. At least as I read them, clichés make it more difficult to elaborate a singular and unique persona since they come with so many specific prior associations. An artist can construct a unique persona out of clichés, but there is always the feeling that the personal identity of the artist is being obscured. This appears to be the case for many rock listeners of the 1960s and 1970s, and we have already seen the concern about authenticity which arose in connection with Young's more extreme use of clichés. What I would now like to present is a selective discussion of some traditions Young has signified in his work, identifying those clichés and typical features which he has mobilized and commenting on how these have inflected his idiolect considered as a whole.

Folk Revival. Folk revival features mobilized by Young include the basic performing format (solo singer accompanying himself on guitar) and various harmonic and melodic features of folk and old-time musics, all of which are in evidence throughout his career. Young was never a folk revivalist as such. However, his early work in Winnipeg was notable partly for his interest in playing traditional folk songs in a rock band format. Several of his later songs display clear borrowings from traditional folk song paradigms ("Running Dry," "Captain Kennedy"),[86] and there are many typical features shared between folk revivalism and other traditions in which Young is more directly active (country music and singer-songwriter). Few of Young's performances are narrowly located in the folk revival tradition, and this tradition has not been a dominant one in his work at any particular time, but it remains an important background element in the idiolect.

Progressive Rock. There are a number of progressive rock features that have been mobilized by Young, especially in his earlier work. These include the use of symphony orchestra or orchestral instruments, large sectional forms with marked textural contrast between sections, and passages of linear, contrapuntal through-composition. Young's position with respect to these techniques is interesting because he in no way shares the high art pretensions common among many of the rock musicians who use them. His use of classical formal procedures and instruments is perhaps best described as cinematic—an extension of his interest in songs which relate to some kind of story line and of his involvement with filmmaking. In terms of his work with Crazy Horse, large sectional forms allow Young to explore the epic qualities of his particular brand of garage rock without straying from garage-like timbres, chord changes, and melodies. Young began experimenting with these techniques in the late 1960s, slightly after they were pioneered by artists like the Beatles and the Beach Boys and slightly before they were adopted by the progressive rock movement proper. His use of them remains tied to the earlier frame of reference. Young has never chosen an intensification of the symphonic approach as one of his stylistic directions. He has never abandoned these resources altogether, but he has shown no interest in extending his use of them, perhaps because such a direction would clash too strongly with his consistent emphasis on spontaneity. For all these reasons, Young's continuing relationship with complex and symphonic arrangements stands in an interesting tension with other aspects of his work.

Singer-Songwriter. Neil Young is one of the key figures in the creation of this tradition, along with artists like Bob Dylan, James Taylor, and Joni Mitchell. Early in his career, Young frequently presented himself as a singer-songwriter in terms of musical style, genre, personal image, and performance context. The singer-songwriter tradition was arguably dominant on the *Neil Young* solo album, and it continues to be important. However, despite his status as a singer-songwriter of sorts, Young has always distanced himself from the confessional tone common among others working in this tradition. While his lyrics often convey a general impression of intimacy and he has on occasion revealed the biographical subtext to some of this material, on the surface his songs give away little personal information. This double posture with respect to confessional lyrics was maintained by Young through the 1980s. *Trans* is deeply concerned with Young's adjustment to life with his son Ben, but the story is disguised and coded. More recently, beginning with *Harvest Moon,* Young has begun to record songs which are simply and clearly autobiographical ("One of These Days"), but he also continues to record songs which sit on the border between confession and obfuscation ("Music Arcade," "Slowpoke").

The singer-songwriter tradition has important relationships with other aspects of Young's work. As already noted, material of this kind is often conventionally coded as feminine, placing it in a complex and constantly changing relationship to the other main stream of his work, the masculine-coded garage rock of Crazy Horse. Additionally, there is a close relationship between the singer-songwriter tradition and the soft rock tradition, discussed below. Soft rock settings were typical for early singer-songwriter material, and much of Young's work reinforces this connection (especially on *Neil Young, Harvest, Comes a Time,* and *Harvest Moon*). In summary, the singer-songwriter tradition is an important reference point for Young. It has been active to varying degrees throughout his career, and it engages in complex relationships with other traditions. In fact I would suggest that the core of Young's idiolect—the part of his work which usually seems to be perceived by commentators as the "real" Neil Young—is largely characterized by an ongoing relationship between the singer-songwriter tradition and the garage rock tradition.

Garage Rock. Features of garage rock evident in Young's work include the instrumental lineup of Crazy Horse (two electric guitars, electric bass, and drums), the sonic texture emphasizing overdriven guitar amplifiers, the band's championing of technical limitations, and their emphasis on extended improvisations based on simple song forms. In addition, Crazy Horse is frequently *called* a garage band, and the staging of their tours has underscored this rhetorical move (especially the Rust Never Sleeps tour of 1978 and the Rusted Out Garage tour of 1986). However, it should be immediately noted that garage rock is a tradition which has largely been created in retrospect. Its current sense and status is due in large part to the influence of Jack Holzman and Lenny Kaye's

1972 *Nuggets* anthology and to the views of critics like Lester Bangs. As a result, the role and importance of mid-1960s garage bands was reinterpreted in the 1970s. In the mid- to late 1960s, many bands which are now thought of as garage bands aspired to become stars, but simply failed to do so. And it was not until the mid-1970s, with the punk movement, that groups with obvious technical limitations generally drew attention to the fact as a positive aesthetic value. Crazy Horse was never a technically sophisticated group, but these limitations were not *celebrated* until the mid-1970s, and it was not until the band had achieved commercial success that Young publicly eschewed such success.

The term *garage* is perhaps most commonly used to describe a particular economic and social niche. It connotes an amateur band, limited to a local scene, perhaps with aspirations for but little real hope of success. At certain times and in certain places, there have been typical repertoires for such a group. In the mid-1960s, this repertoire might include blues, British Invasion material, and instrumental rock. Neil Young and Crazy Horse material was a staple for 1970s garage bands, and still is for those of a rock persuasion. Despite the generic, stylistic, and repertorial features of garage rock bands, however, the tradition is defined as much by its economic and professional position as by anything else. In this sense, Crazy Horse is a simulacrum of a garage band. The romantic mythology of garage bands which arose by the mid-1970s allowed Crazy Horse to align itself with a certain kind of rock fundamentalism while at the same time making major contributions to the creation of that mythology. As Hicks notes, the image of the garage is a powerfully homosocial and marginal one, "a place of noise and alienation" which implies a distance from respectability, but also a sense in which garage bands "may have also seen themselves as a new musical elite—authentic practitioners of music on the cutting edge of an emerging culture."[87] While Crazy Horse could be seen as a garage band blown up to epic proportions, it could also be seen as a band which has always been of epic proportions and has helped to elevate garage rock to mythic status as a result.

In this connection, it is interesting to note how Crazy Horse has stretched beyond certain aspects of the tradition in ways that might be interpreted as bringing them closer to other traditions without ever losing touch with a basically garage identity. For example, their extended instrumental improvisations have never seemed to move into the territory of progressive rock, or heavy metal, or jazz-rock fusion, or any other tradition emphasizing extended instrumental passages. Their instrumentals have always been most akin to garage jams. Also, even though some Crazy Horse tours have featured extensive stage sets and props, these have never been theatrical in the manner of glam rock, or progressive rock, or heavy metal. They have been a lavish version of the kind of decorations common in amateur jamming spaces, or, on the few occasions where they have been too elaborate to be interpreted in this way, they have usually been explicitly constructed as surreal enlargements of garage rehearsal spaces. In summary, Crazy Horse relies on the garage rock tradition in three main ways: as an origin myth, an ideological orientation, and a source of theatrical inspiration.

Soft Rock. By soft rock, I mean music which is clearly tailored to a mass market through its intermediate tempos, intermediate dynamics, high production values, pop-like emphasis on melodic hooks and themes of romance, and aggressive marketing. Soft rock is, like garage rock, a fuzzy category at best. It can be applied to any music which displays connections to a form of rock but which is explicitly commercial and which downplays the elements of rock music sometimes perceived as abrasive. In the early 1970s, the term had a fairly precise referent in groups like the Eagles, who were perceived by many critics to be deliberately backing away from the radicalism of 1960s rock music toward a more adult, easy-listening style. However, the lines are easily blurred. For example, CSNY is considered soft rock by some listeners, but folk music by others. Similarly, while *Harvest Moon* is generally considered to be Young's most decidedly soft rock album, the case of *Harvest* is less clear. Historically, it was *Harvest* which brought Young his greatest early commercial success, and which caused him to worry about the possibility of becoming artistically irrelevant. *Harvest* also contained vocal contributions from soft rock icons James Taylor and Linda Ronstadt. But the album still incorporated some harder rock material ("Alabama") and some material with challenging lyrics on countercultural themes ("The Needle and the Damage Done"). As a final complication, it should be noted that while soft rock was, in the early 1970s, associated with commerciality, and while harder rock traditions during this period still had an air of opposition, by the 1990s the lines were no longer as clear. Although it is not common to see rusties or critics suggest that Young is operating from primarily commercial motives, when this accusation is made it is just as common to see it leveled against *Ragged Glory* and *Mirror Ball* as against *Harvest Moon.*

Soft rock is perhaps best understood as the union of (1) a particular set of stylistic and generic features with (2) the ascription by listeners of a primarily commercial intent. There are a number of qualities which might cause a listener to invoke the term: high production values, perceived lack of emotional intensity, perceived use of pop formulas, perceived avoidance of controversial or potentially difficult material in lyrics or music, and a clear marketing strategy aimed at a broad and perhaps older demographic. "Soft" is in many instances almost an accusation, not terribly different from "selling out." Thinking of soft rock as an attributed intention in addition to a specific set of features is especially useful in the case of Neil Young because he so freely moves between the clearly hard Crazy Horse stance and various degrees of softness. The gendered implications of this can be read from my earlier discussion of pop styles, since soft rock is said to be soft to the degree that it displays pop tendencies. At times, Young has been strongly aligned with a soft rock attitude. *Harvest Moon, Comes a Time,* and his continuing association with CSNY are the most commonly implicated here. At other times, he has mobilized a number of soft features while simultaneously refuting or contextualizing them. *Harvest* has already been discussed in this connection, and the first solo album could be placed in this category as well. Since all of Young's softer musical choices converge not just with commerciality, but also with other elements as outlined above, his softer material is usually perceived by rusties and critics as existing on a continuum with his other, more abrasive material. This coexistence of harder and softer material in Young's work is assisted by his frequent movement between the two, never giving the impression that he has left one or the other behind altogether.

Country Music. Many typical features of country as a general category have already been shown to overlap with folk revivalism, singer-songwriter, and soft rock. What I mean to point to with this category, then, is the use of outright clichés, such as the act of recording in Nashville, use of pedal steel guitar, use of established country session musicians in order to highlight their own idiolects, appearances on country-oriented TV shows like *The Johnny Cash Show* and *Austin City Limits,* the use of country-oriented fashion items (cowboy hats, leather vests, cowboy boots), and even something as subtle as Young's pride at owning one of Hank Williams's guitars. Country music has consistently been part of Neil Young's idiolect. Sometimes it has been present only in the form of very general associations, and sometimes it has been present in tight clusters of specific clichés. In other words, Young has always been a country-identified artist, sometimes only slightly and sometimes to the point where he has presented himself as a country artist in a complete and narrow sense. Most of the specific country clichés mobilized by Young are related to honky-tonk and the Nashville sound. In the early years, this was evident in songs like "The Losing End," his cover of "Oh Lonesome Me," his appearance on the Johnny Cash television show, and his decision to record *Harvest* in Nashville and to highlight the pedal steel guitar on that album. In the early years, however, these clichés were counterbalanced by other factors. For example, *Harvest* and *After the Gold Rush* were also strongly identified with the singer-songwriter tradition and with hard rock, as was *Everybody Knows This Is Nowhere.* Also, in this earlier period the specific Nashville clichés were combined with more general associations, overlapping with other related traditions. For example, Young's use of rural imagery and modified farm clothing, as well as instruments such as the banjo and folk-derived styles on the acoustic guitar, could be taken as referring to country music, or to old-time music more generally. The country association was invited through the use of the more specific clichés, but other elements prevented it from being the exclusive interpretation. Some of Young's comments at the time explicitly distanced him from the assumption that he was becoming a country artist as such. He was interested in the particular heritage of Nashville, but located this interest with respect to more general aesthetic considerations.[88]

In the 1980s, with the *Old Ways* album and his work with the International Harvesters, this situation changed. In these projects, Young adopted a pure Nashville country attitude on almost all levels and indeed presented himself *as* a country artist. This intensified use of country codes was interpreted by many critics as less sincere than his earlier, more ambiguous use of them. Many thought it was a joke, or deliberate role play, or were at least unsure on the question. This reaction was due in part to the timing of the move, coming as it did in the middle of Young's most intense period of generic and stylistic play, and hence a time of great confusion in general. The challenge of reading his mid-1980s country allusions is also complicated by Young's battles with Geffen records over the issue. Geffen's resistance to Young's country direction meant that no one could be sure to what degree Young was following his muse and to what degree he was just being stubborn. Whatever Young's feelings and intentions at the time, the more clichéd country direction of the mid-1980s seems in retrospect to be an anomaly. Country music continues to play a key role in Young's idiolect, but the proportions in the 1990s returned to those of the 1970s, country influences being carefully blended and juxtaposed with others.

The foregoing discussion has focused only on traditions which clearly form part of Young's idiolect. There are other traditions which he has at times referenced—especially electro-pop, stage band blues, and rockabilly —which for one reason or another seem more marginal. The reasons for this will be discussed in later chapters.

2 | Unlock the Secrets

Waywardness and the Rock Canon

Surprise is one of the central themes in Neil Young reception. This single word indicates a range of complicated factors: the nature of stylistic norms, the creation of expectation, and the construction of relatively stable or unstable authorial personas, among others. Surprise has in one way or another been associated with Young's work from the outset. The following passage from Holly George-Warren describes such an event:

> It was the fall of 1978 . . . [when] word got out that Young had embraced punk rock as much as I had. . . . To my horror—and surprise—this autumn eve the local FM DJ gleefully announced a preview of Young's upcoming "country-folk album." I had been hoping for feedback and shrieking guitars; instead I heard pedal steel and strings, as the soft sounds of *Comes a Time* came purring out of my VW Beetle's tiny speakers.[1]

The moment of surprise described here is less extreme than some—for example that which greeted the *Tonight's the Night* tour—but is equally central to the listening experience. The example is also interesting because it shows that Young can issue surprises from several different stylistic directions. In 1973, he surprised by being unpolished and rough, and in 1978 he surprised in precisely the opposite way. More importantly, George-Warren goes on to argue that surprises are integral to Young's aesthetic in general, that he has "defied categorization," and that as a result, "unlike any other artist, Young has traveled the often treacherous road from the Sixties to the Nineties, without ramming into a dead end."[2] Here we can see a complex intertwining of elements. Chief among these are the existence of stylistic and generic categories, which in turn play a key role in constructing Neil Young's authorial persona. Rather than tackle the concept of surprise in all its richness, this chapter focuses instead on a subtopic: the nature of stylistic and generic boundaries and the manner in which these provide relative stability or instability for Neil Young as an authorial presence. Specifically, this chapter develops a dialogic perspective on the nature of stylistic and generic categories. This line of interpretation will eventually allow us to describe metaphorical links between the particular natures of the various actors involved in musical practice, both those which are more virtual (styles and genres as described in this chapter, musical personas as described later in the book) and more literal.

George-Warren's reminiscence provides a fine example and summary of the way critics often assess Young's relationship to stylistic boundaries. The relationship is a double one. It includes a tendency to veer between extremes, but also the retrospective judgment that this has, taken on the whole, been an artistic strength. The same considerations, however, can lead to opposite conclusions. Marsh, for example, argues that Young is "less diverse than erratic, his stylistic charms the result of lack of commitment rather than successful eclecticism," and in the end concludes that "Young lacks the coherent, consistent world view that marks the greatest artists, in rock or anywhere else."[3] The unusual career trajectory followed by Neil Young has been described in chapter 1. An impressive range of traditions was touched upon during this journey, and it is this combination of a mercurial career path with an exceptionally wide range of stylistic experiments that has led to the kind of critical disagreement evident between George-Warren and Marsh. Neil Young has arrived at a complex position, by a complex path, and this is one reason he has been perceived as surprising and unpredictable. However, complexity in itself does not necessarily produce surprise. An artist could maintain these kinds of contradictions in a stable form, displaying richness but not change. The Grateful Dead did that for long stretches of their career, and a more recent provocateur like Eminem does it as well. We could even suggest that since the 1990s, Neil Young has done likewise. So we can ask: What mechanisms earlier in Young's career caused the tensions and contradictions in his work to achieve the extra feature of surprise? I would suggest that there are three primary considerations: Young's tendency to juxtapose rather than blend his various stylistic interests, his timing, and the nature of the traditions in which he works.

Young's unpredictability stems partly from his personality, or at least many critics see it this way. For example, Young's continual leaving and rejoining of Buffalo Springfield has often been taken to indicate a personal ambivalence toward stardom. More generally, Young began in the early 1970s to display an aversion to any form of typecasting. This emerges as an explicit interview theme around the time of *After the Gold Rush* and was already evident in his 1969 decision to sustain simultaneous involvement in CSNY and Crazy Horse. It was dramatically highlighted during his "dark period" of the mid-1970s and in the stylistic experiments of the 1980s. Constant movement between bands is also a major element of Young's career. With a few exceptions, such as the Crazy Horse *Sleeps with Angels* album, Young rarely takes a particular backing band in a new stylistic direction, preferring instead to change bands in order to change styles. And while some of his early albums displayed a wide range of styles (especially *After the Gold Rush* and *Harvest*), it is far more common for Young to produce albums which explore one particular aspect of his work in depth. As a result, sharp contrasts occur from project to project. These are not *necessarily* surprising, and by the 1990s many listeners had thoroughly absorbed some of these shifts as routine for Neil Young. However, any surprises which may be lurking will be highlighted by this sort of narrow focus from project to project.

Besides his involvement with a variety of groups and traditions, Neil Young has also been associated with changeability because of the roles he has played *within* each of his bands. In Buffalo Springfield, he created some of the group's most complex multi-section suites, but also some of their most direct rock songs. In the case of CSNY, the meaning of Young's involvement is complex because it changes whether one's frame of reference is within the band itself, in which case Neil Young represents an edgy and pessimistic foil to the rest of the group, or is cast wider, in which case CSNY as a whole represents an alignment with accessible commerciality, especially when compared to Crazy Horse. Similarly, within Crazy Horse there is a constant tension between Young's frequently stated desire to be just another member of the group and the obvious fact that Crazy Horse is in some senses a backing band. In all of these ways, Neil Young's complex roles within various bands provide ample scope for reversals and changes.

Another source of surprise has been Young's frequent divergence from the expected work cycle of a rock star. As Shuker describes it, the usual organization of the rock work cycle involves "creating and working-up new material for performance, studio recording and touring, and once again back to creating and recording to keep the momentum going."[4] There are many variations within this basic pattern, but it was common enough in the 1970s that it formed a core expectation of what a rock performer would do next. Neil Young has frequently disrupted this expectation. He often changed previously announced release dates, sometimes altering an album considerably in the meantime or even releasing something else altogether. As a result, no one was entirely sure when the next Neil Young record was really coming out or what kind of record it would be. Also, Young frequently embarked on seemingly incongruous tours, for example the tour of *Tonight's the Night,* which substantially preceded the release of the album, or the solo acoustic U.S. tour following the release of *Trans.* The expected tour format for such an album, a full band, was presented in Europe only.

Perhaps more interesting than all of these factors, however, is the manner in which Neil Young has been positioned relative to the very nature of stylistic boundaries in rock, his basic stance with respect to territories of sameness and difference. It is this aspect of his work that I would like to consider in depth. In order to do so, it is first necessary to present some theoretical remarks about genre, style, and tradition. These do not constitute a theory as such, but are meant to shed some light on the relationship between stylistic boundaries and authorial personas.

A Dialogic View of Genre, Style, and Tradition

As I argued briefly in chapter 1, it is difficult to provide definitions for terms like *genre* and *style,* since these discursive categories were evolved in practice in many different contexts rather than invented. It was suggested that we may wish to treat them not as textual properties but as schemata for the production and interpretation of musical utterances, and that the question of historicity is of crucial importance here. My principal interest in discussing these terms is not to draw fine distinctions between style, genre, and tradition in Neil Young's work, but only to suggest their dynamic properties as one step toward a dialogic theory of their social entailments. As has been amply demonstrated in popular music studies, style and genre are not just textual categories, but are tools of identity formation and of self-performance. This observation has served to make the study of musical style a central part of sub-cultural studies overall, and while much of value has emerged from the approach, a limitation in some of this work has been the manner in which complex and subtle features of actual texts have become reduced to simple signifiers of broad social concepts. By contrast, recent theories which treat musical works as sites for the production of highly nuanced virtual personas (discussed in chapter 4) provide a more flexible link between textual detail and identity politics, making a metaphorical social actor of the text itself. Under this description, a musical style, genre, or tradition is not just a passive tool of identity politics, but is a dynamic and at times truculent entity with which composers and listeners continually negotiate. The resulting picture may appear bizarre from a literal standpoint, but it is highly effective in illustrating the dynamics which unfold between the identities of texts and the identities of those who make or use them. A full discussion of exactly what I mean by *identity* will have to wait for chapter 4, where I develop a theory of musical personas. For the time being, it should just be noted that the interpretive moves made in this chapter—the emphasis on energetic and spatial metaphors, the attention to the social entailments of generic categories, the use of dialogism as a fundamental mode of description—all anticipate and lay groundwork for this theoretical stance.

The first step was taken in chapter 1, when I argued that general terms such as *style* or *genre,* and more specific terms like *rock* or *blues* or *funk,* do not refer directly to textual features, or even to complexes of textual and sociological features, but rather to schemata which organize practices of interpretation and production. Further, we can note that the concept of a schema relates closely to that of linguistic or semiotic competency. Hatten has defined style in general as a competency in this sense: one which involves a repository of types, and a grammar, but also which "balances constraints with productive principles."[5] My formulation aims to be consistent with this approach, but I will suggest that genres too, in addition to styles, can be described as forms of competency, so that the distinction between style and genre rests with the kind of activity performed by each. Recall that a problem facing the discussion of chapter 1 was quite basic: should words like *rock* be considered genre categories, stylistic categories, or something else? In that earlier discussion, I treated them as signifiers of traditions and pointed out that the same terms could indicate styles, genres, or traditions, depending on their use. It may be helpful at this point to clarify that suggestion before proceeding to a more exploratory discussion of dialogism. Here are a few tentative definitions. Keep in mind that these have been designed to work for discussions of popular musics in North America during the twentieth century. They may work less well for other traditions, although many of the basic ideas will be portable.

I will use the term *style* to mean a conventional or otherwise familiar pattern in structural organization, interpreted as the correlate and distinctive mark of a specific productive context (e.g., of an individual author, a school or movement, a historical or geographical location). Style could also be understood as that component of musical competency concerned with producing and recognizing consistent tendencies in structural organization and interpreting these as marks of origin. There is something personal about style—people and communities *have* their styles—which is not usually present in concepts of genre. I will use the term *genre* to mean a schema for grouping and producing works according to their social function, or according to their expressive and topical features. Genre could also be understood as that component of musical competency concerned with matching stylistic features to social functions and expressive narratives. I will use the term *tradition* to mean a complex discursive category which correlates bundles of generic and stylistic features with specific social groups, places, and histories. Like style, there is a crucial attributive element to traditions; the part they play in individuating people, places, times, and groups is a basic part of their function.

Since these are interpretive and productive schemata rather than fixed properties, the distinction between them is a matter of the description under which a work is placed. For example, the guitar riff at the beginning of "Cinnamon Girl" could be placed under the following descriptions: (i) a loud, distorted riff, with a distinctive start-stop rhythmic design (a stylistic description); (ii) an upbeat gesture to get the song off to a memorable and optimistic start (a generic description); (iii) a song which helped establish Neil Young and Crazy Horse as leaders in 1970s garage rock, and which arguably exerted influence on grunge music in the 1980s and early 1990s (a tradition-oriented description). These descriptions are of course interrelated. For example, the correlation of this sound with garage rock could be part of the stylistic description, and also the tradition-oriented one. Also notice that the same term can function in all three ways. *Blues,* for example, may be used to describe a set of structural tendencies (a style), an affective dialectic between despondency and redemption (a genre), and a specific set of histories (traditions). When an all-purpose term is needed to refer to the set of such categories as a whole, I will say *style/stylistic* if the issue is one of textual detail, and *tradition/traditional* if the issue is one of involvement in lineages, but the fluidity of the boundaries makes this choice somewhat arbitrary. The rest of this chapter, and the entirety of chapter 4, is concerned with further developing the implications of a view under which stylistic, generic, and tradition boundaries are schemata rather than properties, and are not only correlated with specific identities but are deeply implicated in the creation and perpetuation of those identities. With this in mind, I will now move to discuss the specific dialogic viewpoint that will take our discussion back to the specifics of Neil Young.

Boundaries between traditions, styles, and genres are both permeable and perspectivally specific. Any two listeners may display striking differences between their concepts of these boundaries. Styles, traditions, and genres also change frequently, and indeed it is part of their function to provide a basis from which to innovate and test boundaries. However, despite this fluidity, such categories play a powerful role in the structuring of musical practices, providing a shared set of coordinates and a sense of stability. Within popular music studies, in an effort to describe genres with respect to their social function, Walser has borrowed the phrase *horizon of expectations.*[6] The phrase is most closely associated with Jauss, for whom it refers to the ontologically mixed network of expectations (literary, institutional, and so forth) against which new works gain their meaning. Walser's application of the concept is different, since Walser emphasizes the manner in which expectations are applied by individual listeners in practice (whereas for Jauss, the horizon was more closely associated with broader institutional and social expectations). Under Walser's formulation, which he suggests is Bakhtinian in spirit, one could even think in terms of personal horizons of interpretation which would be mobile and specific to individual interpreters, but still defined partly in terms of how they represent a version or inflection of collective, trans-personal discursive categories. This formulation takes into account both the structured, shared nature of genres and styles and their mode of existence as a mobile frame of reference. Such an approach, rooted in practice theory and dialogism, is especially appropriate to the study of Neil Young. Besides highlighting the dual face of genres and styles—fluid and stable, collective and individual—a dialogic theory can emphasize the importance of personal perspective and identity without collapsing into an atomistic view of the subject. Identity is relevant not only because genres, styles, and traditions are the locus of so much social and emotional investment. Identity is also important because these terms *themselves* have identities and social lives. They have histories, personalities, and a quasi-agency of their own.

The personality of any given genre or style comes in part from its prior associations with people, histories, places, and ideas. This is true not just of genres and styles as composite types, but also of any recognizable feature in a piece of music. Even unusual features will have strong connotations. Because of this, each element in a piece of music carries its own cluster of voices, each a kind of autonomous persona, and the piece of music as a whole becomes a dialogue between these voices. Which is all to say that any musical utterance is in fact *inter*musical. This perspective has been developed in detail by Monson, who argues that the idea of intermusicality allows us to highlight the ways in which "sound itself can refer to the past and offer social commentary," and that musical quotations or allusions can construct meaning "in a relational or discursive rather than an absolute manner."[7] Zak makes a similar point when he notes that "the set of qualities that define a musician's recorded persona are immediately evoked by the lexicon of commonly understood musician references, such as the 'Duane Eddy guitar sound,' or the 'John Bonham drum sound.' Each of these refers first of all to a combination of a performance style and a recorded sound, and secondly, is a reference to a group of specific works and a broader musical style."[8] The dialogic relationships are bi-directional, then, with proper names serving in some cases to indicate broad styles, and with broad styles frequently being correlated to particular individuals or communities.

When I speak of a *voice* in this context, I have in mind the presence of a person or community—a specific history—summoned into discursive activity through details of the text. I use the term *voice* rather than something more neutral, perhaps *correlate*, in order to indicate that once a specific history is evoked, it exerts influence on the ongoing negotiation of meaning in a manner which Monson has called "relational or discursive," and which I refer to as quasi-agential, or virtually agential. When stylistic features evoke people and communities, it can feel as if we are negotiating with those people themselves, or, put another way, those elements of the text correlated to the specific people seem to behave as if they themselves were living extensions of those people. I am of course speaking metaphorically and describing the end product of a complicated process, but the illusion can at times be striking. An advantage of the dialogic perspective is that it does not require us to separate or choose between the formal structure of a text and its social life, but rather it highlights the manner in which formal features of a text embody social histories and interactions and in which social practices acquire and deploy relatively stable textual signifiers. In a general sense, this can underwrite the interesting *conflation* of textual identities and "real" identities crucial to the authorial persona of a mass-media figure like Neil Young. This conflation, and its specific implications for music theory, will be further considered in chapter 4.

Monson acknowledges that intermusicality is an extension of Kristeva's concept of intertextuality. While she does not discuss Kristeva's work to any extent, it is worth noting an important link between the manner in which Monson uses the concept and Kristeva's original formulation. For Kristeva, intertextuality is not a simple relation of quotation or allusion between texts in a formal sense, but rather a fundamental process of the unconscious by which the transposition of an utterance from one text to another, or from one signifying system to another, produces a corresponding shift in the enunciatory position of the speaking subject.[9] For this reason, intertextuality has a strong effect on the formation of subjects and identities and is in this sense involved in both the quasi-agency of genres and styles and in the more literal agency of musicians and listeners as well. Monson does not develop the idea along these psychoanalytic lines, but she achieves a similar result by developing the link between intermusicality and Bakhtin's model of *centripetal* and *centrifugal* forces of language, the former being "forces of centralization, unification . . . and standardization," the latter being "forces of decentralization, disunity, and competition among multiple social voices."[10] Every utterance, which includes every text, will be an unstable mixture of such forces, with "aspects that affirm the general category and those that are highly particular to the moment."[11] I liken this formulation to Kristeva's psychoanalytic concept of intertextuality because in both cases it is the coherence and relative position of a speaking subject which is at issue, and in both cases the relevant forces are forces not only of the psyche, but also of subjectivity and social structure more generally. The alignment is not incidental, as Kristeva deliberately modeled much of her early work on Bakhtinian concepts.

For the purpose of discussing Neil Young, the only thing I would add to Monson's formulation is to emphasize the nested nature of the hierarchy. In the case of Neil Young, it makes sense to cast *rock* as the overarching category, exerting a centripetal pull on its various subtraditions, and to cast the subtraditions—for example punk, rockabilly, country, and blues—as the particular, destabilizing forces. In general, any given voice is not inherently centripetal or centrifugal. Indeed, the whole notion of voice or persona may imply a balance between centripetal forces (those necessary to give it some coherence) and centrifugal forces (those which allow for individuation and relative autonomy). A voice, and the tradition it represents, will function in one way or the other depending upon context, and as we will see, the ability of any given tradition to exert either a centripetal or centrifugal force, or both at the same time, is a key element in Neil Young's unique approach to style and persona.

The term which summarizes this perspective, synthesizing the idea of intermusicality with the model of centripetal and centrifugal forces, is *dialogism.* No genre, style, authorial persona, or piece of music can exist without reanimating all the voices implicit in its raw material, and in turn activating the play of centripetal and centrifugal forces implicit in those voices. So music is always a kind of dialogue. This viewpoint can be extended to include the persona of the musician. The creative persona is plural. It possesses a uniqueness and a kind of singularity, but one made up of a dialogue between many other voices. In a situation like this, there are no completely stable or fully defined traditions or authorial personas; they are always falling under the influence of centrifugal forces. However, there is often the *desire* for stability and identity—a centripetal desire—and there are social interests and forces which work to construct these. A dialogic theory can emphasize the togetherness of disparate voices and interests in a situation or a text. However, in discussing any kind of subject formation, it is important to stress that the process proceeds by both inclusions and exclusions, attractions and repulsions. Dialogism involves not only the inclusion of multiple voices, but also an element of distancing and othering. Still and Worton have emphasized that any intertextual reference is "inevitably a fragment and displacement," and that "every quotation distorts and redefines the 'primary' utterance by relocating it within another linguistic and cultural context." [12] The concept of dialogue, likewise, is founded not just on the presence of one text or voice within another, but equally on their mutual exteriority. The other is included, but is constituted as other in the first instance partly through that very inclusion. The pertinence of this to Neil Young's position in rock and related traditions should be immediately clear. A characteristic strategy of Young's is to make use of established stylistic clichés in order to simultaneously assert his place in a tradition, but also his autonomy from that tradition. Each of his stylistic references simultaneously includes the other style and holds it at a distance, underscoring the double-voicedness common to all utterances.

Throughout my discussion of dialogic interpretation, the primary focus is on moments and strategies in which an apparent unity is constructed and maintained not only despite but by means of dialogic forces. By adopting such a perspective, it is possible to discuss apparent unities without reifying them and without losing sight of their inherent dynamism. A dialogic approach similar to my own has been proposed by Korsyn, but our perspectives differ in that Korsyn seems to want to decenter apparent unities of text and subject to a greater degree than I feel is practical, at least when talking about rock cultures. Korsyn argues that dialogic analysis must "reverse the priorities of traditional musical analysis" since attention to heterogeneity makes it impossible to "secure the boundaries of an autonomous, self-identical text." [13] I would fully agree that apparent unities and totalities need to be properly contextualized, denaturalized, and even deconstructed. However, I do not feel that dialogic forces, per se, guarantee the dissolution of these ideological and perceptual effects. A dialogic approach can make us aware of the play of forces out of which texts and personas and subjectivities emerge, and it can even help us to view those apparent unities in their proper light as internally contradictory moments in a changeable situation. However, the analysis and contextualization of such effects does not make them vanish, and more importantly, it does not necessarily diminish their force in discursive practice. My personal interest in using dialogic methods of interpretation is to emphasize the manner in which texts, personas, and subjectivities function as multi-layered homeostatic systems, generally rebalancing themselves, albeit with frequent transformations.

Under the dialogic description, one way of characterizing Neil Young surprises would be to say that these are moments where intermusicality is highlighted. Not every utterance draws attention to its own intermusicality. In order to create the impression of a strong authorial presence—which requires that everything point back to itself, centripetally—the inherent multi-vocality of the utterance is sometimes obscured. In much of Neil Young's work, however, attention is drawn to the play of voices within the work and to the centrifugal potential implicit in every utterance. The impression of a single, coherent author is allowed to weaken, as we can see in the many instances where unexpected stylistic changes were met with the complaint that Young had lost his way, or that he was burying his true self under personas. From a dialogic point of view, there is no charade, or lack, or loss of direction here, but rather a clear presentation of the multiplicity that is always lurking under the surface of every utterance.

That might not be quite the right way to say it, though. Putting it that way almost makes Neil Young sound postmodern, and I would argue instead that he is an arch-modernist in a sense typical of 1960s rock ideology. When in 1983 Neil Young suddenly dressed and sang like a rockabilly artist, for example, previous assumptions about his persona were shaken by the force of this other voice. And yet this moment occurred as part of an utterance made by Neil Young himself, and so a play of alterity and assimilation was set up. When we look at Neil Young reception in the long term, we see that very often this kind of surprise is reabsorbed into a newly stabilized persona. After a while, intermusicality was no longer a destabilizing factor, but became a fixed part of Neil Young. He was *expected* to surprise, and his stylistic diversity was taken as a mark of authorial integrity. There are numerous examples of critics making such interpretive moves (some discussed in chapter 1), all of which nicely display the fine balance between centripetal and centrifugal forces in Young's work, and the manner in which, for the most part, critics have tended to emphasize and reinscribe the centripetal ones.

The Stylistic Family of Rock

In the realm of genre and style, closeness and distance are changeable and relative quantities. However, certain styles and genres share special kinships. For example, there is a cluster of styles which I will call the *stylistic family of rock.* This family includes antecedent musics such as r & b and country as well as the many subtraditions that at any given time form the unmarked core of the family, and also decedents like punk. The concept of *unmarked core* should be used with caution, since every tradition displays a variety of specific incarnations and sometimes these compete for recognition as the principal representative of the tradition overall, as in east coast and west coast rap in the mid-1990s. Nevertheless, there is an important sense in which some musics will as a rule be unproblematically accepted as solidly and clearly part of a particular tradition, especially when compared to other musics which cannot even be considered as candidates for centrality. Some factors that can draw traditions into such a family relationship include hybridization, historical lineages, and stylistic or generic similarity. These are all centripetal forces which can allow an umbrella tradition such as rock to exist and to incorporate many subtraditions into itself. By *incorporate into,* I mean in part that when clichés or typical features of a subsumed subtradition are used in a piece of music, they do not seriously threaten the categorization of that piece as a member of the larger family. More specifically, the subtraditions are represented and understood as components of the larger family and not as autonomous centers of their own. But while centripetal forces hold traditions together, there are always centrifugal forces pulling in the other direction. Part of the reason for this lies in intermusicality. Each of the subtraditions subsumed under rock, and pointing toward it as a center, are also relatively autonomous, with different histories and other possibilities, and consequently with a tendency to draw toward other centers. Country music, for example, can be made to seem part of rock music, but it is also a relatively autonomous tradition of its own. The presence of country within rock is perched between the centripetal force of the rock family and the centrifugal force exerted by other views of country, in which it is not part of rock.

To come back to Neil Young, we can argue that the strong country inflections evident in his early work—for example, "The Losing End" on *Everybody Knows This Is Nowhere* or the cover version of "Oh Lonesome Me" on *After the Gold Rush,* and even subtler features such as the pedal steel guitar throughout *Harvest* or the fact that the album was recorded in Nashville—are kept in check by the overall image presented by Neil Young at the time and by the other kinds of material on the records. Textually, the country references did not predominate, and in terms of persona, there were still more rock star components to Neil Young than there were country clichés. It was not generally surprising to critics that Young should display a relationship to country music in this way, and the lack of surprise is partly because the potentially centrifugal force of country music was being held in check insofar as the bulk of textual and contextual features framing these country moves were linked to the California rock counterculture, and the folk-rock and garage traditions of music.

As with Young's use of the blues, discussed earlier, the process of keeping country references in check is not politically neutral. Fairly or not, country music in the late 1960s tended to be associated with conservatism of a sort frequently assumed disagreeable to the California rock counterculture from which Young first emerged. Young would often toy with the boundaries of countercultural ideology, for example when he said in a 1970 interview: "[If there's a revolution], I'll be in Big Sur with my guns. . . . I'll get a big cannon if they're gonna have a revolution. I'll sit up on top of my studio there with my material gains after the game, and, uh, contemplate my future."[14] At that time, Young's careful treatment of country signifiers could be seen as a part of his careful management of an insider-outsider relationship to hippie ideology more generally. The fact that most rock critics seemed unsurprised by Young's country moves might be taken to suggest that he managed this balance successfully. By contrast, many commentators *were* surprised when Neil Young presented unadulterated country music in the 1980s. Country music was a part of Neil Young from the start, and it did not always threaten the stability of his persona. This point was made at the time by a few critics, for example Christgau, who wrote, "Warners is touting *Old Ways* as [Neil Young's] country move. . . . [But] Neil has been making country moves ever since he put 'Oh Lonesome Me' on *After the Gold Rush*."[15] Nonetheless, many critics saw the album as surprising and unexpected. Country music was not a new element in Young's work, but a change in emphasis or timing or context can lead to a situation in which certain elements seem suddenly ready to fly away from the category of which they have always been a part. The centrifugal potential of country was actualized in this case. And again, there is an interesting correlation between the stylistic features of Young's 1980s country music and his social positioning of the time. Not only did his work during this period use a far greater number of country clichés, alongside a relative disuse of his established 1960s and 1970s rock style, but Young also chose to publicly announce his political support for Ronald Reagan. It should not be suggested that this linkage of intensified country style with intensified right-wing politics is natural (although it *is* naturalized), but rather that Young's decision to mobilize both of them simultaneously tended to play into established stylistic stereotypes and therefore to emphasize centripetal rather than centrifugal forces, and in particular, it flipped the balance between the competing centripetal forces of rock and country as they had been established in Young's earlier work.

Each of Young's 1980s experiments can be read in this way, as a surprisingly direct statement of a tradition which was always present in his work, but not usually foregrounded or left without counterbalances. With the possible exception of electro-pop, and to a slightly lesser degree rockabilly, in none of these cases was a major new stylistic element added. Even rockabilly and electro-pop were not entirely unprecedented. Although these traditions in their stereotypical forms were absent from Young's earlier work, he had from the outset established a clear interest in both technological experimentation and roots musics. So while these traditions were stylistically incongruous, they were not entirely foreign to the spirit of his pre-existing work. Instead, centrifugal elements present in his work all along became overt rather than latent. Which is not to say that there was no tension in the earlier work; the concept of latency does not mean that intertextual relationships are entirely without effect. The richness of a text like *Everybody Knows This Is Nowhere* derives partly from the play of centrifugal and centripetal forces, even if that play of forces is latent in the sense of not provoking a crisis of tradition attribution or of authorial coherence. As suggested in the readings of blues and country clichés offered earlier, latency may sometimes be a sign of an underlying social power negotiation, mostly suppressed or closely managed but still able to inject considerable energy into the reception of a work. From this perspective, we can see why Neil Young can be surprising and can seemingly move outside of his pre-established stylistic profile without in the end being anything but a rock musician. The key to being surprising while nonetheless remaining within a single tradition is to find the centrifugal forces implicit in that tradition. A tradition like country or rockabilly is admitted to the rock family for historical and stylistic reasons, but from the perspective of rock they are captive traditions, to the point that their presence is often masked altogether.

If you emphasize them enough, you can seem to be moving beyond the traditional envelope of rock music, but from another perspective it would be more accurate to suggest that you are simply drawing attention to the centrifugal forces that gave rock its identity in the first instance.

How is it that a stylistic family like rock can both contain and not contain particular subtraditions? Why do traditions like country and pop exist as insider-outsiders to rock? One important factor lies in the manner in which traditions compete with and supplant one another over time. Within a large stylistic family, at any given moment, the member traditions will have differing status, depending partly on their place in the history of that family. Some will constitute, for the moment, the unmarked core. Others will be ancestors, and for that reason marginalized. We can use the term *supplanted* family members to refer to marginalized ancestors. Other subtraditions will be newly emerging as destabilizing factors, working to change the tradition from within. These subtraditions are often *supplanters,* turning the central subtraditions into dated ancestors. Interestingly, Neil Young does not display a consistent pattern of identifying with either marginalized or central subtraditions. And when identifying with marginalized subtraditions, he splits his time between the supplanters and the supplanted. His punk and electro-pop moves, for example, can be seen as siding with supplanters, but his roughly contemporaneous rockabilly phase was a vote for the supplanted. Over the course of his career, Neil Young has aligned himself with both the past and the future of rock music, and in this way he is constantly repositioned at its center.

Neil Young, the Rock Canon, and the Death of Rock

The manner in which Neil Young plays with these sorts of possibilities has given him a distinctive kind of persona. This persona is simultaneously mobile and stable, and with respect to rock music broadly defined, simultaneously critical and celebratory. Neil Young pushes the tensions and contradictions of rock from the inside, but in the end always proselytizes for its aesthetic and social virtues. This puts him in sharp contrast with artists like Roger Waters or Frank Zappa, who have also launched internal critiques of rock but without the corresponding return to celebration. Neil Young questions rock in a manner which ultimately reaffirms its core myths, and during both the late 1970s and early

1990s—the periods following his two great phases of experimentation—Neil Young fully embraced the role of rock icon. We could also suggest that Young's 1980s experiments represented a less profound threat to rock ideology since these experiments were of a stylistic kind, concerned with formal detail more than with the affective or topical associations of the material, whereas the mid-1970s experiments were more generic, attaching as they did powerful images of abjection to familiar rock styles. Despite their differences, however, the timing of the career resurgences following each of these periods is interesting in that it corresponds to two periods in which the "death of rock" was being declared with special intensity by some critics and academics.

There are many centripetal forces at work in cultural practices. In terms of music, perhaps the most important is the nearly universal tendency to make value judgments, and for those judgments in many cases to lead to the formation of canons. Certainly, some figures in rock music have been canonized in that there is a loose consensus among critics that these artists are somehow important. The process of rock canonization arguably began with the first generation of professional rock critics in the late 1960s—some of whom, most notably Greil Marcus, are still actively developing and reinscribing their influential canonical values—and continues into the present generation of critics and listeners. But it must be noted that the qualitative profile of rock canonization has shifted from a celebration and validation of emerging potentials in the 1960s to a more curatorial and historicist flavor in the 1990s and 2000s. As Shaar-Murray has noted, "the offspring of the people who were behaving badly in the sixties are doing exactly what their parents did not do: take on a previous generation's tastes. . . . The consensus seems to be that the sixties represented the Golden Age of pop."[16] Neil Young is frequently cited as a participant in this golden age, and this is an aspect of his career with which he appears to be uncomfortable. By examining the process of canon formation, we are examining a dynamic that has been key to Neil Young's work and reception: the delicate balance between constructing a hagiography on the one hand and attempting to escape or relativize it on the other.

Canon formation is an extremely common occurrence, and although it is generally accepted that the Western art music canon as we know it was largely an invention of the nineteenth century, canons are common in most forms of Euro-American music.[17] This is especially true when we consider that canons are not only, or even primarily, collections or tabulations. More fundamentally, they are processes of valuation which "[tend] to promote the autonomy character, rather than the commodity character, of musical works."[18] As Samson notes, in recent years among scholars of a culturalist bent "the canon has been viewed increasingly as an instrument of exclusion, one which legitimates and reinforces the identities and values of those who exercise cultural power."[19] And while Samson observes that conservative critics such as Bloom and Steiner continue to insist upon a notion of greatness and intrinsic value—as have rock critics since the 1960s—for most cultural theorists this makes canons even more dubious, not less so.

An even more subtle critique of the effects of canonization has been offered by Tomlinson. With respect to present-day recountings of Renaissance music, which tend to pay the closest attention to figures who can be understood as prefiguring later trends in European music, Tomlinson notes that "we have lost the ability to hear less familiar voices."[20] Perhaps even more pressingly, we may also be losing the ability to hear the well-known voices in all their richness, given our tendency to "conflate much of the distance that properly should separate them from us."[21] This could be profitably juxtaposed with Shaar-Murray's observations about the exceptionally long period in which 1960s musicians have seemed to remain current. "We exist in a grotesquely distended cultural *now* which stretches from here (my current *now* is April '89, but the principle remains the same) back to the early sixties."[22] The pseudo-currency of canonized 1960s rock artists has, in Shaar-Murray's view, led to an oversimplified and commodified understanding of their work. In the case of both Shaar-Murray and Tomlinson, a certain kind of canonization is being criticized because it robs the artwork of complexities and of its alterity, which are essential to participation in a genuine dialogue. This can be seen as a large-scale projection of the disempowering effects of typecasting and audience expectation frequently complained about not just by Neil Young but by many other artists as well.

In the early years of the field, and still today, it was thought by some that popular music studies would be an area that must inevitably challenge the habits of canon formation entrenched in the study of art musics. Certainly, the serious study of popular music requires that different processes of valuation be employed and different artists be celebrated.[23] However, the underlying tendency toward fixing value judgments into canons is just as strong in popular music traditions as anywhere else. Within popular music studies, there are scholars who feel comfortable with the formation of canons and whose work reinforces existing popular music canons or argues for new ones, and there are other scholars who continue to be wary of canon formation as an exclusionary and elitist project. When writing about an artist like Neil Young, the problem becomes pressing. My own inclination is to distrust canons when they become inflexible or absolute, but to honor the central role played by judgment and taste in musical life. This not only reflects my own views, but it is also an appropriate stance to take in the case of Neil Young, given his clearly ambivalent feelings about rock stardom and mythmaking. If Frith is correct to suggest that most fans (and certainly most critics) make evaluation a central part of their musical meaning-making, then these evaluations must be acknowledged as a valid part of the culture under analysis.[24] However, it remains important to examine them as contingent and situated discursive practices, subject to constant revision.

It seems clear that by the 1990s, and probably earlier, no rock tradition could sustain easy access to the myths of heroism and rebellion, authenticity and individuality that have marked much of the music since the mid-1960s. These central myths have been seriously challenged, and their claim to constitute a mainstream of popular musical taste, assuming that it ever had any validity, is largely a thing of the past. The challenge is partly symbolic, arising out of the increased importance of other popular music traditions since the 1980s, and partly economic, as the market share of rock continues to decline. According to many critical and academic narratives, the rock era "is a period that starts with the emergence of rock-'n'-roll in the middle of the 1950s and which then 'progresses' through various significant moments or stages until it ends with punk rock in the 1970s."[25] However, as Negus suggests, this is a partial and somewhat misleading viewpoint. "The idea of the 'rock era' involves a particular way of disrupting the dialogues with the past. It entails placing specific boundaries across ongoing musical activities."[26] The most general definition available of rock music comes from Grossberg, who described rock as a technology for empowerment within daily life.[27] In Grossberg's view, rock pretends to be other than ordinary life without actually challenging the structures of ordinary life. In fact it exists within and depends upon them. However, rock is *affectively* oppositional to the boredom of everyday life. "It challenges the particular stabilities or territorializations of the everyday life within which it exists by producing and celebrating mobilities."[28] In order to do this, rock makes use of a wide variety of myths, engaging discourses of gender, power, class, fantasy, virtuosity, and many others. In the case of Neil Young, the idea of mobility is especially pertinent, as is his underlying cynicism regarding its ultimate efficacy. The ability to surprise depends upon the ability to deterritorialize existing stylistic possibilities, rendering them mobile. Or, to use the argument presented earlier in this chapter, to make evident a mobility which they always possess but which is frequently masked. Grossberg's contention that this mobility is limited, and in fact depends upon larger-scale stabilities, also sits well with the fact that Neil Young can remain, in one way or another, a central figure in rock music despite his changeability.

Echoes of rock styles are still heard all over the popular music landscape. However, as already noted, rock is no longer as commercially dominant as it once was, and more significantly, its ability to serve as a vehicle for symbolic empowerment has also come under question. Frith began *Music for Pleasure* with the statement, "I am now quite sure that the rock era is over."[29] Although the decentering and demythologizing of rock has arguably been underway since at least the early 1980s, it was in the 1990s that the issue seemed to come to the forefront in the media. Interestingly, it was also in the 1990s that Neil Young managed his great commercial and critical comeback. While it appeared in the 1980s that Neil Young had finally run out of steam, he became a full-flung rock icon again in the 1990s, often described in terms strongly resonant with heroic rock mythology. However, the number and frequency of these celebrations seems to hint at an underlying uncertainty. No one can simply assume or assert that Neil Young is still important. Young, along with his fans and sympathetic critics, was seen throughout the 1990s working very hard at *proving* it. And despite the shower of positive press and renewed fan interest during this period, it seems that recognition of Neil Young is far less ubiquitous than it was in the 1970s. You don't need to look far to find listeners who think of Neil Young as a relic of the 1970s or who are not even aware that he is still active. Although Young has not become a nostalgia act, the general romanticization in the 1990s of the 1960s has undoubtedly been a factor in the renewal of his career, and therefore this renewal always carries suggestions, however slight, of nostalgia and decreasing relevance.

Negus points out that there have been two general threads running through "death of rock" narratives.[30] One thread is economic, suggesting that although the music industry was for a time centered on rock music, this was a passing situation. The other thread is ideological, suggesting that rock culture encapsulated certain values and beliefs which by the late 1970s no longer appeared tenable. In this connection, Negus cites Frith as having identified three key elements in rock ideology: the idea of the career path, the view that rock is a form of art and a generational expression, and a faith in the possibility of community between rock listeners and between listeners and artists.[31] We have seen that all three of these factors are central to Neil Young reception, and while his unpredictability and stylistic diversity have led him to problematize many specific features of the rock industry and of stylistic boundaries, he has never thrown these central ideological claims into question without later reasserting them. Indeed, his surprising decisions usually give the impression of having been taken precisely to reinscribe these values in cases where they are being threatened. Frequently, then, Neil Young troubles superficial aspects of rock culture in order to realign himself with more fundamental concerns. This observation can help us to understand why Young has survived through many stylistic periods, both in terms of changes in his own work and in the prevailing popular music contexts since the 1960s.

Is this solution illusory? If, in fact, Neil Young survives by highlighting the difference between local stylistic features and the overarching framework of rock ideology, and if his integrity has been consistently rooted in that overarching framework, then shouldn't his continued relevance be profoundly threatened, or even already gone, if rock ideology has become outmoded? Are the fans and critics who still find importance in Young's work fooling themselves? Negus, for one, may not think so. While many critics and academics have suggested that rock is now in fact dead—decentered economically and deflated ideologically—Negus points out that new artists who clearly adhere to versions of rock ideology continue to emerge and continue to find audiences for whom "rock has been experienced as part of a different history, one that doesn't necessarily 'begin' with a revolutionary moment during the middle of the 1950s," and which has not necessarily ended.[32]

Waywardness

Neil Young, then, questions 1960s rock culture in a manner which nonetheless reanimates its core ideologies. This has enabled him to avoid being too closely associated with an increasingly anachronistic style period while still relying upon certain ideological features of that period for validation. He also roams widely within the stylistic family of rock, seeming sometimes to stray outside of it altogether, but again in a manner which ultimately reasserts rock's centripetal fortitude. The word I have chosen to describe this doubly paradoxical attitude is *waywardness*. People may be described as wayward when they follow their own path in a manner contrary to established norms and perhaps to good judgment. The word is often pejorative, but it is also connected to romantic myths of self-reliance and the exploratory spirit. In terms of Neil Young, the most important connotation is that waywardness explores and celebrates a territory at the same time as it evokes a mode of deterritorialization. I use the word to indicate a habit of wandering broadly but within the limits of your home territory, allowing you to be both an insider and an outsider, a nomad and a homesteader.

Of course, as Grossberg has noted, a great deal of rock music has traditionally hinged upon affective resistance to boredom and a degree of alienation from hegemonic culture.[33] I take this to suggest, in part, that restlessness and mobility are core themes in most kinds of rock music, not just in Neil Young. As Beebe has put it, "because it has so successfully incorporated the possibility of its own demise into its discourse, rock might be most accurately described as a paradoxical animal that lives *by dying*."[34] He goes on to describe a dynamic of retrospective restabilization very similar to the one we have already noted in Neil Young reception: "[Rock] narratives generally serve to contain our worst entropic nightmares . . . within a recursive cycle of death and resurrection." Some of the less unusual features of Young's waywardness, those which reflect tendencies widely displayed by rock artists, include his refusal of external definition, his interest in chaos and disorder, his self-reliance, and his ideology of expressivity. More distinctive, but still shared with many rock artists, are his tendency to jump between styles and moods and his uneasy alliance with corporate cultures. But even where he shares these tendencies with other rock performers, there is a question of degree. Neil

Young is wayward with greater intensity and frequency than most other rockers. Also unique is the degree to which Young has allowed these experiments to at times damage his career and put his authorial integrity into question. Paradoxically, this willingness to risk his credibility became the ground on which Neil Young was constructed as an auteur. Auteurship has been a key component in ideologies of authenticity and value among rock fans and critics since the mid-1960s.[35] Neil Young's waywardness, rather than escaping rock ideology, is often cast in terms of integrity, self-reliance, and determination, all of which are central to the ideology of auteurship and to the myth of American individualism that Marcus argues is central to rock overall.[36]

A wayward life is a kind of mobile habitat, one which both evades and relies upon the territory through which it moves. Neil Young has been maximally wayward within the confines of the rock territory, so much so that for some listeners he has seemed to stray beyond it. If he has appeared unpredictable, it is because few rockers wander so far and because some of the subtraditions of rock to which Young has wandered are sufficiently marginal that not everyone even thinks of them as part of the family. However, I would suggest that with a larger view his entire output seems to be contained within the stylistic family and ideological framework of rock. By moving in this complex yet bounded manner, Neil Young has achieved a unique result. No other body of work in rock shows how so many of the paths that appear to lead outwards in fact turn back on themselves. And few other artists have so clearly illustrated the fine balance between coherence and collapse, and the rich intermusicality, contained within a single tradition.

Technology and Rationalization

One theme implicit throughout this chapter is control. The images of authorial control and self-reliance already discussed all suggest an interpretation of Young as powerful and autonomous, and indeed this is a thread which runs throughout his career, as was described in chapter 1. However, we have also noted that he is associated with certain kinds of instability, and this is an equally important theme in his work. Several critics have approached this dichotomy by suggesting that Young's work is forceful because it is instinctive. Such interpretations argue that Neil Young does not calculate or control in a fully rationalized sense, but that he does create situations in which his intuitions can be explored in a manner he finds appropriate. The point is made in its most extreme form by Christgau, who asserts that "with an artist as instinctive as Young, talk of intentions is useless."[37] Although such a statement could easily be read as an indictment, in the case of Neil Young's relationship to rock critics this was not usually the spirit of the observation. More frequently, the word "instinctive" functioned to lend Young a great degree of artistic license. As Fernbacher noted, the perception was often that "Neil Young is an example of real punkhood in action . . . because he never has to explain himself."[38] The theme of instinctuality, and its opposition to careful calculation, is clearly one of the ways in which Young's waywardness is constructed. As an example of rock ideology in action, Young's persona must display a degree of focus and direction, but this focus must not fall too obviously under the sway of rationalization or calculation, since this would introduce a bureaucratic tone counter to the image of the rebellious rock star. Instinct is a stance which performs this function well. Since instinct is in this case explicitly constructed as a force oppositional to rationalization, it is not surprising that it can also allow critics to address the frequent instances in which Young has seemed to go too far in his dedication to experiment, or the instances in which his commitment to spontaneity seems to veer into outright sloppiness. The themes of instinctuality, control, and error interlock in a complicated manner and are discussed at several points in this book. To conclude the present chapter, I would like to focus on one particular aspect of this complex subject: its connection to rationalization and what this might say about Young's use of technology.

Although rock music has been dependent on new instruments and recording techniques at every phase of its development, throughout the 1970s and 1980s rock fans and critics tended to be wary of newer technologies. Synthesizers and drum machines in particular, and styles like disco and electro-pop which foregrounded such tools, were singled out and stereotyped as cold, unexpressive, commercial, and formulaic. This distrust of technology and its scapegoating as a force of standardization seems almost Weberian or Adornian in tone. For Weber and Adorno, technological rationalization is just one manifestation of a set of forces which tend to bureaucratize and standardize modes of production and social practices. Weber explicitly contrasted the forces of rationalization with those of charisma and posited these as two opposed poles of social organization. To the degree that rock culture celebrated charisma as a force separate from and even resistant to technological rationalization, it followed the Weberian paradigm. However, as has been noted especially in recent work on gender constructions in popular music, technology also provides the means toward displays of control and virtuosity central to rock heroism. From a masculine rockist perspective, then, the challenge is to use technology to assert personal power without falling into the standardizing and rationalizing traps which the technology could potentially set.

Neil Young has always been interested in the possibilities presented by new musical technologies. Sometimes this has led to problems, as with the failed mastering of the *Neil Young* and *Comes a Time* albums. In the first instance, new mastering technologies were employed which severely reduced the sonic quality of the album. Young quickly negotiated to have the old version taken out of circulation and replaced with a new version. In the second case, the issue was not new technology, but simply quality control. Young decided, after the initial pressing, that the mastering and sequencing were not up to his standards and had the initial version removed from circulation at his own expense. Both of these incidents illustrate that whatever Young's reputation for instinctuality, he maintains a close watch and considerable control on the technical side of his albums. Technology was also a factor in the first of the 1980s style shocks. *Trans* not only featured synthesizers more prominently than Young had done before, but also processed his voice through a vocoder, sometimes so heavily as to make it almost unrecognizable. And perhaps more interesting than these obvious instances, we should note that there is an important but hidden technological dimension to Young's work with Crazy Horse. As a 1992 *Guitar Player* feature makes clear,[39] Young's supposedly simple garage rock guitar sound relies upon an extensive array of signal processing devices, the precise setting of which requires considerable skill and attention to detail. For example, Young's long-time guitar technician Larry Cragg claims that Young can tell by ear when his amplifier supply voltage is below the nominal 120 volts, 60 cycles.[40]

Yet, despite his sometimes close connection to new technologies, Neil Young also stands for anti-technological primitivism. His guitars are all vintage, as are his amplifiers. And although he is now associated with the use of advanced digital mastering technology, being an early advocate of the High Definition Compact Disc, he only moved in this direction because of his profound dissatisfaction with available digital technologies and in an attempt to retrieve certain properties of older analog technology.[41] With respect to Young's balance between vintage equipment and cutting-edge technological experiment, the case of the whizzer is especially illuminating. The whizzer is a device which remotely moves the controls on Young's amplifier. Through a system of footswitches, Young can send signals to the robotic device, which then physically moves the amplifier's potentiometers. This is a unique piece of equipment, built for and used exclusively by Neil Young. It is motivated by his feeling that no electronic signal processing offers results as satisfactory as simply changing the settings on an amplifier. Most guitarists get around the inconvenience of manually adjusting amplifier knobs by using outboard signal processing devices, in effect abandoning the older, low-tech method. In the whizzer, by contrast, Neil Young has created a new sort of robotic device which allows him to partially circumvent signal processing technology and to modify his sound in the older, low-tech fashion. This is advanced technology at the service of primitivism, or more precisely, it is the strategic use of a new technology in order to halt the incursion of *other* new technologies.

Neil Young's preference for vintage equipment is not uncommon among rock guitarists. Théberge has suggested that old instruments are a way of sonically encoding nostalgia, and he relates this to the nostalgia that has always been common in lyrics. For younger musicians, vintage gear gives a connection to, or allows appropriation of, the past, both symbolically and literally.[42] Instruments represent "a form of knowledge in action," and intrinsically embody certain aesthetic principles, becoming an important element in the accumulated sensibilities of any tradition.[43] The totemic quality of Young's instruments, especially the Gibson Les Paul guitar named Old Black, is frequently clear in discussions among rusties, who often talk about the instrument as a repository of history and power. There is almost a sense of awe that the same guitar has been used in so many of Young's recordings and performances. Since we are speaking here of the particular instrument of an individual musician, the context is slightly more specific than that usually implied by the term *accumulated sensibilities*, which generally refers to properties of an entire class of instruments. However, this draws attention to an important detail of Neil Young's situation. He plays the sorts of instruments which have, in a general way, acquired strong accumulated sensibilities in rock culture, but he is one of the people whose work helped to create those sensibilities in the first place. His gear is vintage, but he has owned much of it since it was relatively new. In this sense, Young's vintage equipment displays a double relationship to his work. The instruments are personal in that they draw Young back into his own past, and they are trans-personal in that they reference (and helped to create) the accumulated sensibilities of rock technology in general. They impose upon him a multi-layered history. But they are also just guitars, tools which he uses in a variety of ways to maintain both the currency *and* the nostalgia value of his work. The relationship here is almost identical to that between Neil Young and established stylistic traditions, as analyzed earlier in this chapter. Just as he maintains an insider-outsider relationship to the rock canon, Young works enthusiastically with new technologies but also cultivates nostalgia.

To return to issues of control and authorial persona, we should consider the claim that new technologies are changing the nature of authorship. Goodwin has argued that techniques such as sampling are having a profound effect on the definition of what a musician is, such that "the old image of musicians rehearsing music and then trooping into a studio to record it is increasingly out of date."[44] Along similar lines, Théberge quotes Brian Eno as arguing that with so many automated tools and pre-made materials available to composers and producers, artists are now people "who specialize in judgement rather than skill."[45] A corollary assumption is that the nature of expressive culture is also changing, with techniques of pastiche, juxtaposition, and irony gaining precedence over the kind of organicism celebrated in rock music of the 1960s and 1970s. The relevance of this debate to Neil Young should be clear. First, he is a prime example of the kind of authorial persona said to be under attack by these new conceptions of creative agency. More interestingly, he has engaged in varieties of pastiche and juxtaposition that can be contrasted with those discussed by Goodwin and Eno.

The first thing to note is that Neil Young's position with respect to existing traditions, and within rock ideology, borrows from half of this equation only. Clearly, pastiche and juxtaposition have been central to Young's work. However, clear-cut irony has been mostly absent, or at least entirely contained to a few years in the 1980s. More importantly, organicism of a sort is consistently celebrated in Young's work and plays a central role in its reception. One lesson to draw from this is that pastiche does not automatically lead to an abandonment of the traditional authorial role, and by implication, even if certain technologies by their very nature encourage pastiche, they do not necessarily force an ideological shift with respect to authorship. This conclusion seems even more compelling when we note the emergence in the 1980s and 1990s of techno-auteurs such as Derrick May or Beck. This is not to say, however, that popular music has not in fact moved in a more intertextual and ironic direction, nor that digital sampling and editing technologies have not played a major role in this shift. The evidence for such a claim is strong, and with respect to these trends Neil Young is a throwback to another era. He is a rock auteur, holding firmly to the myth of the authentic creative individual as well as to the image of the traditional working musician. With respect to recording technology, Young simply uses new tools to continue doing what he has always done. The only obvious exception is the *Arc* project, discussed more fully in chapter 3. This composition is perhaps Young's most technologically daring work, or at least the one in which technological manipulation is most visible. But it is more reminiscent of Stockhausen than of contemporary pastiche. And groups such as Pink Floyd had already by the late 1960s cleared a safe space for this working method at the heart of rock orthodoxy.

However, if we move on to consider Young's use of synthesizers, especially on the *Trans* album, something closer to Eno's transformation of aesthetic priorities may be discerned, at least with respect to the concerns and fears of those listeners who felt deeply threatened by *Trans*. The depth of their reaction suggests that basic assumptions about identity were being challenged by this album. Rock critics in the early 1980s were for the most part wary of synthesizer-based musics, partly because these tools were associated with a more anonymous, producerly approach to music-making. Théberge has noted that this anti-synthesizer sentiment didn't surface until the late 1970s, with the increasing importance of disco.[46] While synthesizers had coexisted fairly well with other rock instruments before this, and while Young himself had used them occasionally without generating much comment ("Like a Hurricane"), in the late 1970s synthesizers and drum machines came to be perceived by many in rock culture as cold, mechanical, and corrosive of conventional musicianship. Perhaps rock fans sensed, as Goodwin and Eno have suggested, that these technologies could be associated with fundamental changes in the nature of artistry. But the aversion is based in more than technology. Dyer has argued that the reaction against disco, for example, was partly a reaction against black culture, gay culture, and other perspectives central to disco but repressed within the rock mainstream.[47] And as Straw has noted in a slightly different context, "[the visual motifs of masculinist hard rock] increasingly stood out against the geometrical-minimalist and retro design principles that became widespread within rock music following the emergence of punk and new wave."[48] Straw is speaking of changes within rock music itself, but the underlying idea—older identities being thrown into uncomfortable relief by the seemingly cold geometrism of newer styles—is also pertinent to the relationship between rock and other traditions.

Given that Neil Young was one of the foremost icons of masculinist rock music, in which new technologies were central but hidden, his move into the electro-pop tradition with *Trans* may be his most famously unexpected decision. Reaction among critics was mixed. Several reviewers felt that Young successfully blended the new materials into his own distinctive working method, producing something which was not in spirit terribly different from his other work. Most of the rusties who have commented on the issue were initially put off by the record, although for many the vocoder in particular was a more serious issue than the presence of electronics per se, suggesting that disruption of a previously "natural" and transparent relationship to Young's voice was the primary issue. If it was Young's intention to problematize the idea of communication and more profoundly to explore a cybernetic state evocative of his son Ben's condition, then his decision to vocode the vocals is appropriate. As Dickinson has noted, within many musical traditions (rock included), "certain vocal conceits are cherished as exceptionally direct conduits to the core of the self," and because of this ideological association of voice and self, "vocoder tracks vividly highlight the inextricable bond between subjectivity and mechanization. They propose a dichotomy between the vocoded voice and the more 'organic' one, which then crumbles under closer inspection, most obviously because both are presented as exuding from the same human source-point."[49] Going further, and picking up on McClary's reading of Laurie Anderson, Dickinson describes a dilemma seemingly similar to that faced by listeners who experienced difficulty in reconciling Young's new, vocoded vocal sound with their expectations: "The key question here is not: where is Laurie Anderson, but, if this is one Laurie Anderson, what can she mean?"

Many rusties and critics report that Neil Young has frequently surprised them and that his work is difficult to characterize due to his tendency to move in unexpected and sometimes radical stylistic directions. However, these perceptions aside, most of Young's stylistic decisions actually do remain confined to a fairly coherent territory, which I have called the stylistic family of rock. This left us with a question: Why does Neil Young appear so flighty and capricious when, in fact, his work taken as a whole sketches out a fairly coherent territory? Or to pose the question another way: How do we account for the manner in which Neil Young is perceived to be both inside and outside the expected norms of rock music more generally? The concept of waywardness provides one way of addressing this insider-outsider status. The nature of generic and stylistic categories becomes especially important in this discussion, and I argue that Young displays an exceptional ability to work with the dialogic nature of cultural fields, effecting a fine balance between centripetal and centrifugal forces. In some ways this could function as a more formal *definition* of waywardness: the ability to fully explore the centrifugal forces implicit in a tradition without completely losing contact with the ideological underpinnings of more centripetal practices.

In truly dialogic fashion, Young can be understood as improvising a distinctive and relatively coherent series of enunciatory positions within the negotiated, heteroglot space of popular music traditions. Many artists have done this, but Young is different in the degree to which he allows gaps and discontinuities to show through and in the degree to which he has highlighted and juxtaposed the two poles of the process—coherent autonomous identity on the one side, contingent and performative identity on the other—without resolving them. This sort of waywardness is a kind of rebellion and self-reliance, unique in some respects but not all. To the degree that it resonates with foundational myths of rock identity, Young's waywardness is centripetal. And since this fairly radical brand of deterritorialization is so consistently applied, it becomes a kind of territory. Young is a canonized figure and an icon of rock music. He has an ambivalent relationship to both of these tendencies, but on balance that ambivalence, even though it exists on many levels, often folds back into a kind of authenticity and reinforces the same ideologies it questions.

3 | The Liquid Rage

Noise and Improvisation

> I say sometimes to guys, don't play music. Play a sound. . . . Maybe it is musical, but maybe it sounds as if you dropped the dobro. . . . Because it's the tone, in some cases, not the music you play.[1]

In chapter 2, I analyzed Neil Young's relationship to tradition in terms of centripetal and centrifugal forces. The feature of the music most closely under examination was its use of conventional stylistic codes. In this chapter, I would like to focus on a different aspect of the music: perceived intensity and in particular noisiness. As was seen in chapter 1, Young's electric guitar playing with Crazy Horse has been noted for its emphasis on raw sonority, extreme volume, and ideologies of transcendence. Again and again, critics will point out that Young is a guitar player who displays little in the way of advanced technique but makes up for this potential limitation with a noteworthy performative intensity. Just as Neil Young's work overall performs a kind of symbolic violence on stylistic categories, much of his electric music performs an acoustic violence. And just as his destabilization of stylistic categories spirals back into a form of reterritorialization, the noise mobilized through his signature electric guitar style also achieves a kind of constructive, stable identity. It is the purpose of the present chapter to explore the manner in which this takes place.

Noise and Oppositionality

Ideas of chaos, noise, and rebellion have been part of rock culture from its beginning, but *noise* as a culture-theoretical term is more recent.

The most widely influential treatment of the noise/music boundary is that of Attali, for whom noise represents a practice in which existing codes of taste—always in his analysis tied to hegemonic power structures —are challenged and suspended. Noise in Attali's analysis is "a herald, for change is inscribed in noise faster than it transforms society."[2] Noisy music is potentially revolutionary since it posits an order outside of the status quo. On the surface it may seem that rock music of the 1960s and 1970s, insofar as it was perceived as both noisy and counterhegemonic, is an ideal example of Attali's model in action. However, as was noted in chapters 1 and 2, the political orientation of rock is far from uniformly anti-establishment, and even though much rock music represents an affective escape from structures of social power, rock as an institution did not ultimately become a significant challenge to those structures. One weakness of Attali's model is that it seems to encourage an all-or-nothing perspective, forcing us to decide that rock either was or was not ultimately noisy in a profound sense. Rather than accept such a simple reading, under which rock culture is either a yet-to-be-fulfilled revolution or a conflicted movement mired in bad faith, we would do better to view rock noise as part of a *temporary autonomous zone*,[3] a practice which allows for the local, contingent, and temporary suspension of hegemonic norms, creating a playful and experimental space for participants which can model unconventional modes of social organization but which does not ultimately unsettle mainstream conventions. In other words, the social and political significance of rock can be analyzed along lines similar to those suggested by Attali as long as we recognize that these effects are not global. The noisiness of Neil Young's electric guitar playing has inspired descriptions which mix metaphors of chaos and instability with those of empowerment, which is precisely the kind of description we might expect if we follow Attali in believing that noise is a form of disturbing violence but also a practice for creating new kinds of social integration. Further, Young's constant frustration of stylistic expectations could itself be interpreted as a kind of symbolic noise. In both cases, we need to retain the insight that these practices go to the core of social order and personal identity, but nuance the question of just how far their effects reach and how long they last. In effect, the concept of a temporary autonomous zone allows us to retain an appreciation of noise's phenomenological and ideological profundity without exaggerating its ultimate political effect.

Rock music is sometimes noisy in all of Attali's senses, and Neil Young aligns himself with these tendencies in subtle ways. In a literally sonic sense, his electric guitar work often pushes the limits of distortion and volume, emphasizing raw sonority over motivic development. This soundscape emerges in part from Young's resistance to more elaborate techniques of performance or composition, and so the work is sonically noisy partly as a result of a symbolically noisy resistance to systems of control.[4] This resistance to established standards goes beyond Young's guitar playing. For example, it encompasses his voice as presented on albums like *Time Fades Away* and *Tonight's the Night,* as will be seen in chapter 5. By normal prepunk rock production standards of the mid-1970s, such imperfections would be removed as a matter of course, but Young allowed them to stand and as a result enhanced his reputation as a disruptive force. Also significant is the correlation between noisy soundscapes and improvisation in Young's work. Crazy Horse is the band with whom Young plays the longest, most exploratory solos and the one most clearly predicated on an improvisatory group dynamic. The conflation of noisy soundscape and improvisatory attitude in Crazy Horse emphasizes the role of noise in discovering new possibilities and foregrounds its effectiveness at constructing group solidarities. In all these senses, Neil Young's noisier music resists established norms and systems of control while emphasizing exploration and discovery. However, it seems doubtful that Neil Young's noise is, in the end, prophetic in the strong sense envisioned by Attali. The non-prophetic aspect of Young's noisiness arises in part from its coupling with ideologies of individualism and self-determination, themselves rooted in traditional constructions of masculinity and conservative politics. Additionally, noise and chaos became Crazy Horse clichés by the late 1970s, another example of a radical style growing familiar, even obligatory, and therefore somewhat disempowered.

Finally, going beyond the specific case of Neil Young, there is a general problem in assuming that rock's noisiness is *noise* in the full sense. Gracyk has argued that while rock's high volume levels are a key source of its reputation as a noisy music, this loudness (and therefore rock's noisiness in general) is a carefully deployed code and not an intrusion of chaos. On an ideological level, "the rock community has reworked the *concept* of noise in a way that converts an epithet of disdain into one of achievement."[5] And the structured use of noise in rock is not only ideological, but it is systematic on a sonic level as well. Until recently, certain distinctive rock timbres could only be achieved at high volume levels. Volume and noise are not in this context direct expressions of emotion or unreflective outbursts, but are rather resources which become the object of sculpting and aesthetic evaluation. It seems fair to ask how, if noise has been so thoroughly internalized as a structural element in rock culture, can it remain noise? I would suggest that it can, but in a relative rather than an absolute sense. As Kahn argues in his analysis of the European avant-garde, "with so much attendant on noise it quickly becomes evident that noises are too significant to be noises. . . . But noise does indeed exist, and trying to define it in a unifying manner across the range of contexts will only invite noise on itself."[6] There are many ways in which the balance between noise-as-noise and noise-as-code may be enacted. For example, a performance may be understood as being *about* noise even when it is highly conventional. I believe this to be the case in many Crazy Horse performances after the late 1970s. Or listeners may choose to pay special attention to features of the music which are more noisy and disregard factors that suggest regulation, in effect suspending their disbelief and allowing a temporary enactment of noise as a phenomenological event (also, I believe, typical of later Crazy Horse performances). Or an event may be noisy relative to other kinds of events. Rock music may have conventionalized noise within its own practices, but it can still be noisy when compared to traditions which have not undergone this exercise. These are not the only possibilities, but they suffice to show that the oppositionality of noise is an even more complex phenomenon than it first appears.

Many of these themes come together in Young's relationship to one of his most important guitars: the Gibson Les Paul named "Old Black," which he began using when Crazy Horse was first formed in 1969 and which remained the principal guitar in his work with that group through the 1990s:

> The guitar came from Jim Messina, who found the instrument's monstrous sound uncontrollable. "Neil's the kind of guy that if there's an old scraggly dog walkin' down the street, he'd see somethin' in that dog and take it home. That's kind of like that Les Paul—I liked the way it looked, but it was just terrible. It sounded like *hell*. Neil loved it," said Messina.[7]

Young's relationship to this guitar displays the key traits of his relationship to Crazy Horse and to noise overall. The instrument and the band have noticeable limitations relative to established norms of quality, which makes them noisy and unruly. Young exploits these properties and by extension gains the ability to signify his distinctiveness and to set up a form of resistance to aspects of the music industry. However, a key part of this story is Young's control. The guitar is noisy, but in a useful way. In a sense, Young's redemption of the instrument pulls it back into the established institutions and limits its oppositional power. By the late 1970s, Old Black had become a powerful totem for some Neil Young fans because of its connection to the history of Crazy Horse and because of the idea, rooted partly in fact, that the unique sound of the instrument was essential to the creation of this unique music. Like any fetishization, this one implies conformity as much as it implies transgression, to the point that by the 1990s some critics were interpreting Young's Crazy Horse projects as concessions to commercial imperatives precisely because they reiterated styles that had been oppositional to commercial norms in the 1970s.[8] This line of criticism draws attention to an important fact about noise: sounds may be perceived as acoustically noisy even if they are not thought to have oppositional force. Crazy Horse still sounded acoustically noisy in the 1990s, as did traditions like punk rock, but this did not prevent them from becoming commodified and standardized.

Young's 1980s output was noisy in a different sense. For a time, his persona was fragmented, and stylistic markers began to float more freely throughout his work, effecting the kind of symbolic murder evoked by Attali when he describes noise as a simulacrum of sacrifice. Neil Young, through the medium of stylistic noise, may be understood as having tried to murder his earlier selves and even to sacrifice his past success in order to gain mobility in the present. However, this potentially radical direction was eventually brought back into line with Young's master persona and emptied of strong prophetic qualities. The noise in Young's music, whether sonic or symbolic, is oppositional but not prophetic. And it is oppositional in a non-specific way. Young does occasionally identify specific targets—for example the Nixon administration in "Ohio" or the debilitating effects of addiction in "Cocaine Eyes"—but for the most part he emphasizes the affect rather than its object. This possibility is implicit in Attali's model, although he does not discuss it, preferring instead to focus on either the strongly hegemonic or the strongly prophetic.

But consider what Attali has to say about the three typical uses of non-noisy, harmonious music:

> We will see that it is possible to distinguish on our map three zones, three stages, three strategic uses of music by power . . . [first] an attempt to make people *forget* the general violence . . . [second] to make people *believe* in the harmony of the world . . . [and finally] to *silence,* by mass-producing a deafening, syncretic kind of music, and censoring all other human noises.[9]

Neil Young has at times made music which quite specifically resists these three actions of power. Against the forgetting of general violence, Young's work has often served to remind listeners of the destructive underbelly of rock culture and North American culture more generally. Rather than believing in social and symbolic harmony, Young's work questions and destabilizes complacency. And against the tendency toward silence, Young's lyrics often foreground characters who speak out against the discourse of established interests. I do not want to suggest by this that we pigeonhole Young as an anti-hegemonic artist. The pitfalls of such an interpretation have already been mentioned, and they include the fact that his individualism is reactionary and his opposition to the marketplace is ultimately marketable. But it is nonetheless striking that Attali's analysis of harmonious, hegemonic music seems to provide a negative template for Young's stance. In this sense Young's work, at least in its stated intentions, contains genuine noise in the oppositional if not the prophetic sense. It is also worth noting that this balance is not really so far from Attali's reiterated suggestion that, as a general rule, *music* is bounded by *noise* and *silence.* To rephrase this, music is always a zone in which absolute change and absolute quiescence are juxtaposed against one another. Young's continual movement between reflective acoustic music and noisy hard rock, as well as the dynamics in his persona between the private individual and the star persona, can be seen as a negotiation of noise and silence, an ongoing opposition to the centripetal forces both of hegemonic power and of any specific revolutionary agenda.

Arrangement and Improvisation

A great deal of the foregoing discussion echoes my earlier remarks on technology in that it hinges on questions of control. Since noise is in some respects a form of violence, its use implies an exercise of power. Unlike displays of technological prowess, however, the exertion of power through noise often presents itself as an exercise in irrationality, as a display of indifference or antipathy toward the kinds of instrumental reason enshrined in technology. This is perhaps less universally true outside of rock music, since certain avant-garde movements have foregrounded technology itself as a source of noise, and in such cases noise is cast against more humanistic values as the ultimate extension of instrumental reason. But in rock culture, noise is generally juxtaposed against instrumental reason rather than aligned with it, although even here there is an irony in that the realization of this strategy requires both the mobilization of technologies and a rationale. Noise must appear within a space and as part of a practice, and these contextual factors continue to display their characteristic structures. Two structures in Neil Young's music which perform such a framing and enabling function for noise are the guitar solo and his general approach to arrangement. In both cases, a framework is provided both for acoustic noise in general and for improvisation, itself an intermediate category between fully rationalized practices and those which are noisy in the sense of being relatively unconstrained. To advance our discussion of noise in Neil Young's work, then, I would like to comment briefly on his arranging practices and to describe general features of his guitar solos before moving on to a general discussion of his stance with respect to improvisation.

In the 1960s and early 1970s, Neil Young in collaboration with Jack Nitzsche was frequently associated with large-scale orchestral-style suites and had a reputation as a perfectionistic and experimental arranger. By *orchestral style suites* I mean multi-section works featuring many elements in the arrangement and frequent changes of texture. As in the work of the Beach Boys and the Beatles, who are generally considered to have pioneered this technique in rock music, the effect was sometimes accomplished literally through the use of an orchestra and sometimes through multiple overdubs of more conventional rock instruments. Often a combination of these techniques was used. Much of the orchestral writing on Young's early records was in addition truly symphonic in style, reflecting romantic and early twentieth-century orchestration techniques. By *truly symphonic,* I mean that the orchestra, or orchestra-like resources, were not simply used as color details over a standard rock song form but displayed features atypical of most rock music, such as chromatic harmony and through-composition. After *Harvest,* Neil Young records would still sometimes feature orchestral instruments, but increasingly in pop-style arrangements.

Both kinds of orchestral arrangement—the more symphonic and the more pop-oriented—have the potential to create the impression of wide and deep spaces. They also allow for great variety in spatial effect, for frequent contrasts, shifts of focus, widenings and narrowings. Increasingly through the 1970s, Neil Young came to favor simpler arrangements within a small-band format, but he would still sometimes use these more limited resources to construct carefully worked-out passages mirroring more elaborate orchestral arrangements ("Albuquerque," "Tired Eyes," "Look Out for My Love," and "Going Back"). Even in his most minimal work with Crazy Horse, timbres are carefully selected and juxtaposed, as is especially evident in the longer songs ("Cowgirl in the Sand," "Down by the River," and "Slip Away"). This attention to detail is also evident in the placement of instrumental resources within more unassuming songs. Some examples of seemingly simple songs which display considerable attention to detail in the deployment of instruments include "Ambulance Blues," "Don't Cry," "Harvest Moon," "Old Man," "Only Love Can Break Your Heart," and "Safeway Cart." In short, Young's more elaborate small-group arrangements sometimes generate the same impression of large space, and the same spatial variations, as do the more orchestral arrangements.

After Young so visibly embraced a minimalist aesthetic with Crazy Horse, the subtleties of his arrangements were not usually highlighted. They often took the form, instead, of a few details not unique or complex enough to draw attention, but still having the effect of contrasting sections, supporting the overall flow of the song, and creating a unique soundscape. Young's awareness of these nuances can be seen in the following quotation:

> If you listen to it, "Round and Round" is one of my favorite songs on the second album, because of some of the things—I guess you sort of have to listen to them, 'cause I didn't bring them out very much—but the echo from the acoustic guitar on the right echoes back on the left, and the echo from the guitar on the left comes back on the right and it makes the guitars go like this . . . one line starts goin' like da-da-daow . . . and then you can hear like one voice comes in and out, and that's 'cause Danny was

rockin' back and forth. . . . Those things are not featured, they're just in it, you know, and that's what I'm trying to get at. I think they last longer that way. Doing it live and singing and playing all at once just makes it sound more real.[10]

Other examples are too numerous to list exhaustively, but would include: the choice of French horn as a solo instrument in "After the Gold Rush"; Ben Keith's distinctive steel guitar on *Harvest;* Molina's signature "cha cha cha" rhythm frequently embedded in the surrounding back beat in a way that just barely draws attention to itself ("Don't Cry No Tears," and "Drive Back"); the emphasis on one rhythmic cell, reminiscent of modal rhythm, in "Don't Let It Bring You Down" and "Only Love Can Break Your Heart"; the atypical cowbell and fuzz-laden riff of "Drive Back"; the distinctive instrumental combinations of "For the Turnstiles" and "Motion Pictures"; the continual subtle changes of signal processing in "Will to Love"; and many others. In all these cases, the arranging decisions create a distinctive texture but in no way draw excess attention to themselves. Increasingly, Neil Young's arrangements through the 1970s appeared to be conceived as frameworks for performance rather than structures to be emphasized in their own right. This can be seen clearly in the quotation given above, where Young discusses in detail the specific sonic effects allowed for by a particular performance context. Arrangement for Young involves careful preplanning, followed by a willingness to find and seize the right moment to realize the song. For example, *Tonight's the Night* has become famous partly for the manner in which it was recorded (described in chapter 1). By contrast, Young let it be known that *Zuma,* the album which marked his emergence from the mid-1970s dark period, was recorded only during the daytime. Other examples can be found, but these serve to illustrate the principle. Even when Young launches projects that are largely improvisatory in nature, he carefully selects times and contexts which are likely to produce a particular sort of result. Young's work makes use of both spontaneity and deliberation, each at their appropriate time. The category of *arranging* draws attention to this relationship, since it is by nature intermediate between composition and performance.

Young's interest in controlling the context of recording is hardly unique, and neither is his belief that this context exerts considerable influence on the final artistic product. In this he is closely linked to the general melding which occurs in rock music between composition, arrangement, and performance. For example, as Zak notes, "over the course of rock history . . . an increasing number of artists have adopted synergistic creative approaches where song-writing, arranging, and recording proceed simultaneously," such that "the simultaneous consideration of music and audio amounts to an integrated kind of arranging where musical parts and actual sounds are interdependent."[11] This last remark brings to mind Young's comment, quoted at the beginning of this chapter, that the acoustic properties of a sound are often its most salient musical feature. When Young distinguishes between "the tone" and "the music" in this context, he draws a line similar to that drawn by Barthes between the grain of a performance and more rationalized musical content.[12] Without wanting to perpetuate problematic separations of form and content or to suggest a simple hierarchy of rationalization, we can still note that Young often treats arrangement as a framework for the encouragement of performances, and that his primary interest is with the particular properties of these specific performances. Given a forced choice, the concept of noise must attach to the particular, to the unrepeatable, and to this extent even Young's more formalized arrangements, when they are treated as frameworks for performance rather than ends in themselves, display a commitment to noise. It must be noted however that this reading, suggestive as it may be, does not accord with Young's reputation as a strict and exacting bandleader. While his work with Crazy Horse is marked by a degree of laissez-faire, he is known with other groups to hold, and to insist upon, very particular expectations. In the last analysis what matters most is that Young enacts a dynamic relationship between control and contingency, and that while the exact ratio varies from project to project, the underlying dialectic is a continual theme.

For an artist like Neil Young, arrangement is necessary but problematic. Improvisation is another musical practice which requires a similar balance of planning and spontaneity. The level of improvisation involved in Neil Young's music varies considerably from project to project. Crazy Horse, especially in the 1990s, is founded largely on group improvisation, and Crazy Horse live albums are in part a document of these improvisatory explorations. At the opposite extreme is material containing almost no improvisation, also well-represented in Young's output. For our present discussion, it is interesting that Crazy Horse, Young's most consistently noisy band, is also his most deeply improvisational one. The chief improviser is almost always Neil Young on guitar. His coguitarists will often play solos as well, but these are never as long as Young's and are usually less flamboyant. Young also improvises on harmonica, and other supporting instruments will sometimes take solos as well (especially the steel guitar). But it is Neil Young playing an electric guitar solo with Crazy Horse that stands for most listeners as the central improvisatory framework. I'll be focusing, then, on one particular subset of Young's solos: the extended guitar jams most commonly associated with Crazy Horse.

It is in these solos that Young's desire to foreground sonority comes most clearly to the forefront. The solos place little emphasis on the working through of motivic or rhythmic ideas, although this does occur, and tend instead to be structured around gestures and textures. The solos are similar to *musique concrète* in that timbre and density become key materials for manipulation, and Young's approach could also be compared to that of John Coltrane. Indeed, Young has occasionally mentioned Coltrane as an influence, although he has never elaborated on the connection. However, Young's almost exclusive emphasis on texture, rhythm, and gesture places his solos in a different category from those in a tradition such as jazz—in which both virtuosity and motivic development tend to be important—or heavy metal—in which virtuosity is likewise highlighted. Although space doesn't allow for an exhaustive analysis of Young's improvisational vocabulary, a few of the most striking features should be pointed out:

1. There is a tendency to use rhythmic and melodic material primarily as a basis for timbral and gestural exploration. Young's solos are usually based around a central motive, which is used as a framework but is not subjected to methodical exploration.
2. The solos tend to explore a wide dynamic range, which has the effect of varying the amount and kind of distortion applied to the guitar (i.e., the wide dynamic range also produces a wide timbral range, given the nature of tube amplifiers).[13]
3. Young employs a variety of signal-processing devices which vary the tone of the instrument but rarely draw attention to themselves as special effects (with noteworthy exceptions, such as the octave divider used for "Like a Hurricane").
4. There is a tendency to gradually explore registral space, often starting low, slowly moving up, and then returning.
5. Young uses slides more predominantly than any other ornament

and generally reserves bends for climactic moments. This point is subtle but is one element that makes Young's style stand apart from guitarists who make a greater display of technical proficiency.

6. When an especially dramatic effect seems to be intended, Young produces extremely wide and rapid vibrato with the tremolo bar.[14]

7. Young frequently uses repeated chords or repeated notes to explore textural variation and to build intensity.

8. There are long pauses in which the guitar will complete a large section, then drop back into a rhythm function for a few measures, and then begin again in a solo function.

9. There is no virtuosic playing in Young's solos, but a density similar to that created by virtuosic scale or arpeggio passages is produced by stretches of what I will call *frenzy*, which combine rapid pick movement with deep vibrato and seemingly random note choices within certain boundaries.[15]

Any given solo is distinguished by its combination of these factors, as well as by the particular thematic material it uses as a framework. Partly because of the emphasis placed on timbre and dynamics and partly because of their generally high volume level, Young's solos achieve an impressive degree of physicality both in terms of his performance style, which involves a great deal of movement and dramatic facial expressions, and in terms of their impact on listeners. Young has spoken about the necessity for his Crazy Horse solos to achieve a powerful physical presence:

> It's the consciousness of playing the guitar in a stadium setting; it's a different way of playing. Not so much playing more from your soul, 'cause I always try to do that. But with rock 'n' roll you've got to throw the notes against the back of the building. You have to reach the people in the gray seats . . . [you] actually have to project the guitar like a missile.[16]

Published reactions to Young's solos are full of references to intense overwhelming sonority. Of course it is not necessary that a solo designed for maximum projection in a stadium should go as far as Young's do in emphasizing the physicality of sound. Other rock guitarists also project to fill large spaces while still placing an emphasis on technique and motivic development. So Young's own approach is a result not only of the performance context but also of his aesthetic, which precludes virtuosic display, and of his interest in conveying an impression of direct emotional expression. In chapter 2, I borrowed Monson's concept of intermusicality in order to discuss Young's use of stylistic codes. Monson developed the idea as a way to analyze the complex systems of reference and motivic development typical of the jazz solo. Strikingly, although intermusicality was such a useful concept for illuminating Young's stylistic experimentation, there is little hint of it in his guitar solos. In Neil Young's view, his solos are less a cerebral exercise than an opportunity to explore an altered state of consciousness:

> [Interviewer: What do you look for in a solo?] Elevation. You can feel it. That's all I'm looking for. You can tell I don't care about bad notes. I listen for the whole band on my solos. You can call it a solo because that's a good way to describe it, but really it's an instrumental. It's the whole band that's playing.[17]

> [Interviewer: Can you tell us what goes through your mind on stage?] No, not if it's good. If it's bad I can say that I'm listening to one of the other guys in the band, trying to figure out what the hell's wrong with the sound. . . . Good is no memory at all. It's trance-like.[18]

This emphasis on what Young calls *elevation*—involving as it does a reliance on instinct rather than calculation and a deliberate avoidance of technical awareness—is mirrored in the general working method of Crazy Horse while in concert. It is not only Young who has spoken of the experience in these terms, but other members of the band as well:

> [Frank Sampedro] Once we get going, anything can change at any time, and you just have to keep your head up rather than down. You just have to be really there with each other. . . . [Interviewer: How do you know when Neil's solo is ending? Billy Talbot answers] It's like the wind is blowing, and you're at the beach, how do you know when the wind is dying down and the end of the day is coming? Do you know what I mean? You just feel it. . . . [Interviewer: That thing you all do, gravitating towards each other in the centre of the stage . . . instinct or choreography? Ralph Molina answers] It's the pocket of sound. It's not just us wanting to be really close together, although that's what happens and we want to be close together to feel the vibes. [Frank Sampedro] It's the centre of energy too—you just want to get in there. You can hear the sound of all of us together and we're right there together. I don't even realize it's happening.[19]

Although there is little in these improvisations which could be called intermusical, they are dialogic in another sense. They place great value on the group dynamic and on the collaborative nature of the improvisation. This attitude toward performance, emphasizing as it does intuition over technique, relates to themes beyond the context of the improvised solo. In terms of songwriting, for example, Denski has shown that many rock musicians take a mystical view of composition, feeling that the song is not a product of their own ideas and work but something for which they are only a conduit.[20] For artists who take this view, there is a strong desire to retain an instinctual dimension in the music, and Neil Young is one of the several artists quoted by Denski who feel this way. This theme of openness and surrender to outside influences is also evident when Young discusses the live performance context as a whole, not just the solos. For Young, performance is about getting outside normal frames of mind. The solo is perhaps the most extreme expression of this experience, but it is part of a continuum which also includes composition and non-improvised elements in live performance. This is of course a statement of Young's ideal rather than a description of any particular listening experience. For listeners who strongly favor the live performance context, one reason seems to be the powerful experiences of elevation possible during Young's solos. But not all listeners share this preference. Those who do not favor live performances over recordings either do not have this experience or do not value it as highly as others. Also, not all of Young's solos are equally improvisatory, and the dividing line is in any instance vague between spontaneous improvisation and reflective composition.

Bailey argues that improvisation is difficult to study since it is by nature dedicated to spontaneity and change.[21] Improvisation is valuable because it can take one beyond familiar systems and ideas, even though it clearly relies on rehearsal, habit, and formula, and for this reason often fails to surprise or elevate. In all of these ways, the improvised solo is a fitting emblem for the experience of live performance as Neil Young speaks of it. However, as Bailey notes, improvisation has an ambiguous relationship to audiences. Some artists see the audience as essential and rely upon audience reaction to fuel the improvisation process. Under this view, improvisation is a matter of responding to an overall context, of which the audience forms an important part. Other artists find audiences inhibiting. Even positive audience reaction can discourage exploration, for example when it leads to repetition of a successful formula. Neil Young has expressed no misgivings about audiences insofar as improvisation is concerned. He has, however, often expressed unhappiness about the inattentiveness and prior expectations of audiences where the composed portions of songs are concerned, especially in acoustic concerts where improvisation is much less in evidence. He has, on many occasions, berated audiences for not listening closely enough or for insisting on hearing songs other than those he has chosen.

Bailey also cites certain objections to the whole notion of improvisation as an aesthetic strategy. Gavin Bryars, for example, feels that improvisations are necessarily tied to particular times and places and therefore cannot achieve generality of significance. Performing an improvisation in his description is like standing a painter next to the painting so that the two are always seen together.[22] For a composer who seeks to create seemingly autonomous music, such an effect is undesirable. However, when considered as a positive value, this foregrounding of persona and context can help explain the special place of improvisation in rock aesthetics. The solo can highlight the immediacy of the concert experience, deliberately heightening the very non-conceptual and place-bound aspects objectionable to Bryars. The solo is also an opportunity for the centrality of the star persona to be expressed. Fans who come to a concert expressly to see Neil Young do not generally object to finding him foregrounded, and indeed since a great deal of the musical interpretation practiced by fans unfolds through a process of identification with the artist, the significance of the music may be intensified rather than lessened by any factor which seems to bring listeners into closer contact with that artist. Also, as we have already noted, improvisation is a social event not only between performer and audience, but also among performers. Taking this concept to its limit, Monson has argued that improvisation is as much a mode of interpersonal exchange as it is a musical device, and that for jazz improvisers the creation of an overall groove or feeling is the most important goal.[23] Monson phrases this in a way that implicitly responds to Bryars and is also appropriate to Neil Young and Crazy Horse. "On the one hand, the aesthetic of [jazz] is centered on the inventiveness and uniqueness of individual solo expression; on the other, climactic moments of musical expression require the cohesiveness and participation of the entire ensemble."[24] Following this insight, Monson develops at length a metaphor of *conversation* to describe the improvisation process.

This is all relevant to the relationship between Neil Young and Crazy Horse during extended guitar solos. Young is clearly the central figure, but the overall sound of the band is crucial. They provide a shifting back-drop which continually adjusts to and enhances Young's playing, and he in turn adjusts his playing to highlight details within the band texture. While the metaphor of conversation seems apt in this case, the physical behavior of Neil Young and Crazy Horse points out another, even better metaphor: *circling*. It is common for Young, Sampedro, and Talbot to huddle together in a circle onstage during solos, creating a collective physical space which seems oddly intimate in the large arenas where they perform. The importance of this physical and musical circling is under-scored by the cover design of the *Year of the Horse* live album. The front cover features a photograph of Crazy Horse in this physical configura-tion, with a bold white circle imposed over them. This is not to say that circling is the only way in which Neil Young and Crazy Horse relate to each other during extended improvisations. At times, Young will stand markedly off to the side, clearly in his own space, as the band supports him. This is especially visible in the *Weld* concert video. Also, while Neil Young and Crazy Horse appear together in the circle on the front cover of *Year of the Horse*, on the rear cover Young appears alone in the circle. Nonetheless, circling is a prominent and distinctive Crazy Horse con-figuration. The metaphor of circling is perhaps more appropriate in this instance than that of conversation because, as already noted, Molina, Sampedro, Talbot, and Young do not describe the process of improvisa-tion as one of exchanging ideas or developing a structure, but rather of creating a center of energy and sensing each others' mood.

Neil Young's identity as an improvising musician reinforces his asso-ciation with surprise and changeability. This becomes even clearer when we notice that Young's tendency to work quickly on some projects is also a kind of improvisation. Young has on several occasions chosen to record a band in what would be considered by some the early stages of rehearsal, and then released these recordings as an album. Good examples include *Everybody Knows This Is Nowhere, Tonight's the Night, Eldorado, Mirror Ball,* and *Greendale.* This working method, besides being an extension of his improvisatory activity, resonates with Young's occasional rejection of music industry norms. It also allows for projects to be completed quickly, which can at times enhance their surprise value (enabling, for example, *Everybody Knows This Is Nowhere* to be released in the midst of Young's early CSNY involvement). To go deeper into the vocabulary of chapter 2, I would suggest that improvisation in these instances provides centrifugal effects in Young's work, creating a space in which set forms can be momentarily suspended. However, while the idea of centrifugal forces does seem to encapsulate the affective language in which some describe the process, that characterization is too simple. Indeed, improvisation has in some senses been as much a source of centripetal as centrifugal forces in Young's work. For example, most of his extended improvisatory activity has been confined to Crazy Horse, and it quickly became something of a cliché. Also, some of the most characteristic aspects of Young's solo guitar style were absorbed by fans and critics through album versions of the songs. There is a tendency for solos to ossify once they are recorded, with later performances being compared to the recorded solo or even using it as a template. Finally, the elevation Young seeks in a solo does not always allow for performances to be clearly distinguished from one another, or at least not distinguished on as many different levels as is possible, say, in jazz music. There is a sense in which the solos are all the same utterance, spaced out across songs and across the years. In fact, this can become a positive aesthetic force, and Young seems to cultivate it as such. In a famous live concert moment, recorded on *Year of the Horse,* an audience member yells out that "they all sound the same." To which Young replies, "It's all one song."

Solos, *Arc,* and Free Noise

In Young's own comments, and in those of rusties and critics, there is a tendency to interpret his style of electric guitar improvisation as being about raw sonority, even noise, and to contrast this approach with styles that emphasize harmony, melody, and rhythm. According to a persistent cultural habit, commentators still frame the former style as more intuitive, intense, and chaotic, while the latter is often seen as more cerebral. This dichotomy is evident in Young's comments on "tone" versus "music" cited earlier in this chapter. By aligning himself with less obviously rationalized parameters in this way, Young aligns himself with noise, but again turns it into a structured expressive resource. Having begun the discussion with Young's distinction between tone and music, it seems appropriate to conclude with a consideration of *Arc:* a sound-collage album released in 1991 and assembled from live recordings of feedback and other concert sounds which would be considered extra-musical under Young's tone/music distinction. It is on this album that

Young allows himself the most latitude in removing timbre and gesture from the confines of traditional song form. *Arc* shows the degree to which Young is interested in these resources, and it provides clues as to how he visualizes the place of raw sonority in the larger field of popular music styles.

> It's just sounds. That's the essence of it. It's like new age metal. You could play *Arc* in a heavy metal club as music between bands, and it wouldn't get in the way. It has no genre or attitude; it's not like it's coming from this place or that place. It's just metal. And it's exploding, it's molten, it's happening. . . . There's no rhythm in *Arc*. It's 35 minutes without a beat anywhere. It just keeps changing all the time, instead of the music we've got nowadays, which is an hour of music all with programmed beats. . . . So it's refreshing in that way. It's completely free.[25]

For Young, *Arc* presents an intriguing double identity. It is clearly identified with certain hard rock styles, and yet is not a token of any type. In describing the connections between *Arc* and heavy metal, Young interestingly reaches back to a metaphor which could underlie the name "heavy metal" itself, aligning *Arc* with that tradition in a manner that is both indirect (it's not literally heavy metal, it's just like heavy metal) and profound (it is like heavy metal in the most important way: by being metallic). Young is struggling with the same problems of terminology and family resemblance that motivated my distinction between genre, style, and tradition in previous chapters. Young is using the word "genre" in exactly the way I was using the word "style," and although the word "attitude" may be similar to what I meant by "genre," Young seems to intend by it something more like "tradition." The fundamental point is that *Arc* achieves a high degree of liminality, clearly mobilizing elements of particular genres, styles, and traditions but not sitting comfortably in any of them. It may be for this reason that Young characterizes the work as totally free while at the same time drawing attention to its associations and origins. These origins are interesting because they show how the work evolved as an expansion of the raw-sonority orientation already discussed and because they show Young's willingness to follow the suggestions of younger musicians:

> Something I heard in my head were these parts of the songs that I wanted to isolate. . . . We'd been playing *Arc*-type instrumentals for the last five or six years. We really enjoyed the hell outta that. . . . Eventually what it became was, we'd play the song, but the essence of the song was in the

ending. Just the passion of the song, only. So I did a tour with Crazy Horse back in 86, and I made a movie of it myself . . . during the movie itself was when we started doing these long endings and beginnings. So the soundtrack is all that—it's just noise and distortion. . . . So I said to Thurston [Moore, from Sonic Youth], 'What do you think of this music'? Because I knew he was into that kind of stuff . . . [and he said] yeah, you ought to go ahead and put all of it out on a record. . . . I looked at myself and said, 'That might be an idea, but how the hell could I do that'? Then the more I worked on *Weld* the more I realized that it was all there. I heard . . . all these wild things. So, I made *Arc.*[26]

Here Young links passion to noise, as we have seen before. But interestingly, the passion in question is the "passion of the song." The noise is transgressive, and foregrounding it is a liberating experience. Yet the noise is clearly situated as a component in the overall musical order and is not a dissolution of that order. In Young's description, there seem to be two mechanisms underlying this effect. On the one hand, noise is already a structural feature at certain moments in the performance, and may be prolonged like any other structural feature. On the other hand, noise can be an entirely new sign for an affective state signified in different ways by other parts of the song. In this instance, the noise remains closely connected to the song but in a semantic or intentional rather than a structural sense. Under the latter interpretation, both the song and the noise attached to its performance may be understood as signs for a more general set of feelings or ideas which are in some sense more primary.

Another interesting feature of *Arc,* also hinted at in the last quotation, is the question of how it relates to Young's working method more generally. One aspect of this question has already been discussed: the project clearly intensifies certain improvisational and exploratory aspects of Crazy Horse. However, this observation has more to do with the source of the project's raw material and with the character of the end result rather than the manner in which the piece was composed. In realizing *Arc,* Young seems to have adapted with ease to the rigorous process of constructing a large-scale electro-acoustic work. This is a reminder that even in the midst of his Crazy Horse primitivism, Young is the same artist who was famous for orchestral pop and elaborate arrangements earlier in his career:

There is an order to it. I took 57 pieces that we called "sparks." We took them out, numbered them and disassociated them from the concerts that they came from. Of those 57 pieces, I chose 37. I had them all on a data-base and I had all the keys and the lyrics that were in each piece all written down, and the location of the pieces so I could tell what hall it was from, so that I could move from one hall to another so the sound wouldn't change so radically. . . . If you listen to it a few times, you will see that it's almost like a song. Things come and go, hooks come back, it all cycles around. But it seems to degenerate also. By the time you get to the end, it's a little more frantic, a little more out of touch. It's starting to lose its mind a little [grins]. . . . If you look at my music over the last 30 years and want to see where I'm at now, this is it. And it happens as soon as we lose the beat. We break it down, and then we're gone. Nothing else matters. It's like jazz or something.[27]

In some ways, *Arc* represents Young's finest balance between spontaneity and deliberation. The material is subjected to rigorous organization, but it would not exist without the non-deliberative improvisations of Crazy Horse. Similarly, the systematic and mechanical process of assembling the work takes many cues from Young's subjective feelings about particular moments, as well as the contingent acoustic qualities of different concert halls. Some of Young's excitement over the project, and the degree to which he tries to relate it to existing traditions—something he has never done with any other album—may be related to this rich and, for Young, unique working method. Interestingly, given the amount of thought he has given to the project, Young does not seem aware of or interested in the history of such work in experimental classical music. This even though Sonic Youth, the partial inspiration for the project, are themselves rooted in the New York City avant-garde. Nor does Young mention the closest parallel to *Arc* elsewhere in rock: Lou Reed's *Metal Machine Music*. Although he does not refer to it, Young's feelings about *Arc* are similar to the ideas expressed in the liner notes to *Metal Machine Music* (1975), where Reed suggests that he has created a new style of rock and roll, one which is in some ways a distillation of the chaotic essence of the original. It seems likely that Reed's liner notes were intended at least somewhat ironically, and it is unclear to what degree Young is also playing with interviewers in his descriptions of *Arc*. Nevertheless, the surface similarity between Young's and Reed's comments is worth noting because it throws light upon the general role of noise in rock culture.

That an artist like Neil Young is able to produce such work without feeling the need to situate himself in the avant-garde says something about the current relationship between popular culture and high modernist experimentation. Gendron has noted that the kinds of prestige afforded by association with the avant-garde are typically limited to small, specialist markets. He goes on to argue that "popular music has reached such a critical mass in its own cultural empowerment that it no longer needs alliances with high culture to further its interests. In the cultural competition between popular music and high art, popular music has won, not by rising 'higher' than high-cultural music . . . but by making the latter less culturally relevant where it matters."[28] Gendron's argument is perhaps too sweeping, and the fact remains that many of the rock artists who regularly work in these sorts of experimental forms remain closely connected to "high art" contexts. However, his comments do resonate with the fact that Neil Young can make extensive comparisons between *Arc* and other musical traditions without any reference to experimental classical music and that he can describe groups such as Sonic Youth in entirely rock-centric terms. Seemingly for Neil Young, and for many other listeners, this sort of noise is not a borrowing from avant-garde classical traditions, but has become a possibility inscribed within the rock tradition itself.

A Trip Through a Power Chord: From Noise to Song and Back Again

Arc is like being inside of a very big thing. I equate *Arc* to that movie *Fantastic Voyage*—it's like a trip through a power chord. The chord may last like five or six seconds, but it takes *35 minutes,* at the size we're reducing ourselves to, to go through it.[29]

Simultaneism in the avant-garde was closely associated with noise in two ways: as the product of an instantaneous awareness of numerous events occurring at any one time in space . . . and the product of an additional collapse of time into that already collapsed space.[30]

Besides its political significance, noise has cognitive implications. In transgressing established categories, noise can allow for the formation of new conceptual resources. By this I mean not only the kinds of alternate social organization described by Attali, but also a multitude of more subtle effects in perception and cognition. The collapse of time and space described by Kahn, for example, involves the participation of linguistic categories, cognitive schemata, and affective qualities. More to the point, such a description places less emphasis on the disruption of an established order and more emphasis on the unique perspective opened by such a disruption. This kind of image emphasizes dimensions of noise relatively neglected in Attali's analysis in at least two respects. First, it invites us to view the effects of noise from a positive perspective, as sometimes constructive rather than always disruptive. Without such an understanding, it would be tempting to see Young's image of a "trip though a power chord" as unrelated to noise, which would remain connected only to his remarks about abrasiveness. We would then have missed the fact that noise functioned in this case not only to produce oppositional qualities, but also to open the way for a more neutral or even positive representation. Second, such a description invites us to treat noise from a cognitive perspective since it tends to emphasize the effects of noise on basic perceptual and conceptual categories. The view of cognition and musical meaning to be developed in chapter 4 places great emphasis on metaphor and conceptual blending, processes which make creative use of the disruptability of conceptual categories. Under this sort of reading the image of a trip through a power chord, relying as it does on schemata of spatial organization, can form a bridge between the code-centered mode of analysis pursued in my first two chapters and the more metaphorical direction pursued in later parts of this book.

The image also draws attention to further links between *Arc* and the rest of Young's work. When Young discusses the more structured features of *Arc,* he says that it is "almost like a song," implying that for him the terms "song like" and "clearly structured" would be vaguely synonymous. But *Arc* is not ultimately a song because it does not follow the same conventions of temporal and spatial organization. It loses its mind and suggests a radically altered sense of scale. I would suggest that in Young's more conventional Crazy Horse performances, especially live in concert, there is a deliberate back-and-forth movement set up between the relatively structured time and space of the vocal passages and the comparatively free framework of the solos. Young generally uses songs as an occasion for exploring texture and gesture (as a chance to play solos), but he also uses the solos as a device for going deeper into the song (for example by intensifying its overall mood or adding extra weight to structural features when they re-emerge). The image of changes and reversals in scale is therefore not just a convenient metaphor for a working method, but also for an important phenomenological aspect of Young's overall performance practice. What makes *Arc* distinctive, then, is not that there is a relationship enacted between freer and more constrained structures, nor that the freer structures are associated with perceptual and cognitive effects like reversal of scale or suspension of time. What distinguishes *Arc* is that the structured method exists *only* to allow the trip into the power chord, whereas in many of Young's other projects there is greater give and take between the various sorts of awareness. I believe this is one thing Young means when he describes *Arc*-style instrumentals as "the passion of the song . . . only." The comment is not only about structural devices or the intent of the players, but is also a description of the kind of metaphorical journey to be undertaken by listeners: a one-way incursion into a surreal landscape rather than the usual give and take.

In an acoustic sense, *Arc* is a distillation of the noisiest aspects of Crazy Horse. In a stylistic sense, this leads to an interesting double identity for the album. In Young's comments, the dichotomy becomes a narrative. At first, the material was seen as standing too far outside expectations and therefore as almost completely unassimilable. However, upon further reflection, Young began to feel that the material was entirely consistent with the spirit of his other Crazy Horse projects. Under this reading, *Arc* stands apart from the rest of the Crazy Horse repertoire only because it summarizes overall properties of that repertoire in a way that no other individual piece could do. This is a complex relationship—to escape identification with a context by virtue of encompassing it—and is an apt metaphor for Young's relationship to noise and oppositionality overall. Of course, in terms of sales and the amount of attention it received from critics, *Arc* may as well not exist. It is another of Young's peripheral projects, as far as I know included by no one in their list of the most representative or important Neil Young albums. This does not, however, suggest that Young is wrong is his assessment of its significance. *Arc*'s marginality may suggest instead that in Neil Young's work, especially with Crazy Horse, noise is constantly subjected to a dual demand. On the one hand, it must be genuinely noisy, the kind of transgressive, surprising soundscape which finds its ultimate distillation in *Arc,* and for that reason continues to fall outside the commercial mainstream even when presented by a mainstream artist. On the other hand, it must simultaneously find a working place in Young's overall persona, reaching an accommodation with contrasting elements of control, conservatism, and musical niceness (his pop and folk dimensions, which never entirely disappear). Perhaps the key argument of this chapter as a whole is that although the noise in Young's work is not entirely revolutionary or prophetic, it is nevertheless truly oppositional and refreshing. In sociological terms, we could make the point by speaking of how it opens up temporary autonomous zones, and in cognitive or semiotic terms we could point out the ways in which noise supports this temporary autonomy by transgressing established boundaries and encouraging new metaphors. In order to pave the way for more detailed interpretations of this second kind, I will now move on to a general consideration of musical signification.

4 | Have You Ever Been Singled Out?

Popular Music and Musical Signification

This chapter is not specifically about Neil Young. Elsewhere in the book, theory and application are developed in parallel. By contrast, in this chapter I would like to present some very general remarks about the nature of musical signification. The result will not be a systematic theory, but rather a series of refinements to existing models, with two goals in mind. First, I would like to show how the specific concepts developed in chapters 2 and 3 take their place in a broader orientation toward meaning. Second, this chapter lays the groundwork for more detailed engagement with musical sound in chapters 5 and 6. Although Neil Young's music does not arise explicitly here, my theoretical orientation has been deeply influenced by my encounter with his music. When conceptual paradigms are brought to bear on specific repertoires, there is a possibility that those repertoires will be reduced to mere examples of the theory, and there is also a possibility that the coherence of the theory will break down in the face of complex social facts. Like most theorists who choose to write about a particular artist or tradition, I hope that the relationship between theory and application in this book is more symmetrical. I have been led to develop or adopt a particular set of concepts in large measure because of my need to say certain things about Neil Young. And while the theoretical framework will subsequently take on a life of its own, it will always reflect the repertoire that inspired it, just as that repertoire will never look quite the same to me as it did before the theory was developed.

My emphasis is not on uncovering new areas of speculation, but on demonstrating the possibilities implicit in a certain combination of existing approaches. Specifically, I will draw upon the following traditions: (1) Peircian semiotics, which provides a high-level typology of signs, and especially theories of iconicity and indexicality; (2) theories of musical persona, which can dramatize the links between human agents and the quasi-agential frameworks (social and stylistic) within which they operate; (3) conceptual metaphor theory, which provides an explanatory model of how the semiotic relationships described above are organized and function; (4) cultural theories of popular music (such as those thematically deployed in chapter 1), concerned with the historical and social situations in which this all unfolds. Besides drawing from all these traditions, I want to show how they are on some levels complementary. Most simply, I will suggest that spatial and energetic metaphors drawn from embodied experience provide a framework within which we can describe three crucial factors in musical practice: (1) musical sounds; (2) identities (textual, personal, and social); (3) the activity of discursive formations in constraining and enabling practices and institutions. If all these elements are described in similar terms, it becomes easier to demonstrate their many subtle interrelationships, because of course they are not really separate, but represent various aspects or moments of music as a heterogeneous social fact.

This sort of orientation has already been displayed in chapters 2 and 3. For example, the dialogic theory of genre accords with a general perspective under which social conventions and frameworks of all kinds are described as quasi-agential. In treating stylistic and genre norms as fields of force and as virtual personas, the argument presupposed a more basic theory of meaning, identity, and text, which this chapter aims to furnish. Some questions addressed by the semiotic and cognitive perspective of this chapter include: In what sense can a partial or virtual persona be said to exist, and in what does its character subsist? Why is music an especially powerful medium for creating such effects? And how may the personification of textual features aid in explaining the ways that particular kinds of music do particular kinds of cultural work? The most basic claim in the chapter, expressed in both semiotic and cognitive terminology, is that a common set of conceptual metaphors and schemata underlie many different instances of spatial and energetic iconicity, which in turn are fundamental not only to musical meaning but to identity formation and social structure in general. This argument will allow for a perspective in which persona and text, subject and environment, art and other social practices all relate to one another in a constant and fluid structuration.[1] The overarching phrase under which I've placed all these elements is *poetics of energy*. One constant feature in this book is a tendency to read everything in terms of spatial and energetic metaphors, and in turn to treat these as always displaying expressive properties to some degree. Under such a view, energy is always poetic because it is never far from an expressive reading, and poetics revolves around concepts of energy. In making this suggestion, however, I am not proposing to develop a systematic poetics, but rather to signal that I find something poetic in the interplay of these concepts. The title was chosen partly through intuition and will perhaps be justified that way as well. I recognize my aspiration in what Zak has called *resonance* (although he raises the word in an entirely different connection), a suggestive fit "at once impressionistic and precise."[2] In the end, I hope that the theoretical apparatus I construct will be resonant with Neil Young's music, with the discourses surrounding it, and with other theories of musical meaning.

It must be acknowledged that such a program involves a fair bit of appropriation and often combines concepts in a manner not entirely consonant with their respective source traditions. Most pressingly, there is a tension between the relativism implicit in my neo-pragmatic view of interpretation (discussed in the introduction) and the scientific roots of the cognitive and music analytic vocabularies deployed in those interpretations. Consider, for example, the manner in which I will use formal musical analysis in chapter 5. Although the situation has changed somewhat in recent years, there is still a tendency among music theorists to regard formal analysis as a kind of discovery procedure in which consistency and clarity are required if the apparatus is to produce correct information. By contrast, my work proceeds from the belief that it is equally valid to use formal analysis simply as a descriptive language. It is possible to choose analytic techniques not for their systematicity, but because they encapsulate culturally pertinent ways of hearing and representing acoustic events. For example, if there are reasons to believe, based upon cultural practices and discourses, that some people think and hear through metaphors of harmonic distance or tension and release, and if a given analytic method encapsulates this perspective, then this method may be used as a way of exploring and describing that way of listening. The method may not be consistent or entirely systematic, but it must be arguably pertinent. But this is not to say that analysis should be limited to describing impressions that someone has actually had. Since analytic techniques are in some instances algorithmic —some of them can be set up and left to run themselves without direct intervention—an analysis may turn up a wealth of material not yet perceived or thought of by anyone. This is part of the purpose of doing analysis: to discover novel descriptions which may later be judged pertinent. However, I would suggest that the value of the process is not determined by the systematicity of the analysis, but rather by the aptness of interpretations which the analytic vocabulary can express. In other words, I aim to use analysis as a *signifying resource,* treating each analytic technique as a method for placing musical sound under a description.

The problem enters with expectations that trail in the wake of systematic vocabularies. Even when systematicity is not foregrounded, there will be many systematic elements in my analytic practice. An analytic vocabulary will not yield its distinct perspective if we *completely* fail to honor its systematic requirements. This could lead to misunderstanding, since the presence of any degree of systematicity has traditionally been understood as a commitment to complete systematicity. However, if we consider analytical systems as analogous to mathematical logics, there are precedents for seeking a balance between systematicity and intuition, especially where the object of analysis is a lived cultural practice. As Bourdieu notes, "practice has a logic which is not that of the logician."[3] Practices are not illogical, since they generate and employ organizational schemata. These schemata may satisfy requirements of mathematical logic to a certain degree, but there is nothing in the nature of most cultural practices requiring them to do so altogether. The message here is that rules of logical systematicity are not an all-or-nothing affair in cultural practices, and so their use should be similarly flexible in the interpretation of such practices. To use them doesn't always oblige one to use them completely, and to transgress them doesn't always mean that one has abandoned them altogether. I have directed these comments to formal musical analysis, but they would also hold with respect to my use of models from the cognitive and social sciences.

This chapter is designed to first address general disciplinary questions, then to elaborate on selected core concepts, and finally to present an overview of my interpretive practice. It will begin with some remarks on structure and semiosis as framing concepts, moving later to consider the different traditions of semiotic work that have developed in the study of popular music and Western concert music. I feel that these traditions need to be brought together, not only for my own project, but simply because they have much to offer one another. I will then discuss particular topics which concern both traditions and which are also of central importance in my reading of Neil Young: conventional correlations, iconicity, the body, and identity. This will involve a consideration of conceptual metaphor theory and the theory of embodied image schemata as frameworks that can highlight and further develop these areas of common interest. Finally I will sketch out a program for interpretive practice which incorporates all these elements. Readers who are less interested in the detailed history of musical semiotics and would prefer to just scan the main argument may wish to skip ahead to the section titled "Cognitive Theory and Signification."

Structure and Semiosis

Even though semiotic terminology is not used extensively in this book, I would suggest that my interpretive agenda is for the most part a semiotic one. This is not only because the literature on musical semiotics was my primary inspiration in framing questions, but also because my most general objective for the book is to describe some of the mechanisms which have caused Neil Young's work to be interpreted in particular ways. Concepts such as noise and dialogism, developed in previous chapters, are implicitly semiotic since they are concerned with the nature of cultural meaning systems and seek to describe ways in which specific texts and identities can be individuated with respect to these. However, given that semiotics has never acquired a standard methodology or a common set of concepts, it is important to say what kind of semiotics I have in mind. So before returning to more specialized topics in which the semiotic connection may be less evident, I would like to situate my work in the semiotic field.

My central suggestion is this: semiotics remains useful as a high-level descriptive and interpretive framework for theorists who seek to explain the social formation of meaning and who wish to do so in a manner both systematic and non-reductive. Conceived in this way, semiotics is similar in spirit to naturalism as described by Flanagan: a doctrine rooted in science but which does not favor reductive explanations, arguing instead that higher-level phenomena require higher-level vocabularies for their description.[4] In saying this, it is not my intention to argue that semiotics is a master key which unlocks the other disciplines. I simply want to suggest that a semiotic vocabulary remains consonant with more specialized approaches to cultural forms—especially linguistics, philosophical logic, cognitive science, critical theory, hermeneutics, and cultural studies— and that just as naturalistic models can summarize and interpret specific results from fields like biochemistry, genetics, and geology, semiotics can provide a high-level interface for a range of specific results in these cultural sciences. The closeness of fit will of course vary between theorists, and there will be semiotic theories which do not accord with my model at all. It should be understood that I am describing a particular perspective—one that could be called semiotic—rather than offering a program for semiotics as a unified discipline.

It may seem circular to suggest that semiotics be understood as a high-level vocabulary for synthesizing results from these intellectual traditions, since semiotics was itself a foundational influence on most of them. However, we should not assume that because semiotics bore a particular relationship to certain disciplines in the past it will continue to bear the same relationship in the future. In some respects the old relationships will persist. For example, semiology of a Saussurian kind has a systematic origin in phonology, and although contemporary linguists do not make explicit use of its vocabulary the basic spirit of Saussurian structuralism continues to accord well with linguistic theory. Similarly, although the structuralist approach to culture in general now constitutes only a part of contemporary social thought, within those boundaries its fundamental features remain fairly intact. But in other respects, the relationship between semiotics and its source traditions has changed. Peircian semiotics, for example, has been largely abandoned or ignored by the pragmatist philosophy with which it was first associated. Indeed, the more idealist elements of Peirce's system have elicited bewilderment or even hostility from contemporary pragmatists.[5] And even though Saussurian terminology and models survive in the field of cultural studies, they are nearly always combined with elements from practice theory and other critical perspectives, crucially undermining the early structuralist faith in holism and completeness. As my own analyses throughout this book show, I am similarly selective in my borrowings from the Peircian and Saussurian traditions. However, certain concepts from these semiotic traditions are still among the most powerful available for talking in a general way about the structures and practices which generate and organize meaning.

When making this suggestion, the two umbrella concepts I have in mind are *structure,* treated in a Saussurian manner, and *semiosis,* considered from a Peircian perspective. By the concept of structure, I mean arguments which incorporate the following kinds of claims: (1) that it is the form rather than the content of communicative systems which must be studied; (2) that meaning is relational and conventional rather than immanent or natural; (3) that contrast (difference in a discrete parameter) is the fundamental mechanism of value within cultural systems; (4) that continuous phenomena can be segmented so as to participate in an ordered system of differences; and (5) that it is in general possible to create synchronic formal analyses which demonstrate the fundamental terms and relations of a cultural system at any particular moment. This kind of structuralist program is so familiar that I will not discuss it at length, but it should be noted that any time I speak of codes or hierarchies or deal with conventionalized systems of difference, I am doing so with such a framework in mind. However, there are crucial elements of the structuralist program which are absent from my work insofar as some of the other models I deploy—practice theory, dialogic theory, and intertextuality theory—are overtly poststructuralist in their origins. For example, although differential formal structure is a key determinant in all kinds of meaning, an intertextual perspective abandons the idea that such a structure can be closed. Similarly, there are many shades and kinds of difference besides binary opposition, and in some cases sameness and repetition will be as important as difference. Finally, the doctrine of pure conventionality in the signifier-signified relationship will be retained for some purposes—for describing cases in which the correlations are, in fact, based almost entirely on convention—but will be juxtaposed with Peircian concepts of iconicity and indexicality, in which meanings are shaped by factors additional or even foundational to convention.

The Peircian model is probably less well-known to most readers. As a philosopher interested in logic and scientific investigation, Peirce provides a concept of *semiosis* as a dynamic process highly complementary to the more static structuralist model. Peirce's thought is complex and arguably stood unfinished at his death. His ambition was to create a complete philosophical system, and in doing so he positioned himself between idealism and materialism, trying to reconcile them in a pragmatic theory of knowledge as habit. The exact nature of his program, not to mention its success, remains a matter of debate among specialists, but Peirce unquestionably succeeded in sketching out a broad orientation toward signification with important features for both cultural studies and for aesthetics. For Peirce, *semiosis* is the activity or life of signs. At times, his view of semiosis seems almost animist, even mystical, treating signs as entities which elaborate themselves in fluid chains leading toward preordained ends. This is the idealist Peirce, although paradoxically these views are also closely related to his practice as a scientist since he usually seems to hold natural law to be the driving force behind long-term semiosis. At other times, Peirce treats semiosis as a social practice of knowledge formation. In either case, semiosis is a concept which emphasizes the dynamic unfolding of signification.

Another crucial feature of Peirce's thought that it highlights what I will call the *ontological heterogeneity* of semiosis. For Peirce, as for Saussure, signs are relational rather than material entities. However, unlike Saussure, Peirce emphasizes that the semiotic relation emerges from a coordinated activity of three basic categories (in the Aristotelian and later Kantian sense of ultimate classes). Although Peirce's categories are not exactly ontological, I am taking the opportunity to highlight the manner in which his triad of categories includes between them the mental and the material, the ideal and the particular, relations and singularities, so that when he proposes a semiotic system that relies on all three categories the result is ontologically more diverse than the Saussurian model. For Peirce, the sign is an event in which the particular qualitative, material, and relational features of a given moment interact. But rather than say more about Peirce's categories, which are not easy to gloss in contemporary terms, I will move on to his triadic concept of the sign.

My description is modeled on that of Lidov.[6] For Peirce, a sign consists of an irreducibly triadic relationship between three relata: object, representamen, and interpretant. The *representamen,* without too much distortion, can be understood as analogous to the Saussurian signifier. The *object* is analogous to the signified, but here the differences require immediate attention. The object is something with which the sign user is already familiar, for example, a physical thing, a state of affairs, a text, a theoretical model. The activity of semiosis transforms or extends the sign user's experience of the object. Unlike the Saussurian view, in which a signified is simply correlated to a signifier, in the Peircian model the object of the sign is actively changed by the activity of semiosis, and indeed the purpose of semiosis is to bring about such change. The third element in Peirce's triadic sign, the *interpretant,* is the most distinctive. The interpretant is a bridge phenomenon—for example a further sign or chain of signs, a physical reaction, a habit—which instantiates a particular kind of connection between representamen and object. The interpretant is a process, unfolding in time, but structurally serving a singular mediating function in the sign. According to Lidov, where art is concerned, "principally, the interpretant is our awareness and understanding of the object in the light of its representation."[7] In other words, due to the activity of the interpretant, "the sign is biased. Representation is of something *as* something. Turkey and pumpkin pie signify Thanksgiving as festive."[8] This, too, is unlike the Saussurian model, in which the creative combination of distinct terms, representing something *as* something, is allowed at higher levels but is not a basic component of the sign itself.

In summary, there are two features—dynamism and ontological heterogeneity—which allow Peirce's system to address aspects of social practice and especially aesthetic experience not well-served by structuralism, yet to do so in a manner mostly compatible with structuralism. In one sense, then, my interpretive practice is a blend of Saussurian and Peircian elements. From Saussure we can adopt a model of structure and apply it to cultural systems such as style, genre, and ideology. From Peirce we can adopt a perspective on the ontological heterogeneity and dynamism of structures in practice. Since much of the existing work in musical semiotics is expressed in Peircian or Saussurian terms, this way of describing my program can help situate the work with respect to existing musical semiotics. It should also be noted that my perspective bears a close resemblance to Bakhtinian social linguistics (as deployed in chapter 2) and to the practice theory of Bourdieu. Both of these traditions, in different ways, retain crucial elements of the Saussurian perspective while allowing a foundational place for the situated activity of real subjects. Indeed, they tend to define subjectivity itself as a process in which individuated positions and identities are improvised within cultural structures of constraint. This is a crucial point because persona and identity are central issues in my work on Neil Young and are not well-treated in either the Saussurian or Peircian traditions, which tend to either grant the subject an unrealistic degree of freedom or, alternatively, to reduce subjects to epiphenomena of cultural systems. Practice theory and dialogic theory, by contrast, specialize in analyzing the various shades of subjective freedom and the many different positions that can be occupied between full individuation and pure tokenhood. For these reasons, and also since both traditions have been widely influential on recent cultural theory, there are times that my analysis will deploy terms or general concepts from Bakhtin and Bourdieu (explained as needed where they are used).

A Very Brief Overview of Musical Semiotics

The literature of musical semiotics can be loosely divided into three groups, according to whether a given work is most concerned with ethnomusicology, popular music studies, or Western concert music. Although there is some overlap, for the most part these three literatures have proceeded in isolation from one another. Writers in any one area rarely cite the others, which is unfortunate because in many instances similar topics are being addressed using similar theoretical models. Although I did not make a special project of uniting the traditions of musical semiotics, I ended up doing so incidentally, having been profoundly influenced by works in all three areas. In order to describe my orientation it is necessary to briefly describe each tradition and to make explicit their points of congruence and difference. Specific theoretical areas of interest are described more fully later in the chapter. What follows here is a very condensed overview of the field as a whole.

Although theories of musical meaning can be found among the very earliest writings on music, the discipline of musical semiotics proper can be traced back to the work of Ruwet, and very shortly afterwards Molino.[9] Ruwet's special interest was in developing a structuralist poetics for music, with special emphasis on the repetition of melodic units (paradigmatic repetition). Molino's basic orientation was similarly structuralist and linguistic, his most influential contribution being the idea of a tripartition of the musical fact into three levels: a process of production, a process of reception, and a structured physical artifact. Both Ruwet and Molino, apart from being fully committed structuralists, sought to establish methods of analysis applicable across different cultures, as did their chief follower, Nattiez.[10] There were other early semiotic theories of music in addition to the structuralist ones, for example the aesthetic philosophies of Langer and Epperson, the quasi-linguistic correlational scheme of Cooke, and the behaviorisms of Coker and Boilès.[11] However, these were not as widely influential, and for the most part early musical semiotics was concerned with adapting structural linguistic methodology to musical contexts. The questions of interest centered around segmentation (as an analog to phonology and morphology), the nature of musical competence (as an analog to Chomsky's linguistic competence), and musical syntax. The question of semantic fields and reference was also raised, although interestingly it did not receive much systematic treatment. As a rule, early musical semiotics was purely formal.[12] The question of what a musical *meaning* might be like was not systematically explored by musical semioticians during this period except insofar as the structural nature of the theories implicitly or explicitly endorsed a formalist, self-reference view of musical semantics.

At around the same time, semiotic methodology was being taken up by popular music theorists. Early examples are Tagg and Stefani,[13] both of whom were also structuralists (although Tagg's early work also includes an interesting use of the centripetal/centrifugal force schemata to be discussed later in this chapter, and draws upon certain aspects of perception and temporal experience which go beyond traditional structuralist concerns). However, the influence of British cultural studies caused semiotics of popular music to move in a sociological direction, and there is a political and cultural-theoretical dimension to popular music semiotics which remains mostly absent in semiotic theories of Western art music. Crucial here was articulation theory as developed by Stuart Hall.[14] This approach is basically Saussurian in its assumptions, but places emphasis on the social and pragmatic dimensions of sign manipulation. Closely related is the treatment of style in subcultural theory[15] and the treatment of competence as a question of the pragmatic deployment of various levels of code.[16] In all these cases, a basically structuralist view of sign systems is mobilized for the purpose of cultural criticism, and the result is a model similar in its formal features to other musical semiotics but quite different in ultimate effect. Later extensions of this approach include Middleton and Shepherd.[17]

The 1980s marked a radical shift in semiotic methodology in all three traditions. In ethnomusicology, and in anthropology more generally, there was a shift away from structuralist abstraction and toward the interpretation of lived experience in terms more closely resembling the vocabularies and priorities of social actors. For example, Feld developed a theory of *interpretive moves* which blends elements of pragmatics with textual formalism, and some workers began to emphasize the importance of iconicity.[18] The interest in iconicity is crucial because it marks a shift away from the Saussurian doctrine of unmotivated signs.[19] In my own study, the balance in practice between conventional signs and motivated signs, interpreted largely through metaphors of subjective freedom and constraint, is a central consideration. In the semiotics of Western art music, around the same time, there was a similar move toward iconicity, and especially icons of embodied experience. Lidov was an early worker in this area, and the theory is currently being developed by a number of workers, including Lidov and Hatten.[20] Ideas of gestural meaning and iconicity were also being developed by popular music theorists, especially Middleton, along with Shepherd and Wicke.[21] This approach, besides acknowledging degrees of material and psychological motivation in semiosis, is distinctive in treating the signifier as a *time form,* thus granting a crucial role to the perception of temporal unfolding, unlike the structuralist approach in which the value of a signifier is essentially atemporal.

The idea of competence continued to be important into the 1980s, but it was more frequently conceived in hermeneutic terms or in terms of genre. Both tendencies were evident in Hatten, and in ethnomusicology Rice has promoted a hermeneutic orientation.[22] The idea of code also survived, but it tended to be developed under the rubric of topic theory.[23] For many of the aforementioned theorists of Western concert music, Peircian semiotics came to displace the Saussurian model as a central reference point, and the Peircian perspective appeared in ethnomusicology as well.[24] The other prominent development of the 1980s was the widespread adoption by many European semioticians, especially Tarasti, of Greimassian narratology.[25] I would suggest that the narratological model and work on embodiment and iconicity are complementary insofar as the latter provides a model of the mechanisms by which the former operates. Similarly, I will soon argue that recent theories of cognition provide an explanatory framework for theories of iconicity.

In summary, despite considerable areas of overlap between the semiotics of Western art music and of popular music, these literatures have not for the most part engaged with one another. Part of the reason is institutional, with differences in repertoire and allegiances to different cognate disciplines serving to divide workers. Part of the reason is doubtless ideological, since popular music studies in the early years was largely dedicated to challenging the canonic and normative assumptions of more traditional musicology. In recent years, however, the differences have perhaps been lessening. For example, where early popular music studies was hostile toward aesthetic philosophy, some recent popular music theorists have begun to take more interest in aesthetic experience (for example Gracyk and arguably Krims). And while the semiotic study of Western concert music sometimes relied heavily on the concept of an ideal listener, some recent work in the area has been more reflexive and more deeply engaged with specific histories.[26] Most importantly, there are new areas of convergence emerging since the 1980s, which include topics such as embodiment, metaphor, and identity (although, again, workers in the two fields almost never acknowledge that they share this territory). I would now like to look at these topics of common interest in more depth in order to begin sketching the details of an interpretive practice which borrows freely from all existing schools of musical semiotics.

Potential Points of Convergence: Topic Theory

Topic theory as such cannot be called a point of convergence between semiotic traditions since it has developed entirely within the literature on Western art music. Nonetheless, topic theory encapsulates many of the assumptions and methods typical of recent literature on popular music as well and so deserves attention as a potential meeting ground. Topic theory was first developed by Ratner in his work on the classic style.[27] A topic is a particular musical figure or schema which has acquired a conventional correlation. Hunting fifths are a good example, and distinctive dance rhythms such as a tango or waltz are another. The concept of a topic involves the idea of music being "appropriate to its subject," but is more developed in that "certain portrayals are conventional . . . part of a semantic universe within which the music is composed. Thus, no text or title is necessary for musical topics to carry signification."[28] One crucial feature of topics is that they extend beyond the musical. There are, for example, military topics in music which form a part of the broader cultural concept of the martial. The theory can thus address both the nature of fit between music and text or narrative, and also the ability of absolute music to achieve, in some cases, fairly specific connotations. Another important feature of topic theory is that it achieves a balance between conventional signification and more motivated iconic or indexical signification. Topics themselves are conventional, but in many cases the conventional topic when studied historically turns out to be a conventionalized icon or index or, in other words, a conventionalized representation of a more motivated relationship of resemblance or physical connection.[29] This raises a third crucial element of topic theory: since topics are culture-specific, they must be studied in context. Topic theory borrows from structuralism the idea of stable correlation and invites formal analysis, but it insists further that the *specific history* of a correlation is fundamentally pertinent to the analysis.

A caution is in order here. Ratner's work made extensive use of the writings of contemporaries to establish topics, and in one respect this is a commendable feature of the theory. Indeed, if topic theory is ever directly applied to popular music then the reports of musicians, critics, and listeners will be a crucial factor in discovering topics. However, as Monelle points out, the opinions of contemporaries are not infallible in this respect since "contemporaries are engaged in the *justification* of their music and thus in concealing vital features."[30] Similarly, a central claim of topic theory is that "certain musical styles and figures were understood to signify particular cultural units, wherever they occurred," and this is sometimes explicitly denied by contemporaries, who may wish to argue for the autonomy or exceptionality of certain musics.[31] This is to be expected, given that all conventional signification is to some degree ideological. The essential point is that topic theory requires that a topical universe be described through minute historical or sociological study and that this will involve both taking seriously the reports of contemporaries and digging for crucial unstated or even repressed correlations.

In this respect, it is clear how a critical project, for example McClary's work on the gendering of musical style,[32] can be akin to topic theory in the way it treats conventional correlations according to their balance of the spoken and the unspoken, the public and the hidden. More directly, the similarities between topic theory and a correlational study in the style of Tagg should be evident. In general, topic theory provides a framework within which we can model conventional correlations, thus preserving some key concepts of structuralism, in a manner which takes account of history and pragmatics. Topic theory has not yet been directly applied to the study of popular music, but much of the existing work on popular codes and discourses is compatible with it. In the present study, I do not directly develop a list of topics in 1960s and 1970s rock music, but the manner in which I choose descriptive metaphors, based as it is on highlighting those themes which seem conventionalized or nearly so, is directly inspired by topic theory, as is my treatment of conventional correlation as a historically specific process connected to, but distinct from, more materially motivated factors in sign formation.

Potential Points of Convergence: Homology and Iconicity

In the semiotics of both popular music and Western art music, recent theorists have paid attention to the variety of ways in which correlations and meanings may be established. As we have seen, even the fairly straightforward notion of conventional correlation has, in topic theory, been expanded to include degrees of motivation. It has also, within cultural studies, been connected to the idea of discourse as a kind of force, a structuring of communication which is simultaneously an exertion of social power. Beyond these expansions to the theory of correlation, both popular music and Western concert music researchers have begun to explore non-arbitrary mechanisms which underlie some kinds of sign formation. In Birmingham subcultural studies and much subsequent popular music sociology, for example, the cultural logic of homology is taken to be a strong force in style formation. The concept of homology addresses situations in which many different codes in a subculture—musical style, fashion, bodily deportment, dialect, etc.—display a similarity of form and tend to connote similar kinds of meaning. The theory of homology strikes a fine balance between motivation and convention, since under homology theory it is largely the structural logic of existing conventions which exerts force on subsequent sign formations. In other words, convention becomes a motivation.

An even closer fit between workers on popular and concert music, and possibly a stronger concept of motivation as well, can be found in theories of iconicity. One kind of iconicity which concerns workers in both areas is that of energetic and spatial configurations in general, and bodily states in particular. Details will be discussed shortly, but the argument in outline is that musical sound, being an energetic phenome-non, can display energetic configurations which literally resemble those found in bodies, and more generally in many kinds of physical states. More subtly, the theory of homology can itself be understood as a special case of iconicity, as is suggested by the fact that some theorists have used the term *structural iconicity* in a manner almost synonymous with ho-mology.[33] This sort of iconicity relies upon Peirce's notion of *diagram-matic* resemblance, an iconicity where similarity rests not in properties but in the structure of oppositions.[34] Thinking of homologies in terms of diagrammatic relationships takes us away from simple mimetic con-ceptions of iconicity and allows us to conceive similarity of logical struc-ture as analogous to visual resemblance, an interpretation which will be strengthened in our discussion of conceptual metaphor.

Potential Points of Convergence: The Body

Most current work on musical icons tends to emphasize gesture and other bodily states. Indeed, the emergence of embodiment as a cen-tral focus is another important unifying theme in the semiotics of popu-lar music and Western concert music. The iconicity in question here is not a visual one, but rather one of kinesic sensation and temporal shaping. It is a similarity in the topology of energetic states and in the time forms through which they display change, expressed in terms of bodily posture, movement, affect, or more generally in terms of cogni-tive schemata which require a body for their orientation (high/low, near/far, contained/free, etc.). So before discussing this work in more depth and making clear exactly how I intend to relate these theories to ques-tions of persona and identity, a few general remarks about body theories are in order. The literature on embodiment is too vast to be summarized, so my emphasis will be on identifying some of the body theories which have been most influential on musicology and which can contribute most directly to the semiotic interpretation of rock music as a cultural practice.

Much early work on musical embodiment seeks to find a code in the body insofar as it views the body as a source of discrete states which may be correlated to particular meanings. In the search for a code-like body, there are at least two possible strategies. Some, for example Clynes,[35] seek a code *in* the body, beginning with a materialist and normative view of the body and concluding that within such a body there must be code-like systems. In the case of Clynes, a finite set of temporal envelopes is said to be found in the central nervous system, and each of these time forms is argued to be correlated to a specific basic emotion. Others take a more moderate view, although one based in the same sort of materialism, and look for uniform effects of the body *upon* systems of code. An example of this sort of approach would be the work of Stefani, who in one article wishes to find somatic factors underlying the codes that mark certain vocal genres as popular.[36] One could also note the code-like attitude toward the body in early cultural studies. In much of this work, the body was treated as a visual surface which offered certain possibilities for displaying discrete and articulated behaviors of fashion, proxemics, and so on.

Some researchers have resisted this code-like approach to the body. Possible objections include its tendency toward essentialism (Clynes is especially vulnerable on this count) and that such theories do not for the most part address the unique properties of embodiment, preferring to emphasize parallels between the body and natural language (in this connection, Clynes has made an important contribution by refusing to separate felt affect from the formal structure of his code). One such code-resistant theorist is Keil. He does not present a theory of the body as such, but the body is strongly implied by his focus on musical participation. Keil's approach, often called grooveology, is rooted in the materiality of the body but is nonetheless very far from the deterministic models favored by workers like Clynes.[37] Keil borrows Meyer's term *embodied meaning* for syntactical configurations (embodiment here refers to the instantiation of a formal relation in a piece of music, not directly to the bodily experience of listeners or performers). To embodied meaning, Keil adds the concept of *engendered feeling*.[38] Keil is aware that "the metaphysical specter of mind-body dualism seems to emerge from these polarities," but he is quick to agree with Meyer that the debate on dualism is non-productive and circular.[39] Keil does not seem to favor an equal partnership between the two, however, and I would suggest that there is an ideological dualism here if not a metaphysical one. Keil celebrates the body in an openly polemical fashion as part of his celebration of popular musics and of highly participatory traditional musics, and I believe that a comparison with Clynes, whose work often reads like an argument for the exceptionalism of Western concert music, is instructive. The theories of Keil and Clynes articulate opposite ends of a continuum from elitism to populism, yet they both use a theory of the body to do so. Clynes seeks to rationalize the body, viewing bodies as the source of strict codes, whereas Keil seeks to use the body as an escape from excesses of rationality. Both views are essentialist in their way, and both are centered on the body. If there is a message here, it is that the body as a theoretical object has served varied ideological ends.

The phenomenological approach to embodiment, shaped by the work of Merleau-Ponty, is another orientation which has had influence in musicology. Merleau-Ponty distinguishes the physiological body from the phenomenal one, although awareness of one's own materiality is sometimes a part of phenomenal body awareness. The phenomenal body includes bodily sensation, conceptualizations of the body, the practical experience of being in the world as an embodied being, and in general all the ways in which one's sense of self is intimately connected with one's sense of having a body. The phenomenal body bears an extremely flexible relationship to the physiological one, and for this reason much phenomenological work on embodiment may not at first appear to be about bodies at all in the narrower sense. As a result, the perspective can be of use when we wish to discuss selfhood, identification, and affect. In addition, the phenomenal body provides an important model of how virtual bodies and personas may be constructed in music, since it allows for an experience of embodiment not tightly coupled to the immediate presence of a physical body. Something like a phenomenological dimension is of crucial importance in studies of the body and music for several reasons: (1) it deals so closely with how it *feels* to have a body; (2) it shows that the body serves as a conceptual structure as much as a physical one; and (3) it offers a framework for discussing the particularity of individual selves. Although my own work does not engage directly with phenomenology, I want to point out that many of the assumptions of conceptual metaphor theory, discussed shortly, are compatible with phenomenology in a broad sense.

And since I have already described parallels between my own approach and the practice theory of Bourdieu, I should mention that conceptual metaphor theory also shares certain things in common with Bourdieu's theory of *habitus,* although not the same features as it shares with phenomenology. For Bourdieu, habitus is "the system of structured, structuring dispositions . . . which is constituted in practice and is always oriented towards practical functions."[40] Habitus is a state of embodiment insofar as many of its structures and dispositions are physio-logical ones. As with Butler's constructivist position (much more influential on musicology than has been Bourdieu's theory of habitus),[41] the body is the self as constructed by the social conditions of its life history. A body which has been constituted in a particular manner subsequently orders and orients all practices engaged by the subject (although for Butler, much more than for Bourdieu, the socially constructed body often includes within itself a variety of possible selves and the possibility of movement between them). Habitus resembles the phenomenal body in that it is not coextensive with the physical body, but is better understood as a set of dispositions of that body in practice. However, it is unlike the phenomenal body in that it is never the object of direct awareness. What habitus shares with conceptual metaphor theory is the emphasis on pre-conscious structuring phenomena, which are largely excluded from phe-nomenology. In short, as we will see, conceptual metaphor theory ad-dresses two key features of embodiment which are treated separately in the theory of habitus and in phenomenology: how the body functions as a preconscious mechanism, and how the body feels to consciousness. Conceptual metaphor theory cannot *replace* either of these other theo-ries because it lacks the aesthetic dimension of phenomenology and does not share practice theory's powers of sociological critique. However, the fact that it is consistent with both of them makes conceptual metaphor theory a powerful tool, and it will allow me to borrow selectively from both phenomenological and practice-theoretic authors without stepping outside a relatively coherent paradigm.

When we speak in more detail of icons and indices of bodily experi-ence, we will need to keep these various aspects of the body in mind. There is a tendency in much musicological literature to begin discussion of body topics such as gesture without first specifying a theory of the body itself. As a basic framework, then, I want to stress the following points which can underlie the more specialized discussions that follow:

1. The body is material, but not in a single or simple way. It is ma-terial because the body as a mechanism is material, but the body as we live it is not coextensive with this material body. However, a concept or experience of materiality is usually implicated in the phenomenal body as well, helping to give it a distinctive iden-tity among other phenomenal entities.
2. The body is a profound locus for our sense of self, both because

it provides some of our most intense experiences and because it is our means of being in the world.

3. Bodies are socially constructed, and this constrains the options available to us. Conceived as habitus, a particular body is the result of a cultural system's self-reproduction. So our body becomes the site of profound self-ownership, but also profound self-alienation.

4. Because it is material, the body is continuous yet also amenable to discrete articulation (possession of both these features is typical of material continua in general). There are powerful forces acting to articulate and code the body, many of them social and many biological. However . . .

5. These biological and cultural systems of articulation do not exhaust the potentials of the body. The body has features and can enter into behaviors which are not regulated or recognized by these biological and cultural functions. This aspect of embodiment is not well-treated by habitus theory, but is a key component in the late work of Foucault, and also in psychoanalytic work such as that of Kristeva.

All this needs to be kept in mind as we now move on to consider the theory of conceptual metaphor, which will enable us to return to specific questions of musical sound and musical persona.

Cognitive Theory and Signification

In recent years, an interest in theories of cognition has been growing in many branches of musicology. Much of this work is focused on experiences and conceptions of embodiment, making it amenable to synthesis with semiotic work on musical iconicity. More specifically, the theory of cognitive semantics as developed by Lakoff and Johnson has been of interest to many music theorists. McClary was an early advocate, and in popular music studies the approach has been adopted by Fast and myself.[42] Among theorists of Western concert music, the theory of cognitive semantics and other closely related methodologies are developed by Brower, Cox, Larson, Saslaw, and Zbikowski, among others.[43] For the purposes of my analysis, what is significant about all these approaches is that they share the following core concepts: (1) embodied experience is at the root of many cognitive processes; (2) schemata of spatial relations (also known as image schemata) form one of the most fundamental layers of cognition; and (3) processes such as cross-domain mapping and conceptual blending are vital in explaining the way music is conceptualized. I would like to describe each of these claims in some detail, in the process also describing what I take to be a complementary relation between cognitive theory and semiotics.

As described by Johnson, "a schema is a recurrent pattern, shape, and regularity in, or of, [our] ongoing ordering activities. These patterns emerge as meaningful structures for us chiefly at the level of our bodily movements through space, our manipulation of objects, and our perceptual interactions."[44] Schemata develop early in life, abstracting frequently met patterns of spatial experience. For example, a schema develops which describes elements fundamental to the experience of being *in* something, and another for the basic structure of *in-out* movements.[45] Such schemata are gestalt structures, designating the form of a recurring spatial organization. Crucially for musicology, Johnson argues that "image schemata transcend any specific sense modality, though they involve operations that are analogous to spatial manipulation, orientation, and movement."[46] They are not best understood as fixed forms, but rather as recurring dynamic and cross-modal patterns in conceptualization. Although schemata emerge from embodied experience and can be understood in visual and spatial terms, they are in fact more abstract and in effect this is a theory of how bodily experience may be understood as the root of all cognition.

Such a perspective is clearly stimulating for music theory and has prompted much research. However, a caution is in order. Given the seemingly immediate applicability of image schemata to music analysis, there is a tendency to employ them in a manner which suggests they are on the forefront of awareness, in effect treating them as phenomenological entities (my own earlier work sometimes fell into exactly this trap). Such a reading misconstrues the cognitive level on which schemata operate. As Zbikowski puts it, "by definition, image schemata are preconceptual: they are not concepts, but they provide the fundamental structure on which concepts are based. . . . Whatever actually occupies our thoughts is not, by definition, an image schemata."[47] This is not to say that the fundamental properties of schemata—spatial and bodily origins, analog and flexible structure, intermodality—do not manifest themselves at conscious levels. It is just that image schemata are not the appropriate level of analysis if we are most interested in conscious experience and social discourse.

Having made this argument, I also need to acknowledge that any talk of fixed levels must be taken loosely. Even among cognitive scientists and philosophers of mind, there is no consensus about how to define basic terms like concept, category, or conceptual model.[48] However, it seems reasonable to posit a rough hierarchy beginning with the physiological body, so long as we keep in mind that social conventions and representations on the "highest" level in turn feed back onto and influence the structure of this body. At the next level would be schemata and other basic categories. Then would come conceptual models and, slightly higher, metaphors and conceptual blends. It is the level of metaphor and blend that I find most useful for work on musical discourse, since it is at this level that cultural work of a dialogic kind begins to be manifest, although here as well we must keep the interconnectedness of levels in mind. It is the lower-level concepts and schemata which structure and generate basic sensations and habits of force and space on which these higher-level formations depend.

For Johnson and Lakoff, *metaphor* refers not to novel or counterfactual uses of language, but to conceptual cross-domain mapping. "The essence of metaphor is understanding and experiencing one kind of thing in terms of another."[49] A classic example would be a metaphor such as MORE IS UP, which explains all manner of increase as a spatial event (such that, for example, the stock market can rise and fall).[50] As described by Zbikowski, "cross-domain mapping is a process through which we structure our understanding of one domain (which is typically unfamiliar or abstract) in terms of another (which is most often familiar and concrete). For example, one way to think about the elusive concepts of electrical conductance is in terms of a hydraulic model."[51] Notice that since the theory already assumes spatial and bodily concepts as the simplest and most familiar, a frequent effect of cross-domain mapping is for abstract and not inherently spatial or bodily phenomena to be understood in spatial or bodily terms. The importance of this kind of metaphor for music should be immediately clear, and is explored in some depth a little later. However, it is important to note at the outset that cross-domain mappings are not arbitrary. As Zbikowski argues, "mappings are not about the *imposition* of the structure of the source domain on the target domain, but are instead about the establishment of correspondences between the two domains. These correspondences are not haphazard, but instead preserve the image-schematic structure latent in each domain."[52] In other words, a concept similar to iconicity or homology is required here if we are to explain why some metaphors become more widespread than others. In addition, some theory of social discourse is also required since it seems clear that beyond any formal resemblance, the perceived appropriateness of particular mappings is guided by "the global conceptual models we absorb from culture and that supply critical support for the preferred mapping."[53]

For my own synthesis of cognitive and semiotic theories, the final concept to be explained is the *conceptual blend*. Conceptual blending is similar to conceptual metaphor in some respects, and probably equally important.[54] It also resembles the phenomenon of *troping* as described by Hatten, showing that there are important overlaps between the theory of conceptual blends and existing semio-hermeneutic models.[55] Conceptual blending hasn't been given as much direct application to music as have conceptual metaphor and image schemata, but this is beginning to change.[56] While conceptual metaphors attribute new properties to an existing domain by mapping another onto it, conceptual blends create new entities by blending elements from previously existing source domains. For example, talking animals are a conceptual blend. They reside neither in the space of animals nor of people, but represent a blended space (a new entity) which combines elements from each of these input spaces.[57] For my own analysis of music, the crucial feature of blends is that they create new conceptual entities, and perhaps even perceptual ones. For example, consider an instance of Palestrina's text painting as described by Zbikowski. Rather than saying pitches are heard as falling, which would be in accordance with conceptual metaphor theory (and also Peircian semiotics), Zbikowski suggests that there is a blend between a textual space (containing references to "descent from heaven") and a musical space (containing "descending scalar passages") which produces, as the blended entity, "pitch objects that descend."[58] In other words, blending here serves to help produce virtual agents in the music. As Zbikowski's analysis makes clear, this is an additional step beyond simply mapping between conceptual domains, since that mapping must have happened at a prior stage in order to initially understand pitch change in terms of spatial movement. I would suggest that this view of conceptual blending—as a process which creates new mental or even perceptual entities endowed with the properties of various source domains— is crucial to the anthropomorphic hearings of music posited by my interpretive practice. This becomes even clearer when Zbikowski later refers to a more general kind of blend, under which a rule of mapping entities onto entities and states onto states allows the domain of human entities and non-human entities to be blended, creating "non-human entities endowed with human characteristics."[59]

A final note is required before moving on to synthesize the various theories described to this point. If we are to simultaneously accept semiotic theory and theories of cognition, it is important to mention the problem of essentialism. There is a sense in which cognitive science presumes a universalist perspective, positing as it does a level of basic physical influences which are presumably the same or very similar for all humans. However, it is also important to note that there is an epistemologically relativistic reading of cognitive theory available to those who, coming from a background in social theory, may be uncomfortable with this implied determinism. Because, as Zbikowski argues, "conceptual models do not give us access to deep, timeless, and immutable truths about musical structure. They instead offer us an image of how we construct our understanding of music."[60] The key word here is *construct*. Even positing a basic level of embodied experience, the level of consciousness on which musical experiences and social discourses unfold is extremely flexible and extremely sensitive to context. We can presume a level of physical and neurological fact, and allow it a great degree of general applicability, without disallowing a high level of cultural and personal specificity in the particular conceptualizations of those facts. In much existing musicological work on image schemata and metaphor (my own earlier work included), not enough attention is paid to this point. There is sometimes the presumption that because basic neurology and basic laws of physics condition the form of schemata, more abstract conceptualizations based on those schemata will continue to be determined by those factors. This is not necessarily the case. Indeed, a central point in the theory of image schemata is that highly elaborated conceptualizations will display a general schematic form clearly related to physical facts without being determined by those facts.

A General Perspective on Musical Spaces and Forces

At the beginning of this chapter I suggested that spatial and energetic metaphors provide a framework for describing three crucial elements of musical practice: musical sounds, various sorts of identity, and the activity of social discourses. I argued that by describing these three factors in similar terms, we can highlight their interconnectedness, and that two ways this happened in previous chapters were with the personification of genres and styles and with the reading of cultural conventions as forces. In other words, underlying much of my specific analysis of Neil Young is a view about how personas, both real and virtual, are constituted through music and how musical personification is connected to broader social processes of individuation and subjectivity. The semiotic and cognitive vocabularies outlined earlier in this chapter provide most of the tools required to give a fuller description of this claim, and so I would now like to proceed with a synthesis of those arguments, with special attention to how they might coalesce into a perspective on musical persona.

Music is able to construct uniquely effective icons of gestural and emotional states because music, like the human body, is an energetic configuration changing in time. As Shepherd and Wicke point out, sound is a *medium*, a physical continuum whose parameters can be shaped in accordance with a code, but which also affords certain applications more readily than others.[61] The acoustic medium is not limited in principle to conveying only certain kinds of meanings, and indeed a social convention could be established to correlate any meaning to any sound. Recalling our capsule history of musical semiotics, the point to bear in mind is that earlier work on codes and syntax remains relevant. By specializing my study in the newer area of iconicity and embodiment I do not wish to entirely lose sight of these other levels of musical signification. However, musical sound does in fact seem especially inclined to be read in terms of spatial and energetic metaphors. One result is a notable discursive entanglement between musical vocabularies and vocabularies of space, energy, and affect. And the entanglement is not only discursive, but perceptual as well. In semiotic terms, we could say that various factors converge to produce a powerful experience of resemblance—an iconicity—between musical sound and spatial or even animate states.

The basis of this resemblance becomes more obvious if we choose a sufficiently general definition of human gesture, for example the one offered by Hatten when he characterizes gesture as "expressively significant, energetic, temporal shaping across all human modalities of perception, action, and cognition."[62] When human gesture, and the range of experiences accompanying it, is conceived this broadly, we are invited to explore the significant areas of overlap it shares with other varieties of energetic and temporal shaping. Up to now, I have been conflating the concepts of "spatial" and "animate" or "agential" without explaining the ground of that connection. Having established reason to believe that music will be heard spatially, the rest of the chapter will now try to say why hearing-as-space, hearing-as-affect, and hearing-as-agent display such a close relationship to one another.

In recent work influenced by Cumming, Lidov has modified his theory of music-gesture iconicity to place more emphasis on the links between musical movement and persona, referring to the movements perceived in music as its *motional object.* Motional objects are one reason that "music confronts us as an acting subject, a persona with whom we identify."[63] As noted earlier, the theory of motional objects relies on a concept of the iconic sign. It is because energetic configurations can be diagrammatically similar or identical to other energetic configurations that they can so easily be read through metaphors of spatial movement. We should also, however, notice the role of *indexicality* in this process. Stated at its simplest, an index is a sign which functions by virtue of there being some real physical connection between the representamen and the object. The classic example is smoke and fire. Smoke does not signify fire arbitrarily, nor by resemblance, but because we know that fire is usually accompanied by smoke. In musical terms, this adds another level of motivation to certain signs. For example, anxious performers will tend to play faster than they would in a calm state, and this fact helps to make a fast tempo an especially apt sign for anxiousness. Of course, music is generally a symbol for affective states, not a symptom of them, and so the indexicality does not usually function on a literal level, but as one piece of contextual knowledge which can assist the interpretation of symbols and icons. Beyond this, though, there is an important nuance to incorporate from Peirce's conception of the index. For Peirce, indices are closely aligned with the category of secondness, which is to say with the brute fact of otherness, the encounter between two entities in which one cannot deny the existence of the other. As a result, indices *compel* attention but do not offer further interpretation. "The index asserts nothing; it only says 'There!' It takes hold of our eyes, as it were, and forcibly directs them to a particular object, and there it stops."[64] Peirce characterized this kind of relationship as an "Outward Clash," and in a slightly later formulation suggested that "any fact is in one sense ultimate,—that is to say, in its isolated aggressive stubbornness and individual reality. . . . Why IT, independently of its general characters, comes to have any definite place in the world, is not a question to be asked; it is simply an ultimate fact."[65]

In musical interpretation, I believe it would be wrong to understand this kind of compulsion in terms of determinism or a simple trigger theory of musical affect. Most fundamentally, this concept of the index highlights the manner in which certain features can create an irreducible sense of otherness, the impression of a real, inescapable "isness" possessed by the music and by the other people involved in its production. There is not just an abstract resemblance, but a *particular* entity which resembles (even in cases where the objects resembled by that particular entity are general or indeterminate). A theory of iconicity can help explain why a passage of music may demonstrate particular qualities, but a theory of indexicality is necessary to explain why we sometimes feel, in an immediate way, that these qualities compel some form of *relationship* with the music, why they are particular experiences rather than just instances of general ideas. Such a theory is also necessary if we are to explain the intense identification that listeners can feel with music, an identification which suggests they sometimes hear the music as a particular, irreplaceable entity toward which one may feel powerful emotions and even certain ethical responsibilities. Finally, a theory of indexicality can take account of the unyielding quality of certain musical experiences, the feeling that a particular piece of music is imposing itself on us, that it will not alter itself to suit our tastes, that it was made completely without our input.

All these examples represent the kind of effect included under the Peircian concept of the index and represent important dimensions not included in iconicity. I would not necessarily want to suggest that the index is as important as the icon in a functional sense, because in fact many of the effects I have described may be explained as habits or conventions rooted in, but relatively autonomous from, earlier experiences of indexicality. Nonetheless, it is important to make the initial distinction between iconic and indexical influences in order to throw into relief special musical effects dependent upon indexicality on whatever level. Also, the two may be drawn together in another way since with both kinds of sign it is often musical *movement* which is the crucial phenomenon, whether interpreted in iconic or indexical terms. Later I will expand this view slightly, describing other factors in addition to musical movement which contribute to the appearance of musical personas. However, before doing so I would like to briefly review some of the ways in which motion, space, and energy—crucial building blocks of personification—have been theorized in cognitive accounts of music.

The tendency for listeners and performers to talk about music in terms of movements and spaces is so widespread that many theorists feel justified taking it as a datum. Since the concepts, metaphors, and blends involved in this interpretive move are extremely basic, it would perhaps be fruitless to try and analyze them past a certain point, since they are so closely related to preconceptual categories and schemata. However, it is instructive to identify some of the primary metaphors that underlie these more complex ones. To begin with, consider the following three primary metaphors proposed by Lakoff and Johnson:[66]

CHANGE IS MOTION
TIME IS MOTION
STATES ARE LOCATIONS

Taken along with the fact that temporal unfolding is one of the most important dimensions of musical experience, the result is a network of primary factors—some conceptual, some related to the nature of the medium—strongly encouraging us to hear music as a form of movement through space. This much was already implied by the semiotic theory of iconicity, but the cognitive level of description contributes a degree of generality. Motional objects and relationships of iconicity are elaborate manifestations of these basic processes and so gain a kinship with other manifestations of the same underlying mechanisms. This will be a crucial point when I argue for the synthetic and emergent nature of musical personas.

One thing which makes music distinctive is the specific network of more elaborate metaphors it constructs above this base. For example, music does not move through just any space, but through a pitch space in which VERTICALITY and SCALE schemata are of special importance. And beyond this kind of spatial metaphor, there is the more complex field of forces implied by tonal hearing. Tonic function can be described in at least two ways: TONIC-AS-GROUND and TONIC-AS-CENTER.[67]

What both descriptions share is the implication of force—downward in the first instance, inward in the second—which begins to evoke ideas of consonance and dissonance, tension and release. An image-schematic analysis such as this is suggestive since it restates, in cognitive language, many of the traditional descriptive tendencies in tonal music theory. However, there are two things that must be remembered. First, although image schemata are extremely helpful in clarifying these aspects of music, they may not always be the most appropriate level of analysis. One author who has written extensively about musical forces but has not made much use of image-schematic vocabularies is Larson. He is concerned mostly with melodic expectation and prefers to speak in terms of three more elaborate metaphors: *gravity, magnetism,* and *inertia.*[68] The advantage of these terms is that, being at a higher level than image schemata, they are closer to the terms used in common speech but lose no analytic power as a result. And in fact, although it seems tempting to translate them into primary metaphors and image schemata, it can be difficult to do so. On the one hand, their application in practice is so nuanced that a long string of metaphors would be required to do justice to their various applications. And on the other hand, the primary terms upon which they rely—such as *force* or *change*—are so basic as to be pre-conceptual.[69]

The second thing to remember is also related to an aspect of Larson's work. Although tonality is the central focus of most theories rooted in Western concert music, there are many kinds of pitch-related force in addition to those of tonality, just as there are many different kinds of musical force in addition to the pitch-related ones. To name just a few, we could include melodic inertia, rhythmic inertia, an attraction to lower pitches, perceptual gestalt principles, motivic coherence, general principles of voice leading, and the force of generic and stylistic expectations. It would be a mistake to assume that musical forces are not extremely various just because they can be described with a relatively small collection of primary metaphors. This is one feature of conceptual metaphor theory which strongly resembles older semiotic models: in both kinds of theory the emphasis is on showing how a finite generative system can produce a possibly infinite series of forms. The other thing to note, however, is that certain primary metaphors from Lakoff and Johnson *can* be seen to lurk in all these cases, especially CAUSES ARE PHYSICAL FORCES and the closely related CAUSATION IS FORCED

MOVEMENT.[70] In other words, any factor which may be said to cause or condition a musical event will tend to be interpreted as a kind of force.

A General Perspective on Musical Personas

The ubiquity of conceptual metaphors such as those described above creates a situation in which music is heard as a form of movement in space and in which musical norms are made analogous to physical, social, and psychological forces. Taken together with the kinds of conceptual blends described earlier, in which new entities come to exist, it is a short step to suggest that music may in some cases be heard as an agent in its own right, or at least as a kind of field in which virtual agents appear and live out their lives. As Turner puts it:

> One type of extremely fundamental projection projects action-stories onto event-stories. George Lakoff and I named this general pattern EVENTS ARE ACTIONS. An action is an event with an actor. EVENTS ARE ACTIONS guides us in projecting familiar action-stories onto event-stories with or without actors.[71]

In other words, all the foregoing metaphors, having described music as a form of movement and as a series of energetic events, tend to imply that these events must be symptomatic of the actions and states of some actor. However, the identity of this actor is a complex question. Contemporary semiotic approaches to the issue often follow, implicitly or explicitly, from Cone's work on "the composer's voice."[72] Although Cone was primarily concerned with the traditional question of how a composer's artistic identity may best be described, his work was innovative in pointing out both the profound connection and the profound disconnection between features of music, heard anthropomorphically, and the composer's persona. On the one hand, it is tempting to interpret seemingly agential features of music as symptoms or intentions of a composer. On the other hand, there is no literal way in which the composer places a piece of himself or herself into the music. Rather, the persona of the composer is an inference derived from more basic features of the music and strongly cued by contextual and social factors. As Cumming puts it, "Cone's reflections do not suggest that a listener ought to be listening *through* the music, as if it were a transparent vehicle of the composer's voice. They imply only that an agency emerges in the themes as 'gestures' accorded individual instruments within a work."[73]

This much would be true of any formalistic approach to music. What makes Cone's approach so distinctive is that while he maintains a division between subject and text, he makes full use of the subjective *appearance* of the text. To borrow a word from Alexandra Pierce, any given passage of music will display a *character,* which is to say a distinctive combination of affective and gestural implications.[74] The word is instructive because it can be taken variously to refer only to a set of qualities or, additionally, to a situation in which these qualities cohere into a stable and individuated persona. In my final position, I will further emphasize the dual applicability of this word. For now, we can simply note that the complexity of the situation has caused theories of musical persona to move in a variety of directions. Some theorists, such as Lidov, have tried to describe the lower-level mechanisms upon which these effects rely. Others, notably Abbate, have moved in a hermeneutic direction, and in work by Cumming all these trends are combined within a more explicitly philosophical perspective. In addition, narratological approaches such as those of Tarasti rely on music's ability to be heard anthropomorphically, and Brower makes clear the manner in which a narratological perspective can be linked with a cognitive one.

Let me return once more to the title of this book: poetics of energy. The central role of energy (and space) in conceptualization should now be clear. What is *poetic* in this view? I do not mean poetic in a structural sense, but rather in terms of factors which create layers of connotation and richness, polysemy and affective resonance. One factor is the seemingly magical appearance, from conceptual blending, of music-beings, music-spaces, and music-stories. Beyond this is the rich interrelationship and slippage that can occur between different kinds of agent and force in musical personification. To elaborate, I will return to the semiotic vocabulary of interpretants and objects. There are two kinds of slippage or interrelationship I want to examine here: the blurring between human and non-human objects and the question of what it might mean to call the music itself a semiotic object.

First, the blurring of human and non-human. Many authors have noted that iconicity allows a wide range of natural phenomena to be represented in music (landscapes, storms, galloping horses). In addition, it is possible to suggest in music a human affective state or action without implying a full-blown persona. The point here is not only that different objects may be implied, but that they are implied *through the same basic means,* and as a result they can imply or resonate with one another. Hatten has used the term *flow event* to describe the low-level conceptualization of a series of percepts as a unified singular event.[75] This kind of event is often further interpreted as the trace of some actor or object, and what I wish to highlight is that various higher-level conceptualizations may serve as correlates to the same flow event. For example, we earlier discussed Zbikowski's analysis of a blend in Palestrina producing musical entities that fall. Falling can be done by a variety of objects: conceptualizations of a falling leaf, a falling human body, and falling spirits all share certain schemata and metaphors. When such objects are individuated though the addition of extra information, they do not lose their lower-level connectedness, and so many kinds of resonance and connotation can be constructed between them. More powerfully, the modularity of their substratum allows for partially individuated entities—most generally, a *character* in the sense developed above—to be constructed which may develop into any one of several different objects, or a blend, or simply hover as a sensation of potential. Because conceptual blends are able to create new entities recognizably akin to familiar ones yet not fully bound by the same rules, they can produce a dreamlike space in which things are both familiar and strange. I would suggest that there are at least two processes at work in music which can create this kind of resonance and slippage. One is conceptual blending as described by Turner. The other is the presentation of what would be components of a fully individuated persona (gestures, affective characters, and so forth) without these cohering into such a persona.

Second, what might it mean to call music itself a semiotic object? If music is the object, then the various properties projected onto it must be interpretants: we hear the music (object) *as* jagged or sad or in some other light (interpretants). This interpretation is favored by Lidov and Cumming, and I would suggest it is consonant with a generally formalist approach insofar as it keeps musical sounds themselves at the center of attention. While this kind of hearing does in fact occur, I want to stress that it is not the only possibility. For example, in many cases it seems as if the persona of the composer is the semiotic object under elaboration. We come to understand the composer *as* the person who created the music, and whatever qualities we perceive in the music come to be associated in one way or another with the composer. Current research into the listening habits of popular music fans places great emphasis on identification with artists.[76] In cases of powerful identification, it seems most natural to think of the artists' personas, as conceptualized by fans, as being the object of semiosis.

In such cases we should perhaps think in terms of a chain of signs. For example, in the case where a listener hears a jagged quality of movement in a song by Neil Young and concludes that Neil was feeling agitated, we do not assume the listener literally felt as if she was hearing Neil Young move in a jagged manner. Sometimes of course she might, if the jagged acoustic quality is clearly a direct result of Young's performance practice. It is often more coherent, however, to suggest that in the first instance the *music* is heard as moving jaggedly. Then, the sign of music-as-jagged is taken up to elaborate the subsequent object, Neil Young *as* someone who for some reason produced jaggedly moving music. Why, then, have I used the word *slippage* in connection with this sort of event? I use the word because such a situation does not make for clear-cut divisions between various objects. The effect of elaborating Neil-Young-as-object through the music-as-object is often to blur the boundary between Neil Young and the music, to see them as extensions of one another. Indeed, the concept of object itself becomes slippery in instances of this kind. If we define the semiotic object as the entity which comes to be cast in a particular light through semiosis, in effect transformed, then we should notice that transformations move in both directions. For example, consider a case in which a jagged quality is perceived in many of Neil Young's guitar solos. Under one reading, Neil Young is the object because the jaggedness of the solos changes our conceptualization of him (we now think of him as someone who plays jagged solos). However, it is equally true that our conceptualization of jagged solos is transformed, because they are now thought of as, among other things, typical of Neil Young. In other words, there is a symmetricality in the interpretant-object relationship. It is not possible to say in a final way that the music is the object or that the persona is the object. Nor would it be possible, if we wanted to pursue the analysis, to assign absolute roles to virtual musical personas relative to more literal human ones. This does not mean that specific roles do not emerge in specific instances of listening. It is only to suggest that different kinds of listening are allowed within our basic set of concepts.

In general, then, the difference between an isolated affective tone or gesture and a full-blown persona is one of degree and not of kind. Icons of affect and gesture can be perceived and can markedly influence the character of a piece, whether or not these cohere into a persona as such. Similarly, even when we perceive the presence of a musical actor, there are many factors that can blur or complicate the identity of that actor. Since a great deal of my book is dedicated to making claims about Neil Young as a sort of authorial persona, this situation leaves us with an important question. When can we, in fact, speak as if there is a clear-cut persona present in the music? As an indirect strategy for addressing this question, I will make a few remarks about identity in general.

Identity, Persona, and Synthesis

In a recent survey of work on musical identities, it is suggested that we need to distinguish between *identities in music* and *music in identities*. The first has to do with "those aspects of musical identities that are socially defined within given cultural roles," and the second with "how we use music as a means or resource for developing other aspects of our individual identities."[77] With respect to my own study, I might prefer to call the first kind of identity *role identities in musical practice* because the phrase *identities in music* seems to evoke what I have been calling virtual musical personas. The authors of this distinction are presuming from the outset that identity refers in some way to a human characteristic, and so neither of the identities they describe are actually in the music. The situation in my analysis is more complicated because I am interested in how styles, genres, traditions, and individual pieces can be said to have identities. Terminological squabbling aside, this simple formulation begins to hint at the great variety of concepts which have gone under the name identity. In my own discussion, I will touch upon several different kinds of identity—social, personal, phenomenological, philosophical, and practice-theoretic—and this really only begins to scratch the surface. Sketchy as this discussion will be, however, it tries to respond to the call for distinctions between various sorts of identity.

Perhaps the minimal sense of identity is that employed in analytic philosophy. In this context identity is conceived as a kind of self-sameness, the relation which every entity bears only to itself. Closely related to this concept is the issue of discernibility and the generally accepted proposition that indiscernible entities are identical. Such a definition stands in stark contrast to a dialectical view, in which entities are often said to differ from themselves. And it also differs from a structuralist view, in which the concept of *value* is substituted for identity, such that an entity can bear no relation at all to itself since it is entirely described by its relation to other elements in the system. Rather than pick between these broad orientations, I would like to suggest that each can add a crucial dimension to our understanding of what it might mean to have an identity. First, notice that they all presume, in various ways, that identity involves a kind of *synthesis*. For example, in order for entities to be indiscernible it must already be decided which properties belong to which entities. Similarly, there can only be dialectic tension within an entity already designated as containing particular contradictory impulses. In her work on musical affect and selfhood, Cumming has emphasized the importance of synthesis. In terms of music listening, she described the process as follows:

> The temporal dimensions of gesture, of phrase rhythm, and of larger-scale tonal processes are concurrent, but moving at a different pace, so that larger frameworks could be seen to create a "perspective" on more local events, framing them in the context of broader purposes. The process by which signs of different kinds are related to one another may be termed as kinds of "synthesis."[78]

Cumming goes on to note that "a synthesis of musical elements can form a uniquely complex affect, which yet has an element of simplicity or immediacy about it, just because it is resolved in the mind as 'one thing.'"[79] It is here that the influence of her work on my theory of identity should be evident. The process of synthesizing various elements into a singularity which displays complex affective and intentional states is in effect the formation of a musical identity, and further tends to imply a persona or self behind that identity.

Beyond the shared feature of synthesis, we can borrow further details from the three contrasting philosophical approaches to identity. From the perspective of analytic philosophy we can borrow the idea that uniqueness is crucial. Identity is always, in one way or another, about being recognizably one thing and not another. However, from a dialectical perspective we can add to this that such uniqueness does not ensure self-consistency. An identity is singular only by virtue of presenting a unique multiplicity. Further, the dialectical perspective requires us to notice that such uniqueness is not unchanging. An identity is a process. And from a structural perspective we can suggest that uniqueness is not necessarily an intrinsic property, or, more radically, that uniqueness does not imply the existence of anything apart from a unique set of coordinates. Having said all this, there are good sociological reasons to be cautious about extending the word "identity" too sweepingly to non-human objects. This is because while identity can refer to any kind of distinct and recognizable entity, recent work in cultural theory has been most interested in the kinds of identities that define *people* and over which people struggle. Although I am complicating the picture slightly, I want to hold on to this nuance, since when I speak of musical identities it is in order to help personify the music. In order to avoid confusion, though, it may be useful to distinguish several closely related terms: *identity, self, persona,* and *subject.* I have already indicated roughly what I mean by identity, so now we need to explore the other three.

The concept of *self,* related as it is to consciousness, is both extremely clear and notoriously obscure. For our immediate purposes we can keep to its most basic features: self refers to the feeling of ownership and privileged epistemological access we have toward our own body and toward certain mental events. In other words, among all the identities we can recognize only some will seem to be ours, and similarly, we always tend to presume that other people have a similar feeling of ownership over their own selves. When an identity is understood as a "way of being in the world,"[80] associated with and experienced by only one person, then we are speaking in terms of a self. In order to avoid some of the thornier epistemological and ontological problems of selfhood, I am speaking of it here only as a psychological state. The problem of whether people really have individuality, and whether sensations or mental events can ever be truly private, is more closely related to the question of the *subject,* discussed below. But regardless of how we conceptualize the ontology of the subject, we can note that people do experience a sense of self, even if the mechanisms which allow for it "remain a central unresolved theoretical question."[81] By referring to *self* in this manner I am following workers like Cavicchi, who acknowledge the slipperiness of the concept but argue that it is nonetheless essential to studies of lived experience.[82]

By *persona* I mean the outward appearance, semiotically constructed, of a subject, whether or not that appearance corresponds to an experienced self or even the existence of a real subject. Personas in this sense are textual entities, distinctive patterns of signs. They are also synthetic entities, requiring for their emergence a multitude of textual signs on many levels. So in my terminology the "sonic self" described by Cumming, since it is primarily an arrangement of textual elements, would be called a sonic persona. But as Cumming makes clear at many points in her study, there are intimate links between personas and selves. Interpreters construct their sense of other selves largely by reading into personas, and, conversely, subjects can only project their self-image into the world by attempting to create personas which are homologous with that self-image. As Cumming puts it, outward identity is a kind of personal style in the sense of being "the perceptible result of an individual's patterned choices within a social domain."[83] Cumming notes that there are many potential frustrations inherent in this process, partly because the very potentialities in musical sound and syntax which allow for the construction of personas guarantee that musical personas will sometimes pursue their own logic, separate from the agenda of a self trying to project itself musically. This is, in microcosm, the general problem of the subject.

The *subject* as I use the term is primarily a social position, a set of potentialities in various cultural fields. This definition is of course structuralist, and if taken too far leaves no room for selves of any kind. Ultimately, I want to frame the subject in a manner similar to what is found in the late work of Foucault, or most of Bourdieu. Subjectivity is a social function and in that sense both impersonal and constraining. To a large extent, individual subjects are formed by transpersonal systems and do not have the kind of freedom implied by more humanist views of the self. However, subjects do have a sense of self, and because of overdetermination they also have unique identities even within the constraints of the social systems which produce them. As a result, subjectivity is not *just* the state of occupying a given position, but more profoundly the experience of improvising and negotiating selfhood within the constraints of available positions. It is for this reason that I call the subjectivities heard in music itself *virtual*, because for all of their metaphorical life-like character, they cannot be presumed to have this kind of self-awareness or to be consciously trying to improvise their identities.

To further highlight links between selfhood and subjectivity, we can refer to Berger's phenomenological model of musical practice. Berger frames his ethnography around a concept of *experience* as the site in which particular subjects live their lives in particular social and historical frames.[84] What is most significant for our purposes is that he combines phenomenological selfhood with a sociology of institutions inspired by Giddens, in effect redirecting our attention to the fact that selfhood, as the experience of being-in-the-world, involves an awareness of one's own constraints, one's own zones of unfreedom. When we consider "the immediate givens of experience, our attention is first drawn to the situated context and the subject's engagement with the world."[85]

Understanding the subject in this way, and emphasizing the ongoing negotiations between subject, self, and persona, helps to broaden our conception of musical forces. If the subject in general is defined as a play of personal and impersonal agendas, and if the boundary between the individual subject and the social context is not clear, then we should also be looking for expressions of this process in and through musical personas. In other words, we should expect social forces to appear as persona types in musical interpretations (which was the intention of my dialogic treatment of genre and style in chapter 2). DeNora, for example, uses a broad metaphor of musical "force" and "power" to encompass the various kinds of social work performed by music.[86] In order to connect this orientation with the cognitive model developed earlier, we could suggest two new metaphors: SOCIAL ENVIRONMENT IS PHYSICAL ENVIRONMENT and SOCIAL FORCES ARE PHYSICAL FORCES.[87] Keeping in mind that the domain of physical force has already been identified as crucial to the formation of personas and that personas are both a tool and an impediment for selfhood, we can move toward a vision of the complicated interactions between selves, personas, subjects, and broader cultural systems, all expressed through iconic and metaphorical processes in music.

An Overview of My Interpretive Practice

As noted at the outset, this chapter is not meant to justify the interpretations of Neil Young presented elsewhere in the book, but only to put them in a broad theoretical perspective. It would be misleading to say that the material here constitutes a *method,* at least with respect to this present study. Rather, it represents an orientation and a set of interests which have directly shaped the questions I chose to ask and the general sorts of answers I have offered. Just as I have chosen to empha-size resonance rather than correctness as my goal in offering specific in-terpretations, I have tried to create a similarly flexible relationship be-tween my description of a general theoretical perspective and the more particular theoretical claims made in other chapters. To conclude, then, I will briefly summarize the main points of this chapter with respect to how they position the interpretive practice unfolding in the rest of the book.

1. The central focus is on *elaborating semiotic objects*. This has two aspects. On one hand, the interpretive work is descriptive in a sociologi-cal or historical sense, dedicated to identifying semiotic objects that have been of most importance in Neil Young reception. To establish these, it is important to look at actual reports from critics and other listeners and to sort them into distinctive categories of interpretive move. In another sense, however, the most vital work for an analysis is not to describe and categorize the discourse, but to participate in it, in the process offering its own idiosyncratic transformations of those objects already deemed important by collective interpretation. On this level, even more clearly than on the descriptive level, the individual interests of the interpreter will be evident. In my case, that involves choices of methodology (semi-otics, cognitive science, social theory), and subject matter (energy and space, selfhood and persona, resonance and connotation).

2. One level of the analysis should focus on *conventional structure*. This is to say both textual and social structures, with special emphasis on codes, topics, and hierarchical value systems. At this level the many existing formal models of social structure (for example theories of hege-mony and articulation), language (conventionalized correlations, quasi-phonological modes of organization, syntax and rules), and textuality may be employed.

3. Another level of analysis should focus on *motivated production of new meanings*. The separation between this category and the preceding one is perhaps arbitrary because as practice theory makes clear, conven-tional structures are the framework within which new meanings are improvised. However, while processes such as iconicity, indexicality, con-ceptual metaphor, and conceptual blending have a place within conven-tional structure, they also have a striking processual and creative char-acter which can be highlighted in its own right. More importantly, the theoretical models created to address these topics are generally not the

same as those evolved to discuss conventional structure, and so a conscious methodological choice must be made to adopt both.

4. Another level of analysis should try to *clarify the identities of different kinds of subject and persona* and explain their interrelationships. This is the level on which the kinds of analysis artificially separated under the two previous points can be combined, by paying special attention to models that highlight the interlocking and slippage between various levels of identity and actoriality, and consequently between text, subject, and social framework. Such models might include the theory of habitus, practice theory more generally, and dialogism. A central strategy on this level can be to highlight the flexibility inherent in musical *character.* Since the concept of character includes a range of referents—the connotations or affective qualities of fragments, the activity of virtual personas, and the traces-in-persona of human subjects—it can be a bridge between various kinds of subjects, their component parts, and the general forces with which they interpenetrate.

5. Finally, I am always seeking to *find common ground between aspects of music theory and social theory.* The basic strategy in this regard is to redescribe core concepts in each area in terms of iconicities, metaphors, and blends common to them all. In the case of this study, that has meant an emphasis on space and force (which I often collapse together into the concept of energy) and on the personification of spaces and forces (which helps to lend them a poetic quality).

In the next two chapters, I will focus more closely on particular musical details, and so I should conclude this chapter with a few notes on the use of existing music-analytic techniques. My discussion of musical details is meant to provide another perspective on general questions of persona and expressivity raised in other chapters, and so I will be placing special emphasis on those features of the music which seem immediately relevant to metaphors of space and energy. In a recent survey of popular music analysis, Burns emphasizes that the application of existing music theory to popular music requires both the reinterpretation of existing methods and the development of new ones, in order to do justice to those features of the music that are most pertinent in lived practices.[88] In my own study, the emphasis is more on reinterpreting existing methods than developing new ones, and the question of pertinence is addressed indirectly, although it is still of central importance. I begin with metaphors and other interpretive moves that are clearly pertinent based on Neil Young reception history, but I then explore their links to specific musical details in a more speculative manner. Nonetheless, the spirit of Burns's remark is applicable here because it is necessary for me to say how my interpretation of certain existing parameters and methods in music analysis is different from the norm. Rather than attempt an exhaustive overview, I will offer a few comments on two areas in which existing techniques can be redeployed to advance the study of spatial and energetic icons, metaphors, and blends: (1) texture and the sound box; and (2) large-scale formal structure. These are far from the only areas in which we can adapt existing analytic categories, but they can serve as examples.

I use the term *texture* not only in the sense of a deployment of voices (as in homophonic, polyphonic, etc), but to denote the overall quality and spatiality of a passage. As Zak describes it, "on records, this overall quality involves timbre, relative amplitudes, rhythm, ambience, frequency range, chord voicings, spatial configuration, and so forth," all coordinated "with the aim of developing a unique sonic presence for the work at hand."[89] Although texture in this sense involves more than timbre, it resembles timbre in that it has a certain immediacy and physicality. I have in mind here the distinction made by Shepherd and Wicke between timbre and syntax. In their view, timbre establishes the basic material presence of a sound, and this basic material presence makes the sound analogous to other bodies in time and space. Syntax then brings this presence alive through gestural icons.[90] Texture, although similar to timbre in its seemingly immediate spatiality, has a more prominent syntactical dimension since a texture is a distinctive deployment of timbres and the notion of deployment is a syntactical one. But the central point can still be stressed: texture is closely related to an immediate sense of physical presence and therefore is crucial to the notion of a virtual space. Notice that in this connection, there is not much distinction between the space itself and the presence of a texture in that space. Indeed, in a perceptual sense the music *makes* its own space as it goes along. When the music feels comparatively spacious or narrow, for example, it is not being directly compared to other spaces of which it represents a part. It is, rather, presenting the impression of a spatial quality without the necessity of further specifying a more general spatial framework.

The space created by textures is, then, phenomenological and therefore variable. It is also, when we are speaking about sound recordings, the result of production techniques. When we wish to discuss a textural space as the product of particular recording and signal processing techniques, we can follow Moore in adopting the metaphor of a *sound box:* "a virtual textural space, envisaged as an empty cube of finite dimensions, changing with respect to real time."[91] The overall size of the sound box at any moment indicates the spaciousness of the music, and the deployment of elements within the box indicates more subtle features of the particular space. By combining an expanded idea of texture, as described above, with the specific metaphor of the sound box, we can begin to discuss the wide range of spatial effects heard in rock recordings (and in many other kinds of music). More importantly, we can make a link between conceptual metaphors of spatiality and specific techniques of production and composition.

In terms of conceptual metaphors, and especially with respect to the formation of musical personas, it is instructive to notice that the mechanisms underlying texture are very similar to those considered in the study of auditory stream segregation, which is "the perceptual organization of a complex acoustic signal into separate acoustic events," such that "each stream will represent one sound source or event."[92] An important unaddressed question in musical semiotics and narratology is how perceptual processes of streaming play a role in the perception of musical actors and personas. In other words, besides the semiotic synthesis we have been describing, there is a perceptual synthesis to be considered, and the two are likely related since both are premised in part on distinctions between the qualities of different textures and spaces. In this connection, it may ultimately prove helpful to adopt the metaphor of *staging,* suggested by Lacasse in connection with the recorded voice.[93] By staging, Lacasse means to include all the various production and compositional elements which help to individuate and give character to a vocal performance conceived as integral to a recorded space. In Lacasse's work there is no immediate need for a concept of virtual persona since his emphasis on the singing voice tends to provide a sense of literal actoriality. However, by dramatizing techniques of texture and the sound box, and linking them to nuances of vocal personality, the metaphor of staging may suggest ways to integrate semiotic, sound engineering, and cognitive perspectives. Seen in this respect, the metaphor of staging is closely related to that of the auditory scene as used by perception researchers.[94] In both cases, a technical study of sound manipulation offers insight into the individuation of musical actors and scenes of action.

The second general point I want to make about existing analytic categories is that large-scale form, although sometimes conceived in purely static or spatial terms and therefore as different in kind from local gestural features, can itself be understood as an energetic and even a rhythmic construct. At any given point of formal division there will be a sense of return, or of beginning, or of rupture. In short, formal articulation points are *events* with distinctive characters. Similarly, between such articulation points a formal unit will display an envelope of changing character, memory, and expectation. In both cases—experiencing a formal division or experiencing the stretches of time between formal divisions—conceptual metaphors of space, movement, energy, and character are appropriate, and so the distinction between large-scale form and local gesture may seem less pressing. In addition, besides having a general character and displaying an overall spatial-energetic profile, a large-scale form can be thought of as a rhythmic construct. A technical description of the rhythmic quality of forms is offered in the theory of hypermeter, as applied to rock music by Moore.[95] Hypermeter is an intermediate structure between what we might call meter and what we might call form, and it helps to illustrate how form can be energetic or gestural.

In this connection, it is interesting to note that the centripetal/centrifugal terminology which was central to my dialogic description of genre has been applied by Tagg to the analysis of large-scale formal structures.[96] Besides demonstrating the analytic flexibility of these schemata and drawing attention to the spatial-energetic features of large-scale form, Tagg's analysis reveals an interesting difference between the literal temporal center of a form (for example, roughly the B section in an ABA structure) and the "center" implied in the centripetal/centrifugal schemata, which would be the state of stability and fulfilled expectation often experienced in the A sections of that same form (in temporal terms, the beginning and end of the piece, not its middle). This analysis not only demonstrates the wider utility of the centripetal/centrifugal schemata, but also reminds us that although many of the physical terms arising in this sort of analysis derive *part* of their significance from their relationship to more literal applications of the same terms, we always need to pay close attention to the idiosyncratic, specific features they acquire when mapped into a musical interpretation.

In short, it is possible to view large-scale forms as possessing an overall spatial-energetic character, and sometimes even as enacting rhythms and gestures over a broad temporal span. One application of this approach is suggested by Cumming in her model of synthesis. Under that view, long-range musical relationships can participate in the formation of a musical persona, for example by setting a general texture or character which then conditions our interpretation of more local gestures. In this process, the energetic and rhythmic character of large-scale formal relations becomes one component of a persona which is only actually active on the local level, that is, its actions and the events in which it participates are all conceived on the motivic or melodic level, whereas persistent elements of its character or mood pervade larger passages. In effect, large-scale relations are shrunk to map back onto local activity. Another, quite different application would be to allow large-scale characteristics to map directly onto a large-scale actor of some sort. I mean large-scale in the sense that the longer-range formal relations, which take more time to complete, are considered to be the actual salient movements of that actor or to be events relevant to it. Since this level of movement takes too long to be directly perceived as gesture of any kind, it could tend to signify trans-human scales of reference, the scale on which landscapes or large weather systems or supernatural beings operate. In this case, synthesis would operate in the opposite direction: shorter local gestures and characteristics would be assimilated as just tiny components of an entity which is conceived to exist on a higher level.

These comments are of course highly speculative, as were my remarks on space and texture. They are not designed to establish anything in a final way, but rather to suggest how existing analytic categories and techniques can be reinterpreted within the general perspective I've outlined in this chapter as a whole. When I pursue detailed analyses of various kinds in chapters 5 and 6, this is the sort of reinterpretive process I will rely on in my deployment of existing analytic techniques. Given that the emphasis in this book is on presenting interpretations rather than developing a comprehensive system, much of the analytic reinterpretation will be topical and will be presented without detailed justification. However, I hope that this chapter as a whole can begin to suggest the motives and goals behind this sort of practice.

5 | You See Your Baby Loves to Dance

Musical Style

This chapter offers an overview of four key aspects of Neil Young's musical style: his approach to instrumental performance, his melodies, his harmonic vocabulary, and his voice. The emphasis throughout will be on the kinds of feature marked as significant in chapter 4: metaphors of energy and space, the particular textual and performative characteristics which participate in these, and their effect on the formation of personas. I have already, in chapters 1 through 3, given an impression of the kind of personas Young has constructed and how these have been received. The task of this present chapter is to give a more detailed account of how particular musical features fit into this picture. The mode of description will be partly technical and partly impressionistic. I would especially like to emphasize that these arguments are not designed to make sense straight off the page. This chapter is not a self-contained analysis, but rather a collection of suggestions for listening and a general evocation of what I take to be crucial features in the music. In many instances, I simply mention a song in which a particular feature can be heard, rather than providing an exhaustive description. It is even possible that readers will hear features in the music which resemble the ones I had in mind when I offered a particular concept, but are not in fact the same. I would prefer this, were it to happen, over a more exhaustively controlled situation, because it is very much in the nature of schemata, metaphors, icons, and conceptual blends to guide interpretation without constraining it too narrowly. My goal is to offer just enough description that readers can go back to the music and hear, in a general way, the kinds of feature I am pointing to. Neil Young's work can in some respects be read as a continual attempt to slip through interpretive loopholes. It is in sympathy with this spirit that I offer an analysis which is mostly a collection of suggestions and pointers.

In order to get through a large amount of material, the more technical discussions—those of guitar style, melody, and harmony—are divided into two parts. In each case, I present the formal analytic information in a block, followed by a summary of how those particular features relate to broader issues. For the other topics, the discussion is more blended.

Instrumental Performance Style

Rhythm Guitar

Young's guitar solos have already been described in chapter 3, so I will focus here on his rhythm guitar work. While Young's approach to electric guitar solos makes extensive use of the unique textural re- sources of a highly amplified solid-body instrument—in effect placing the most emphasis on features that could not be duplicated on an acous- tic guitar—his electric rhythm parts bear a much closer relationship to his acoustic style. This has the effect both of dividing his electric work into two large categories (rhythm parts versus solos) and of creating connections between his electric and acoustic playing (mostly within the rhythm category).

One of the most immediately striking features of Young's rhythm guitar style, on both acoustic and electric instruments, is the way in which he moves his picking hand and arm. This arm and hand fre- quently move in a regular, piston-like manner, so that whatever particu- lar figure is being played there is always a strong underlying motor rhythm. This is immediately visible and is audible as well. A good ex- ample can be seen in the performance of "My My Hey Hey" in the *Rust Never Sleeps* concert film. This guitar part mixes a single-string riff with varied strumming patterns, but the right hand continues, at least to out- ward appearances, with the same simple pumping movement through- out. The predominance of this arm movement has three effects: (1) the on-beats are often strongly accented, and frequently the low strings will buzz on the downbeat; (2) for embellishment Young emphasizes short clipped notes on the offbeats, which result from the hand moving back up after its downward arc; (3) the resulting rhythmic patterns show a strong motor emphasis on the level of the quarter or the eighth note. Some songs in which these effects are particularly clear are "Harvest Moon," "Heart of Gold," "Southern Man," "Sugar Mountain," "Unknown Legend," and "War of Man."

One hallmark of this hand movement is that it allows for lines which combine features of rhythm and lead playing, in that whatever embellishments are added, the strong rhythmic impetus remains. Young frequently produces acoustic guitar parts which capitalize on this dual character, presenting both straightforward rhythm playing and more subtle countermelodies and embellishments in the same part. Young's acoustic guitar playing here and elsewhere is marked by a fine balance between the kind of percussive, homophonic, or monophonic texture usually associated with flatpick styles and the more layered texture associated with fingerstyle playing. Notice, however, that unlike players such as Jimi Hendrix, who are also noted for mixing aspects of rhythm and lead into one part, Young's models seem to be mostly in the folk and country traditions, in effect an extension of the Travis and Carter styles. Young's usual acoustic guitar style, then, is layered but not ornate.

Besides the style of hand movement, there are other devices which allow Young's rhythm parts to be both layered and simple. Like many folk-rock musicians, Young employs altered guitar tunings to create novel chord voicings without left-hand difficulties. Young uses altered tunings on both electric and acoustic guitars, although slightly more often on the latter. While many comparable artists such as Bruce Cockburn or Stephen Stills use such tunings to create unusual sonorities, Young's use of them does not sound obviously exotic by rock guitar standards. Some extended techniques common in altered tunings include very wide or very close chord voicings, scales and melodies played in a harp-like manner, and the use of a slide to shift entire chords in parallel movement. All of these techniques produce effects quite different from standard tuning, and Young tends to avoid all of them. While his altered tunings will often lend a greater sense of spaciousness ("Sugar Mountain," "Cinnamon Girl") or allow for certain voicings and progressions which would be difficult in standard tunings ("Going Back"), they do not usually draw much notice. (A notable recent exception would be the strikingly low tuning employed on "Bandit").

The same is true of Young's use of color tones in his standard-tuning guitar voicings. Young makes frequent use of major seventh and major ninth triad extensions, but his guitar playing at no time begins to sound jazz-inflected (with the exception of a few moments from *On The Beach* and *This Note's For You*). This is partly because he mostly limits himself to chord extensions played in first position, as modifications of the familiar triadic voicings used by most folk and rock musicians. This means that certain first-position chord voicings become very typical for Young. For example, the first-position CMaj7 (c-e-g-b-e: x 3 2 0 0 0),[1] Em7 (e-b-e-g-d-e: 0 2 2 0 3 0), FMaj7 (f-a-f-a-c-e: 1 0 3 2 1 0), and use of the open top string as a ninth to D are all common in Young's guitar playing, both acoustic and electric. The use of such voicings is as much a physical consideration as an acoustic one. They are the voicings which readily fall under the fingers in first position. This approach to color tones allows for rich chord progressions and a certain amount of contrapuntal voice leading without moving too far from the basic triadic voicings which form the core of Young's style. And since Young uses the same voicings in many songs and on different kinds of guitar, they help to create a unified harmonic and timbral space throughout his many shifts of style.

Neil Young's electric rhythm guitar style is often quite similar to his acoustic style. The same right hand movement is in evidence and the same chord voicings are used. The most typical electric guitar timbre in Young's accompaniments is a *just-breaking-up* distortion, not a fully saturated one. A *just-breaking-up* timbre is produced when a tube amplifier is overdriven to the point that it just begins to distort, so that louder playing or the louder part of the envelope of a single note will produce more distortion, but quieter playing will be less distorted. By contrast, a *saturated* distortion is one in which the level of distortion is very high, so that the basic timbre of the guitar is entirely changed (it generally approximates a square wave) and the signal becomes very compressed (notes do not follow their usual decay envelope but sustain at a fairly consistent volume). The just-breaking-up distortion allows the unique qualities of the electric guitar to come through, but also allows for a playing approach substantially similar to Young's acoustic style. While the timbre is different from that of an acoustic guitar, the envelope and spectral characteristics are similar enough that the sound does not become completely blurred together.

Chords such as those described above will create different impressions when played on an acoustic guitar, or on an electric guitar with the just-breaking-up distortion. The first may be described as reflective and intimate, the second as spacious and nearly chaotic, but both are useable. More saturated timbres, by contrast, do not respond well to full chord voicings. Played with this level of distortion and volume, the voicings become so complex and dense that they approximate white noise. The dual guitar sound common in Crazy Horse is built largely upon the just-breaking-up timbre and upon the kinds of arpeggiated and strummed figures typical of the acoustic guitar. Two other features shared between Young's electric and acoustic guitar styles include an emphasis on clipped offbeats as a contrast to the strong quarter note level pulse ("Albuquerque," "Words") and the blurring together of rhythm and lead work ("Cinnamon Girl," "Down by the River," "Southern Man"). Notice how the just-breaking-up timbre, which distorts louder notes but leaves the quieter ones relatively clean, causes the loud buzzing low string attacks to have a great deal of extra weight and the high string offbeats to be more stinging. These features, already dramatic on the acoustic guitar, create on the electric a layered effect combining long-sustained bass notes displaying a distorted-to-clean timbral envelope, sharp and strongly distorted stabs in the upper register, and a continuously ringing middle register continuously perched between a distorted and clean sound.

The relationship between these various aspects of Young's guitar sound and the piston-like movement of his right hand provides an opportunity for metaphorical interpretation. The hand movement displays a dual aspect. It is a smooth and continuous cycle, but it is also divided into iterated downbeats and offbeats. In general, this produces a feeling of potential, a continuous enablement out of which shapes are plucked. Young's specific guitar figures literally emerge from a less inflected, continually flowing power source, and this gives them some of their impetus. There is a fine balance here between continuity and jarring interjection, and one striking thing about Young's guitar style is that while it suggests in some respects an image of continuous flow, many of the events within that flow are played in a way that draws attention to their transience. For example, a strong attack on low notes tends to make the onset of their decay more evident. More fundamentally, Young's typical electric timbre is defined largely by its decay characteristics, since the just-breaking-up distortion is marked by the transient nature of the distorted part of the signal. There are places where Young makes dramatic use of this transient character. For example, he frequently begins or ends solos or major structural sections by striking a full chord quite hard, then letting it fade. This gesture draws maximum attention to the distorted-to-clean nature of the basic timbre. However, despite the frequent emphasis on interjection or transience, there is also something surface-like in the balance struck between a constant fading of old events and a constant appearance of new ones. In many Crazy Horse performances, this surface-like aspect is embodied in the continual buzz of decaying guitar notes. At one point in my research I produced spectral plots of "Cinnamon Girl" and "Powderfinger," which are acoustically typical of Crazy Horse. I was struck by the fact that for much of the time there was at least a small amount of signal present in every frequency range. This is noisy music in the literal sense that it creates for itself a fairly constant background of nearly white ambient noise, which helps to create the impression of a timbral surface.

Rhythm Guitar: Riffs

The core of Young's guitar style, both electric and acoustic, is the layered approach described above. However, many other elements are also present. For example, within any guitar-based rock style riffs will always be present, and while Young's playing doesn't highlight riffs to nearly the degree that one would find in a tradition like heavy metal, they are still an important part of his music. As Fast notes in her work on Led Zeppelin, riffs can serve many functions in the formal structure of a song. Some crucial analytic questions in this regard include "[D]oes the riff begin the song? Is it used as an introductory musical gesture, thereby foregrounding it, calling attention to its importance? . . . Is the riff heard during the verses or not? During the chorus? In between verses? Is it heard during the outro . . . ? Is the riff heard during the guitar solo if there is one?"[2] Fast goes on to show that in the music of Led Zeppelin there is great variety here and that no one riff function could be isolated as most typical.[3] The same is true in the case of Neil Young, but instead of pursing the formal questions in detail, I would like to develop another angle suggested by Fast. How does the riff function to focus attention and to dominate or to support other elements? Since riffs in guitar-based rock music are usually played loudly, often occupy prominent formal positions, and tend toward a homophonic texture, they can serve as powerful devices for focusing attention. In other words, with respect to musical texture and listener attention, riffs can be powerfully centripetal. This effect depends greatly on a number of factors, however, including the basic structure of the riff, its place in the formal structure of the song, and the degree to which it dominates the overall texture at any given time.

First, the formal structure of riffs. Hicks suggests that we should distinguish initially between harmonic riffs and melodic riffs.[4] This is a useful distinction for rock music in general, and the first thing to note about Neil Young is that he tends to blur it. One of his best-known riffs, "Mr. Soul," is clearly melodic, but it is borrowed from the Rolling Stones, so immediately its intertextual significance may outweigh more subtle dimensions for many listeners. Young has used clearly melodic riffs elsewhere as well ("Drive Back," "Opera Star," "Saddle Up the Palomino"), but generally not in his better-known songs. A much more typical device for Young is to write riffs which blend harmonic and melodic elements. For example, "Cinnamon Girl" is based around parallel harmonic movement (with a heterophonic rather than a strictly homophonic texture), "Hey Hey My My" and "Rapid Transit" juxtapose single-string work against block chords, and "Rockin' in the Free World" juxtaposes parallel chord movement against a repeated pedal tone. As an additional device, besides blurring the line between harmonic and melodic riffs, Young also frequently blurs the distinction between riffs and other kinds of harmonic accompaniment by allowing changes of voicing and ornamentation in a rhythm part to create a texture which is somewhat riff-like, but not entirely so. In some cases the effect seems weighted more toward chord changes with a slightly riff-like quality ("Southern Man," "Heart of Gold"), and in other cases the effect is more like a riff proper, but one clearly constructed from movement within a chord ("Cocaine Eyes," "Fuckin' Up").

As Fast has shown in her work on Led Zeppelin, the kinetic and affective character of different riffs can be described in terms of image schemata.[5] The main point I want to make about Neil Young's riffing practices requires a similar move, but at a higher level of metaphor. I want to make a few comments about Young's relationship to the idea of a rock *anthem* and the manner in which the anthemic involves a concept of the *monumental*. Rock critics frequently describe certain songs as anthems, and this anthemic quality relies partly on the nature of the riff. The image of an anthem is closely related to that of the mass rally and to ideologies of group solidarity. It requires that a high level of energy be generated, but also that this energy be tightly constrained and made to flow in directions which encourage group cohesion and collective experience. Seen in this light, certain riffs—the ones which create both a high degree of energy and a tightly regimented texture—can seem almost totalitarian. An interesting parallel can be found here with Lefebvre's comments on monumental architecture. Lefebvre argues that monumental spaces offer members of a society an image of their membership, and therefore a sense of self-worth and solidarity.[6] This validation relies upon the manner in which the monumental space appears to suspend time, offering a model of permanence and solidity. In addition to the suspension of time, this vastness of space both symbolizes and literally allows for the togetherness of large groups. Lefebvre goes on to note that such solidarity relies upon a generally accepted power structure and in fact contains an element of repression which is inseparable from the element of self-validation. In this connection, it does not seem incidental that one of the distinctive characteristics of a rock anthem is its special appropriateness to the monumental performance space of stadiums and arenas. (One work in which the image complex of rock anthem, monumental stadium space, and fascism is exploited to great effect is Pink Floyd's *The Wall*.)

The riffs in anthemic rock songs not only resemble monumental spaces in an iconic way, but also in the kind of meaning and affect they often create: an empowerment which implies tight control and, to a degree, uniformity of response among a large group of people. In this sense, the anthemic riff seems at odds with the less tightly constrained aspects of Young's aesthetic. Or more precisely, the juxtaposition in Young's persona of hippie and conservative ideologies finds a parallel in the juxtaposition of these two different elements of his rhythm guitar playing. Some of his best-known songs are riff-based and have been described as anthemic ("Mr. Soul," "Cinnamon Girl," "Hey Hey My My," "Rockin' in the Free World"). However, these sorts of concerted, disciplined riffs do not dominate his guitar style overall, but exist in creative contrast with the looser, semi-improvisatory style described earlier. And perhaps more interesting, there are the many examples already described of riffs in which Young adopts some of the typical anthemic traits but blurs them in various ways. Finally, we should consider that although riffs are fairly common in Young's work, most critics consider his electric guitar solos, not riffs, to be his trademark (unlike a guitarist such as Keith Richards, about whom critics generally say the opposite). Fast suggests that it is especially important to note whether a solo is played over top of a riff or over some other accompaniment pattern, because "this is the point at which 'the virtuoso' steps forward, asserting his subjectivity in a profound way," and given the centripetal potential of the riff, playing the solo over something other than the riff can draw maximum attention to the individuality of the soloist.[7] I note this argument because it is rare for Young to play a solo over a clear riff, and this is especially true of the long Crazy Horse improvisations which form the cornerstone of his guitar solo style. This point is crucial because like anthemic riffs such solos could be called *monumental,* but while they suggest a large virtual space and occupy long stretches of time, they do not cultivate the kind of rigid structure linked to more totalitarian kinds of monumentality. This is an example of how two closely related metaphors—the monumental-as-fascist and the monumental-as-sublime—can evoke one another and can deploy similar musical signifiers without being coextensive.

Harmonica

Young's primary identity as an instrumentalist is firmly bound to the guitar. But his frequent use of harmonica and piano at all stages of his career have enshrined these as important secondary instruments. I will not comment at length on Young's harmonica playing except to offer two notes on a generic level and two on a gestural level. On a generic level, the harmonica forms a link between Neil Young and Bob Dylan in the minds of many listeners and is part of Young's involvement in the country-rock and singer-songwriter traditions. Indeed, the harmonica is a crucial symbolic counterweight to the electric guitar in Young's iconography, and so participates in the fuzzy but crucial distinction in his work between softer material and the heavier Crazy Horse material. It is not unheard of for Young to wear a harmonica while playing electric guitar, but for the most part the harmonica symbolizes the kind of quiet, singer-songwriter material usually performed on acoustic guitar. It should also be noted, however, that in a stylistic sense Young's harmonica playing bears little resemblance to Dylan's, although it serves an identical formal function. Interestingly, while it is idiosyncratic by folk standards, Young's harmonica style is strikingly similar to that of Jimmy Reed. As already noted in chapter 2, Young's connections to the blues are substantial but not obvious, and Jimmy Reed is a blues musician who has been mentioned as a direct influence. Reed's harmonica style, however, was not typical of blues harmonica in general, and so in Neil Young's harmonica style we end up with a subtle blend of generic cross-references: a visually powerful but stylistically weak connection to singer-songwriter styles, and a stylistically idiosyncratic but personally crucial connection to the blues.

On a gestural level, the first thing to note is the degree of intimacy between the harmonica and the player. In addition to the direct contact with the mouth, the instrument becomes very much an extension of the player's body when it is worn in a neck brace, as Young always does. Specifically, it becomes an extension of the voice in that it is close to the mouth, has a sound reliant on the movement of breath, and is accompanied by the soloist on guitar in the same manner as is the voice. This interpretation of harmonica as an alternative voice suits Young's use of the instrument. The long harmonica introduction to "Out on the Weekend" demonstrates this property especially well, and the overall approach of this solo exemplifies much of Young's harmonica playing in quieter, slower songs. The harmonica stays close to what sounds like a precomposed melody. The overall texture is monophonic, but dyads are frequently inserted to thicken the line in places. Ornamentation is constant but subtle. Grace notes, slow bends, and a slow medium-depth vibrato are all used, but usually do not dominate the melody. In other words, the unique textural resources of the harmonica are used sparingly, and the overall effect is quite vocal. However, the harmonica is not only an alternative voice. Even in the examples listed above, there are passages where the unique qualities of the instrument come through, especially when Young prolongs notes with very long bends, draws attention to the in-breath, or employs ornaments not possible with the voice. Such techniques are more common in the louder songs, where Young plays harmonica quite percussively, repeating single notes and dyads ("Time Fades Away"). This textural, repetitive approach is also sometimes used in slower songs ("Mellow My Mind"). These general considerations lead me to a second gestural comment: Young's harmonica playing often has a meandering quality also found in other aspects of his music. As we will see in the harmonic and melodic analyses, one typical feature of Young's work is incremental movement and occasionally a prioritization of tone-color over other parameters. In addition, we will see that melodic frames

of a third are especially typical of Young's melodies. The diatonic harmonica is in some ways an ideal instrument for exploring these sorts of
resources, since it offers a limited pitch collection, arranged mostly in
thirds. The harmonica combines a material tendency toward the kind of
melodic frames favored by Young with a considerable range in exploring
variations of tone color. In these respects, it forms a bridge between aspects of his vocal style and aspects of his instrumental work, especially
his guitar solos.

Piano

Some of Young's best-known pieces have been piano songs ("After the Gold Rush," "A Man Needs a Maid"). Other keyboards have been
featured as well, and his use of the synthesizer has been discussed elsewhere. In the late 1960s and early 1970s, Young would occasionally use
electric organ and electric piano, and in recent years, beginning around
the time of *Sleeps with Angels,* the toy-like tack piano has also been an
occasional but recurring feature, as has an ornately carved Victorian
pump organ. Although the pump organ has been known to sit unplayed
onstage for entire concerts, contributing mostly on a visual level, it has
also been used for some memorable performances, perhaps most notably
"Like a Hurricane" on *MTV Unplugged.* Despite this range in keyboard
use, however, the upright acoustic piano is the keyboard instrument
most closely associated with Young on an ongoing basis, specifically
with his singer-songwriter material. A piano is often featured in Young's
harder rock arrangements as well, but in these situations it is usually
played by someone else. When Young plays the piano himself, it is almost always on quieter songs most closely associated with the singer-
songwriter aspects of his work. An important exception is the song
"Tonight's the Night," in which Young usually plays a louder rock-style
piano part with the full band. In these performances, he often sways dramatically, almost appearing autistic at moments, a kind of body movement not seen to nearly the same degree in his other piano performances.
In terms of bodily posture—seated and slightly swaying—Young's piano
performances form a unit with his solo acoustic performances, and both
contrast with his electric performances, in which he is typically very mobile. To distinguish just two broad kinds of Neil Young performance
then—his hard rock and singer-songwriter modes—we need to notice

that there are at least three elements to be considered: (1) repertoire; (2) instrument; (3) bodily deportment.

There are some general correlations between these, but the situation is complex. The first thing to note is that Young almost never moves a song from a guitar-based arrangement to a piano-based one. So the piano songs generally remain piano songs. The guitar-based songs, by contrast, will frequently be played in varying arrangements, from solo acoustic guitar to acoustic guitar plus band to full electric band. So in any given singer-songwriter–style acoustic guitar performance, the distinction from other performances is often in terms of instrument and deportment only, not in terms of repertoire. This being said, there are still broad repertorial patterns in the guitar-based music, since certain songs are always played on acoustic guitar and others always on electric, and in these cases the acoustic songs as a group tend to be the more introspective and melodic of the two. In short, the piano for Neil Young forms part of a complicated system of stylistic and generic distinctions within his work. In a general way, it signifies a less mobile, more melodic, more reflective style, and probably nostalgia as well given its associations with Victorian home life (especially when sharing the stage with a pump organ) and earlier styles of popular music. In this connection, it is significant to note that Young almost always plays an upright piano rather than a grand. This sort of instrument highlights the nostalgic and domestic quality of the upright piano, linking it to clichés of the rent party and the home parlor.

Stylistically, Young's pianism bears interesting similarities to his work on guitar. It does not display extensive technique, but it is strongly expressive. I have already noted that his right-hand guitar technique is marked by a continuous periodic movement which tends to produce a strong motor rhythm. A similar texture pervades much of his piano playing ("After the Gold Rush," "Journey Through the Past"). When I think of Neil Young playing piano, the image that comes to mind immediately is of hands falling with determined regularity, variations arising, but always around a constant mid-tempo motor rhythm. The piano also allows Young to explore the same kinds of harmonic color as in his guitar arrangements: triads with sevenths and ninths stacked on top. Frequently, these colors emerge as Young shifts triads or dyads up and down while holding other notes stationary. This is one of the easiest things to do on the piano, and it produces a sound very much in sympathy with the harmonic vocabulary employed by Young on the guitar. The timbre of the piano also allows Young on occasion to use these chords as much for their textural properties as for their harmonic function. For example, the CMaj7 chord in "Love in Mind" and the 'e' sustained through multiple harmonies in "The Bridge" serve to create a sustained timbral effect. As a timbral resource, Young also frequently uses piano to develop his more elaborate arrangements. The bel canto piano texture at the opening of "Here We Are in the Years" immediately sets the orchestral tone of the arrangement, and the piano part in the instrumental section of "Words" highlights the flowing yet lopsided nature of the asymmetrical meter.

One final point should be made about Young's piano playing: it almost never makes use of stylistic clichés. Some of his piano parts do resonate with established piano styles—for example the classical quality of "Here We Are in the Years," the country overtones of "Journey Through the Past," or the slightly jazz-inflected voicings of "The Bridge"—and the references to existing piano styles are often stronger in songs where the piano is played by someone else. But for the most part, when Neil Young plays the piano the result is stylistically unique. It is almost as if his piano style is a compendium of the more idiosyncratic aspects of his guitar style. This effect might also be partly because Young almost always uses the piano in conjunction with his singer-songwriter performances, which themselves tend to avoid the kind of stylistic intermusicality common in some of his other work.

Melody

Melodic Metaphors

Melody is of great importance in Neil Young's music. Along with his extremely high voice, it was the affective tone of his melodies which was most often commented upon by early critics and associated with adjectives such as fragile, sensitive, and desolate. Young's melodies can be roughly divided into two broad groups, and I will use two core images to describe their dominant characters: *drifting* and *ranting*. I have chosen these images not because they arise frequently in the critical literature (they are not in fact particularly common), but because I feel they summarize families of themes in that literature and can help link those

themes to specific musical features. Reading into the general tone of early
Neil Young criticism, it seems that the image complex I have chosen to
summarize as *drifting* is frequently nuanced with further overtones of
despair or alienation, and in this connection we should recall an observation about lyrics made in chapter 1: Neil Young frequently describes
drifting or flying things from the perspective of a despondent, earth-
bound observer. This is just one example of how a core melodic metaphor of drifting can blend with other elements of his work, acquiring
additional affective overtones. In the melodic analysis that follows, I will
outline formal features which I feel suggest *drifting* as an apt metaphor,
and I will more briefly describe how the rant-like melodies contrast with
these. Before proceeding with analytic details, however, I should clarify
what I take to be the basic structure of each image (I am using the words
"image" and "metaphor" roughly interchangeably). These images to be
mapped onto the melodic data are perhaps the most explicitly phenomenological part of my study. Although they rely in part on general properties of language and the natural world and take their cues from specific
details of Neil Young's music and its reception history, they are ultimately descriptions of my own experience.

Melodic Metaphors: Drifting

Perspective. Drifting often seems to connote the experience of the
drifter itself, to be an image concerned with what it feels like to move in
a certain manner, although images of drifting are also sometimes used
in an evaluative sense to judge or describe the behavior of others.

Energetic state. The drifter itself is marked by its low energy level relative to surrounding forces. The drifter drifts because it cannot or will
not exert enough force to impose a trajectory on the environment and is
therefore mostly at the mercy of outside forces.

Space of movement. Images of drifting tend to strongly connote either
three-dimensional movement in the air or movement along the surface
of water. In the first case, there is a juxtaposition between the freedom implied by three-dimensional movement and the constant if subtle
directionality imposed by gravity and by the location of the ground.
In the case of water, the space is more confining since it is essentially
two-dimensional (if there were large waves, then the image would probably become one of being swept away, or of being violently heaved,

rather than of drifting). Just as an air space can be made subtly vectorial through the presence of gravity, a water-surface space can be given some inherent direction through the presence of currents or winds.

Manner of movement. Consider two particular examples: a dry leaf drifting in a gentle breeze and a ship without sails or motor drifting in the current on a calm sea. In the case of the leaf, the exact path is highly variable, with many twists and turns, surges and reversals, moments of near stasis and rapid accelerations. Gradually and circuitously, the leaf settles on the ground. In the case of the ship, the movement is more steady and linear, but very slow, perhaps imperceptible. The only thing shared by these manners of movement is that the goal to which they tend is not obvious in the movement itself and is not arrived at quickly. In the case of the leaf, the goal is non-obvious because the local movements are so unpredictable, and indeed the force producing these movements (a breeze) is different from that which imposes the ultimate goal (gravity). In the case of the ship, the goal is non-obvious because the path seems so uninflected and deliberate and unfolds on an unarticulated surface. In both cases, however, the drifter moves in a manner not of its own design, toward a goal which is both distant and inevitable.

Affective dimensions. Sometimes, images of drifting convey a feeling tone of liberation and pleasure. At other times, they convey the opposite, a feeling of disempowerment and doom. In both cases, the affective tone is enhanced by the fact that the ultimate goal is distant. In the first instance, the remoteness of the goal can be perceived as the *absence* of a goal, so that the comparative directionlessness of the moment-to-moment drifting is emphasized. In the second instance, the remoteness of the goal makes it all the more threatening, since the experience of gloomy compulsion will be prolonged.

Melodic Metaphors: Ranting

Perspective. In contrast to drifting, I would suggest that images of ranting are most effective when describing how the ranter appears to others rather than conveying the subjective experience of the ranter itself. A ranter is opaque—made psychologically impenetrable by the forcefulness of its expression—and because of its opacity it is the striking character of that expression which becomes the central focus. As with the previous metaphor of drifting, the ranter may be human or may be some other sort of event. The surges of white water around a large rock in a rapids, for example, display an energetic profile similar to what I am calling a rant. However, even more than in the case of drifting, I will emphasize in my comments below the properties of a *human* ranter, because I am especially interested in how the image of ranting can describe a particular kind of uncomfortably intense encounter between a listener and an expressive agent.

Energetic state. The energy level of a rant is very high. This is the single most dramatic contrast between ranting and drifting. The other dramatic contrast has to do with the source of the energy. In the case of drifting, the drifter is dominated by the surroundings. A ranter, by contrast, overwhelms everything in its vicinity. This intense and localized energy is not balanced, however. While the ranter radiates a singular and powerful force, it is not clear whether it is in control. This is again in contrast to the case of drifting, where the forces are less localized but more balanced, producing a gentler energetic profile. A ranter and a drifter are both in an ambiguous position relative to questions of self-control, but this ambiguity is an immediately pressing issue in the case of ranting, whereas drifting is often precisely the process of avoiding such issues.

Space of movement. Ranting, unlike drifting, is not primarily a spatial image, although a few spatial entailment can be identified. Most immediately, if we think about the paradigm case of an observer watching a ranter, the distance between the two will become an issue. The apprehensiveness of the observer, based on the ranter's unpredictability, will charge the space between them, since the observer presumably wishes to avoid direct contact. A ranter has the effect of making itself into a singular point, a center of attention, avidly but apprehensively observed by others.

Manner of movement. Like drifting, ranting combines a stopping-and-starting surface movement with an underlying quality of continuity. However, unlike drifting, ranting is compulsive, or at least the compulsion in a rant is immediate and intense rather than remote and subtle. During pauses in a rant, for example, there is no feeling of stasis, but rather one of building tension, as if a powerful flow of water has been momentarily stopped and the pressure has immediately begun to build. Moments at which the rant recommences after a pause do not feel, as in drifting, like gentle resumptions, but like successive eruptions. This feeling of compulsion applies both to the ranter, who appears to be governed by some unstoppable internal surge, and the observers, who cannot divert their attention. Although drifting may or may not be linear, ranting is always linear in the sense that the pressure is continuous and always palpable. And as with drifting, it is not clear whether the rant is following a particular path. There is a powerful feeling of motive and a linearity in the sense that energy is continually being expended, but there is no overarching goal in evidence.

Motives and affective state. The affective resources of ranting are more limited than those of drifting. The image never seems to convey an unambiguously positive tone, being either cathartic or deranged. One never has the impression that the ranter is in a comfortable or sustainable state, and the observer cannot relax around someone or something behaving in such a manner.

Melodic Analysis

With respect to melodies, drifting could be related to many features. In my own analysis, I discuss the following characteristics: (1) Young's melodies are marked for the most part by incremental movements; (2) there is a tendency toward narrow note frames; (3) his melodies emphasize color tones without moving completely outside the triadic harmonic underpinnings; (4) there is often a rhythmic profile finely balancing movements and pauses. The cumulative effect is one of constant flow and a series of transformations achieved with minimal resources. The presence of these features gives many of Young's melodies a drifting quality, and so my analysis has two goals: to describe in some depth the formal features mentioned above and to give reasons that the image of drifting may be aptly mapped onto them.[8]

As I have already mentioned, an image of drifting only works for some of Young's melodies. In other cases, an almost exactly opposite effect is predominant. In songs like "Rockin' in the Free World" or "Revolution Blues," Young's melodies and their performance are highly charged, nervous, in some ways aggressive. It is for this reason that I suggest the second image of *ranting* to describe this other common character in Young's melodies. The aptness of images such as drifting and ranting derives partly from structural features, but also from performative and contextual ones. In fact, the distinction between these images can in some cases be almost entirely performative rather than structural. A chant-like note frame, for example, can create an impression of relaxed non-directedness in one context and an impression of obsessive shouted monologue in another. Similarly, an oscillating framework can participate in an image of gentle undulation or of frantically running around in circles. In this chapter, in the interest of space and because my intention is to suggest apt metaphors rather than to finalize an analysis, I will focus mostly on structural features that may, other factors assisting, contribute to an image of drifting. The importance of performative features and the relationship between images of drifting and ranting will be dealt with again in the summary section which follows the formal analysis. I should also note that hereafter, when I speak of drifting, I am thinking of the falling-leaf variety rather than the ship-at-sea variety, since it is the former that models the features I want to highlight in Young's melodies.

MELODIC ANALYSIS: CELLULAR STRUCTURE

The idea of a melodic *cell* is intuitively clear but difficult to describe formally. For the purposes of my own work, I mean simply that Neil Young's melodies frequently feature repetitions of a short melodic idea and that these instances of the idea are separated by shorter or longer pauses, frequently with variations upon each repetition. Under this definition, a *cell* is a discrete unit of sound bounded by silences, not a more abstract theoretical construct. I refer to a melody constructed mostly in this way as *cellular*. Two key features of a cellular melody are that it is noticeably constructed of related but isolated fragments and that this creates a fine balance between a feeling of flow, brought about by the continually evolving relationships between the parts, and one of hesitancy, brought about by the frequent pauses. For one example of a cellular melody, see Figure 5.1. Cellular structure is a feature of many popular melodies, but I would suggest that it is an especially pertinent feature in Neil Young's work. Throughout my analysis, I have found that the notion of the cell is an especially helpful one in describing Young's melodies and that many of their formal properties can be understood as operations upon cells. Further, the particular balance between flow and hesitancy which can be constructed through cellular techniques relates well to the core metaphor of *drifting*.

Being cellular is as much a rhythmic feature as a pitch-related one. In

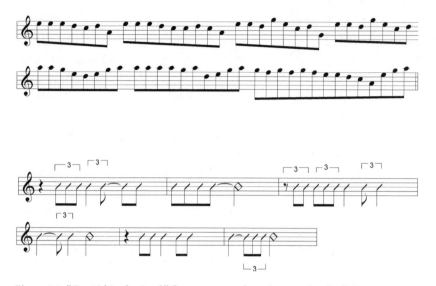

Figure 5.1. "Cowgirl in the Sand," first entrance of vocal, example of cellular structure (*above*). "Love in Mind," first entrance of vocal, example of rhythmic flow (*below*).[9]

a rhythmic sense, Young's cellular structures tend to create what could be called a *flow and pause* effect. Cells are rhythmic gestalts and therefore must flow internally to some degree. Yet their boundaries must be marked by some sort of rhythmic disjuncture. The cellular structure overall, then, balances between flowing and pausing. There is a special sense in which I hear Young's melodies as *flowing*. This special sense of *flow* designates a tendency to use runs of notes with similar but not identical durations, often mixing them to make a rhythmic profile which does not readily break down into simple repeated rhythmic motives, but which does hint at such motives (see Figure 5.1). In addition to *flow*, there are two other common rhythmic profiles in Young's melodies. The intermediate one could be called *motivic*, in which there are clear rhythmic motives, but they are frequently varied ("Hangin' on a Limb," "The Losing End"). Also, several consecutive cells will often flow in a similar manner, producing a kind of motivic effect, but without strong motives within the cells ("Out on the Weekend," "Birds," "Ambulance Blues"). If the cells are short enough, this distinction starts to break down ("When Your Lonely Heart Breaks," "Safeway Cart"). The most extreme kind of rhythmic flow produces another profile, which I will call *speech-like*

("Revolution Blues," "Will to Love"), in which there is very little hint of rhythmic motives, either between or within cells. In contrast to all these varieties of subtly inflected flow, it should be noted that Young does occasionally employ the strict repetition of small rhythmic cells in what may be called *modal* rhythm ("Round and Round," parts of "Ride My Llama").

Young often treats his melodic cells additively, and more rarely, subtractively, transforming them by adding or removing notes on repetition. As one result, it is common for the registral space occupied by a cell to increase or decrease on subsequent transformations. This is not necessary, but it is the normal procedure for Young. Rather than repeating notes within the original registral extremes of the cell, he tends to allow cells to expand or contract registrally as they are varied. Interestingly, while registral expansions are common, Young's melodies do not generally display rhythmic transformations analogous to the registral ones. Usually, if a cell becomes longer or shorter, this occurs through the use of a longer or shorter passage of the prevailing rhythmic flow, not through a rhythmic transformation. Similarly, the basic rhythmic strategy does not notably change for different kinds of framework (e.g., faster or slower, duple or triple, louder or quieter). Any highlighted rhythmic motives will of course reflect these prevailing features, but the overall approach remains the same: mostly flow and pause, with a few highlighted motives on occasion. The *flow and pause* structure of Young's melodic rhythm, along with its generally cellular nature, works well with both of my core melodic images: drifting and ranting. In both cases, there is continual gathering and dispersing of small energy packets within an overall flow. In cases of drifting, this is done in a placid manner, while in the case of ranting it is more intense and driven. The frequently speech-like aspect of this basic rhythmic orientation also works well with the discursive nature of Young's music: the central place of lyrics and of the singer.

MELODIC ANALYSIS: CONTOUR

The basic contour of a melody is crucial to its overall effect. My descriptive vocabulary for melodic contours is based loosely on the work of Middleton and Van der Merwe.[10] Both are interested in how certain melodic shapes have specific histories, but Middleton is much more willing to interpret these in terms of semiotic correlations between melodic contours and other cultural factors. Such correlations are frequently assumed or stated outright in popular music studies: for example, descending profiles are often taken to connote African American stylistic influence, whereas arch forms may evoke the nineteenth-century bourgeoisie. Immediately upon making such suggestions, both the seductiveness and the pitfalls of this kind of analysis become evident. Even more controversial is the idea that particular melodic contours embody temporal and spatial profiles with inherent affective correlations, that in effect they will tend to feel a particular way to performers and listeners and that these feelings are integral to their meaning. Middleton enthusiastically pursues such an interpretive direction, and Van der Merwe avoids it. I will for the most part follow Middleton's lead and treat melodic contour as a crucial formal feature in the analysis both of energetic icons and of conventional correlations.

We can start by looking at scalar frames since they display a balance between stasis and movement similar to that which I described in connection with cellular structure and rhythmic flow. One typical form of scalar frame could be called *wave-like* movement. When such a movement is found in Young's melodies, it usually forms the basis for individual cells, producing an overall melody which sounds like many small waves separated by pauses (see Figure 5.2). *Wave-like* movement is an example of continuous movement producing no net change, which agrees with both the metaphor of *drifting* and with another suggestion that will be central to my harmonic analysis: Young typically creates changes of harmonic color and function in such a way as to maintain an overall impression of stasis or poise.

A second category of note frame, related to scalar movement, is the *fall*. As in all rock music, falling contours are quite common in Neil Young's melodies, and they occur in a variety of ways. Some cells are built on scalar falls (verses of "Cinnamon Girl," first vocal section of "Down by the River"). In one sense, this maximizes the impact of the falling profile in that many local falls are heard in succession as the falling cell is repeated. In another sense, however, melodies built in this way can display a kind of stasis if the falls all occupy the same registral area. In other cases, Young will arrange cells of a different type, for example oscillations, on a larger scalar frame. Here the effect of the scalar structure

Figure 5.2. "Birds," first entrance of vocal, example of wave-like cells (*above*). "Motion Pictures," first entrance of vocal, repeated falls in same register (*below*).

is more subtle, sounding like a series of level shifts rather than a local gesture ("Hangin' on a Limb"). In some cases, Young presents falls which are quite dramatic. Some of them could be termed *plummets* (the end of the verses of "Southern Man" and "Pocahontas"), and others are more extended in time (middle of the verses of "Comes a Time," guitar figure at the end of the verses of "Powderfinger"). Some of Young's melodies are marked by the nearly obsessive repetition of falling profiles ("Don't Be Denied" and Figure 5.2). In these cases, to my ear, the repeated falls usually have the effect of underscoring one of the basic qualities of cellular melodies in general: the continual gathering and dispersion of energy, with pauses in between. Note that cellular structure could easily be associated with other energetic profiles besides this one. For example, cells can be used to incrementally increase tension or excitement. It is more typical of Young's use of cellular structure, however, to constantly gather and disperse energy, with each cell standing as one in a linked series of small energetic pulses.

Falling profiles are closely linked to a number of common metaphors in Western musical discourses. These include the mapping between registral space and physical space, the idea that notes are object-like and therefore subject to the effects of gravity, and the idea that the state of submitting to gravity can be mapped onto affective states of despondency and sadness. These metaphors are useful in discussing Young's use of falling contours. In general, they collectively portray a fall as an anti-drifting kind of event. But many of the specific devices I have described could be understood as balancing this anti-drifting aspect with other factors, for example by repeating the fall often enough that it begins to produce a broader sense of stasis, or by mixing it with other contours so that it does not dominate. In some cases the despondent overtones of the fall create strong melancholic overtones in the underlying image of drifting ("Motion Pictures" is perhaps the best example). It could also be suggested that some of Young's melodic falls are so dramatic and so energetically performed that they acquire the quality of swooping, which is not quite like drifting but is still an air-bound activity ("Southern Man," "Time Fades Away"). At other times, Young uses falling profiles in a manner entirely consistent with the common image of drifting as a gradual fall and a settling to rest. This is certainly the case in the list, given above, of falls used in order to create phrase endings, and it is also the case in a song like "Southern Pacific," in which every melodic phrase is structured around an extended fall over the interval of a minor seventh.

The concept of a note frame involves not only the shape of a movement, but also the distance between its highest and lowest pitches. Frames of a third are especially important in Young's melodies, as in much rock and folk music. Besides the clear-cut third frame, there is a particular interval pattern extremely common in Young's melodies which I also interpret as a kind of third. This is the three-note pitch collection of a third with a second either above or below (for example, d-f-g or c-d-f). I call this the *decorated third* frame, because while it is literally a frame of a fourth, I see it as arising from a third with an upper or lower extension of a second. This note frame is extremely common in Young's melodies. Some interesting examples include "Southern Pacific" (in which the origins of this frame as a decorated third can be clearly heard), "When Your Lonely Heart Breaks" (the frame is repeated with shifting emphasis, sometimes stressing the upper third and sometimes the fourth), and "Down by the River" (much of the melody meanders within this frame). The most common version of the decorated third frame as used in Young's melodies, whether ascending or descending, is that with the second above, and I think it is significant to note that this shape, which gradually narrows in upward movement and gradually expands with played in descending form, strongly suggests metaphors of gravitation. The decorated third frame lends itself to feelings of gentle reaching upwards and gradual acceleration downwards, and does so in a way which balances these movements with a sense of stasis, since they occur over the minimum possible registral range. One could not create these intervallic effects in any smaller a space without introducing a degree of chromaticism inappropriate to the overall stylistic framework.

It is also important to note that the decorated third frame guarantees, when used over a triad, that at least one melodic pitch will be a non-triad tone and at least one will be a triad tone other than the root. This ensures that the decorated third frame will present a continuum of subtle colors relative to the current harmonic root. The decorated third frame is ubiquitous in Young's work, and I emphasize this point because it leads us to an even more general feature of Young's melodies: they tend to emphasize color tones, dwelling upon notes a seventh away from the current harmonic root and, less frequently but still notably often, a ninth away. In one melodic analysis, I counted the frequency of noteheads functioning as particular degrees above their harmonic root (4,968 noteheads in total). The results were as follows (the first number is a degree above the current harmonic root, the second is the percentage of all noteheads matching that description): 1 = 22, 2 = 8, 3 = 23, 4 = 7, 5 = 23, 6 = 6, 7 = 11. In the absence of data for comparable rock artists, it would be difficult to make final claims about the uniqueness of this distribution. However, the relatively strong representation of sevenths and seconds (ninths) seems to bear out the claim that the quality of these intervals strongly influences the sound of Young's melodies. In general, I would suggest that this creates an effect of gentle association between the melody and the underlying harmonies, a continual but sometimes faint mutual attraction rather than strong compulsion.

To return to melodic contour, oscillation is another common framework in Young's melodies, and it appears on various structural levels. There are wave-like oscillations within cells ("Birds," "Change Your Mind"), and melodies entirely based on oscillations which gradually shift up and down ("The Losing End," and Figure 5.3). An oscillation is in itself a fine balance between movement and stasis, and when oscillations are arranged on other long-range shapes, many interesting shadings of this dual tendency are possible. More dramatically, the extreme case of a note frame conveying stasis is that of the chant. Many of the already described aspects of Young's melodies are chant-like. For example, his tendency to stay within narrow registral spans means that he often repeats notes. Similarly, oscillations are very close to chants, since in Young's case they are often oscillations of a second, and even cells displaying more internal movement can begin to create a chant-like effect

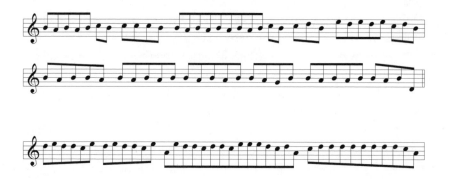

Figure 5.3. "Everybody Knows This Is Nowhere," first entrance of vocal, melody with extensive oscillation (*above*). "Revolution Blues," end of first verse, decorated chant (*below*).

if they are repeated without substantial variation. Insofar as chants are often marked either by a tense energy (a feeling of being confined to the note) or of rest (a feeling of being content to remain on the note), they relate equally well to my two core melodic metaphors of *drifting* and *ranting*. And in fact, Young uses chants in both ways, as well as achieving more subtle effects by combining them with other sorts of movement. The two main chant paradigms in Young's melodies are, first, chant followed by a fall, creating the impression of a relaxed potential energy built through the chant and released through the fall ("Down by the River," "If I Could Have Her Tonight"), and second, decorated chants, which are quite common among Young's louder hard-rock performances. These can suggest a strong central energy from which smaller charges spin off without its being diminished or shifted ("Sedan Delivery," "Cortez the Killer," and Figure 5.3). Comparison of these three examples shows how the same basic melodic approach (which I have called decorated chant) can create a continuum of expressive effects, from gently drifting ("Cortez the Killer") to playfully manic ("Sedan Delivery") to a mimicry of violent psychosis ("Revolution Blues").

Just as falling contours have in the literature on popular music been associated with a particular historical lineage (they are often considered to be Africanisms), so have arch forms, which Middleton has suggested are closely linked to European bourgeois taste in popular song.[11] Energetically speaking, arches are interesting because of their symmetry.

Whatever metaphors are attached to registral movement, the arch moves smoothly between a range of these metaphorical values, and it returns us to where we started. It is one of the ways in which music can approximate circular movement, and it may be the gesture which best combines aspects of circularity with aspects of linearity, since unlike oscillations, arches create a genuine feeling of excursion before their eventual return. Young uses many varieties of arch, most of which combine the standard arch form with some idiosyncratic feature typical of his melodic approach more generally. First, a fair number of Young's arches are quite narrow in register, sometimes confined to the range of a third ("Change Your Mind," "Sedan Delivery"). Second, many of these narrow arches, and some of his wider melodic arches as well, are inverse, moving first downwards and then upwards ("Round and Round," bridge of "Cowgirl in the Sand"). If we assume that Middleton is correct in regarding the upright arch form as an apt image of tension and release, then the relatively frequent appearance of inverse arches in Neil Young's melodies acquires extra importance. The relaxed-tense-relaxed reading of arches relies on the assumption that registers have fixed affective tones, with relaxation and rest being mapped onto lower pitches. This metaphor in turn relies on a terrestrial perspective, which is to say, it is coherent from the perspective of an object which can only go high by being accelerated from the ground. The tenseness of height in this metaphor is secondary, arising from the difficulty of maintaining height if resting on earth is your normal condition. If we invert this perspective and describe the arch from the perspective of a drifting entity whose normal state is to be suspended, a different affective mapping could make sense. In this instance, highness would be associated with lightness and freedom from constraint, while lowness would represent entanglement and being dragged down. Although I would not go so far as to try and suggest a single interpretation as appropriate, this second metaphor seems to be apt in describing the role of inverse arches in Young's melodies. Rather than encouraging a feeling of closure, inverse arches seem almost literally to keep the ball in the air. Experienced from the perspective of a drifter, they could be taken to represent the continual small redemptions which can frame and punctuate a slow descent, and seen from the perspective of an earth-bound observer, they can represent frustration or taunting by a drifter which continually comes almost within reach, only to move away. This is just one interpretation, but it may be an important one given the lyrical themes and affective tone discussed in chapter 1.

MELODY: CONCLUSION

Wearing his rock critic hat in the 1970s, Simon Frith had this to say about Neil Young:

> *Comes a Time* has the romantic innocence of those Sixties folk clubs where I used to sigh over the cool young men who, like Bob Dylan, rooted their personal anguish in the Human Condition, and suggested a life in which, instead of having to go back to school the next day, you could just travel on forever. . . . Some of the lyrics here are dreadful [but] Young gets away with such slop because he doesn't use the other conventions or fake sincerity. . . . It's his folk training again—he sings these songs not as if he wrote them, but as if he plucked them from the air, and his greatest gift remains his sense of melody, his ability to write tunes that sound like they were always there.[12]

Frith does not mean to suggest that Young's music comes across as impersonal, and in fact he argues the opposite. Frith's suggestion is that Young achieves a striking degree of expressive presence by avoiding obvious conventions of expressivity, while still relying on a stylistic framework. A tune can only sound "already there" if it mobilizes familiar stylistic norms, but Frith suggests the fate of "slop" will only be escaped if it uses these norms lightly. His comments also highlight the intimate connection between norms of style, genre, and personal identity, showing how they interact in practice. In this connection, it is important to note that Frith's reaction relies partly on his knowledge of Young's other projects. Elements of certain songs which may seem banal in their conventionality might be given less weight or read more generously if one were aware of Young's more idiosyncratic material. And any tendency toward excessive romanticism or anguish might be tempered by exposure to the broad dichotomy in Young's work between this kind of singer-songwriter material and harder rock.

While Frith identifies melody as one of Young's great talents, Sweeting argues that Young displays *two* main strengths: "an instinctive way with a melody, [and] his love of the sheer *thrill* of brute force and loud guitars."[13] This, too, I would nuance a little. By analyzing melodies both in terms of drifting and ranting, I want to emphasize that the thrill of brute force is occasionally given melodic expression in Young's work, although I choose to place greater emphasis on drifting for the same reasons that Frith and Sweeting correlate melody with a more passive character: Young's characteristic melodic devices emerge most clearly in his quieter material. However, some of the melodic devices I have identified (repetition of substantially similar cells, chants, plummets) are easily deployed as "brute force" tactics. It is this overlap in Young's work between the two broad characters—not only in terms of generic correlation or performativity but also in terms of basic structural devices—that allows a critic like Frith to simultaneously identify Young with clichés of the overly sensitive singer-songwriter and to distance him from them.

I would suggest that the images deployed by Frith demonstrate the usefulness of the correlations I drew between specific musical devices and images of drifting and ranting. Frith speaks of "romantic innocence" and "traveling on forever," which are both images that can be understood partly as specific elaborations of drifting. When we look at the role of devices that maintain continuity in Young's melodies (for example flow-and-pause rhythm, gradual cellular transformation) and which emphasize subtle shifts of tone color within that relatively continuous flow (for example the decorated third frame, oscillating and wave-like note frames, dwelling on sevenths and ninths), the hierarchy of metaphorical interpretation seems fairly clear (although not binding). However, this line of reasoning also points out a potential blind spot in my analysis. Having placed so much emphasis on continuity and subtlety in Young's melodies, how are we to reconcile this with the central importance of *surprise* in his work overall? And what about *noise*? One answer is that the melodic tendencies described in this analysis form a thread of continuity which helps unite Young's persona across surprises and suggest an image of orderliness which counterbalances his noisier moments. Another tack would be to redeploy the concept of waywardness developed in chapter 2 in order to suggest that the delicate balance struck between idiolect and stylistic cliché in these melodies lends to Young's persona a simultaneously stable and unstable character, and that a certain uneasiness will always tinge Young's idiosyncratic take on conventions of melodic and lyrical romanticism. My interest is less in choosing between such readings and more in raising the issues and linking them to specific musical features. As Burns has noted, "while an individual parameter may be isolated for theoretical discussion, its function and meaning are dependent on its context within the remaining musical texture."[14] So, rather than trying to answer such broad questions with respect to the single parameter of melody, I would like to move on and consider Neil Young's harmonic language.

Chord Changes: Gesture and Posture

When I first looked at Neil Young's harmonic language, I was struck by several features, many of which could be described with vocabularies already developed in the literature on rock. For example, many of Young's progressions are modal rather than tonal, a feature with both energetic and stylistic significance to be discussed later. Beyond these sorts of properties, I also felt a subtle effect for which I did not have a ready description. I could not even be sure, however, that it really was one kind of effect I was hearing, since it seemed to arise in different contexts: for example in the long prolongation of harmonies in "The Losing End" but also in the changing yet somehow static chord progression of "Southern Pacific." If these were the only sorts of instance, then I would have simply described them in terms of harmonic prolongation and chord substitution. However, I also felt that what I was hearing in these passages had a kinship with cases that were too brief to be understood as prolongations in the usual sense, for example in places where a highly directed chord sequence pauses only momentarily before its final resolution, as at the end of each verse in "Powderfinger" or in the many instances where Young strikes a tonic chord and allows it to slowly decay before or after a guitar solo. Looking for a general concept that might encompass this diverse range of practices, I began to feel that it would be possible to apply a distinction I had originally developed in connection with the analysis of timbre. As noted earlier, workers such as Shepherd and Wicke have suggested that timbre displays a kind of immediacy in contrast to syntax. In this connection, I began to think of timbres as varieties of *posture* and to contrast them with syntactical *gestures.* The gesture/posture distinction has a far more general applicability, however, and elsewhere I have shown some of the range of questions which it can help illuminate.[15] In the present chapter, I will employ it to explain what I think I was hearing in those Neil Young chord progressions.

After having developed the distinction, I found that Hatten had also used the word *posture* in a similar way, to designate a "frozen motion" which "reverberates with the resonance of the implied gesture of an agent."[16] A posture is a relatively fixed distribution of energy in and upon the body. It does not have the gross temporal dynamics of a gesture, but it does have a distinctive character, recognizable to viewers by its visual form and to the poseur by a particular combination of bodily sensations. There are many instances in which musical events or textures seem to be both static and energized, imbued with the character of a movement without the movement actually taking place. It is this family of impressions to which the term *posture* is meant to apply. In both physiological and musical terms, it is important to note that postures are only relatively static. It is not possible to stand perfectly still, and a perfectly unchanging tone is impossible to create as a percept. However, there are at least two senses in which a musical passage may sound static. It may be relatively static in a literal sense, presenting far fewer changes than surrounding passages or far fewer than a listener may expect within the stylistic context of the piece. Or a passage may *signify* stasis, either by being static in the former sense or in some other way. In the present chapter, I am most interested in the first sense of musical stasis, in which a passage literally presents a smaller number of changes, since this case provides more opportunity for formal analysis.

The tendency in much writing about music and the body has been to emphasize the gestural aspect of musical icons and indices of embodied states, that is, to focus almost exclusively on virtual movements in order to show how musical movement can model bodily movement. By adding posture as an equally important element, we will additionally be able to talk about how music can depict bodies in a state of energized stasis, or how constant affects and feeling tones can run unchanged through otherwise-shifting energetic configurations. Most importantly, by using the words *gesture* and *posture* as a pair, we can show how the mobile and static varieties of musical body signs coexist on a continuum and continually transform into one another. The most illuminating strategy is to show the interrelatedness of gesture and posture as aspects of many musical parameters, rather than to limit any particular parameter to a gestural or postural description. For example, several of the unique properties of timbre are perhaps best understood in postural terms, and a timbre can easily be made iconic with a posture because the spectral properties of a timbre are, like a posture, an energetic configuration. But timbres also display temporal changes which can be more gestural in effect. Walser has noted something similar with respect to the power chord as it is used in heavy metal. "The power chord can be percussive and rhythmic or indefinitely sustained; it is used both to articulate and to suspend time."[17]

This dually static and rhythmic property of power chords is highlighted in the introductory riff to "Cinnamon Girl," in which two beats of power chords in motor eighths are separated by two beats of (relative) silence, followed by a more continuously filled measure. This pattern repeats itself four times to make an eight-measure introduction. The effect of the blocks of motor eighths is striking. On the one hand, next to the silent beats they feel like a continuous presence, some kind of monolithic block of stone. This effect demonstrates the object-like presence enabled by timbre. The blocks of motor eighths also, in the context of the overall riff, produce an interesting rhythmic effect, with the first half of every other measure displaying what could perhaps be called a continuous accent or accent under a fermata (to play with Hatten's description of posture as "gesture under a fermata").[18] And although I have characterized them as in some respects monolithic blocks, the motor-eighth passages also display internal gesture. In this riff, then, postural and gestural potentials are used in tandem to create at least two composite images. First, there is the overall impression which I've characterized as a feeling of large blocks, postural in their solidity, crashing down at regular intervals and making a kind of gesture. Second, there is the dual aspect of the blocks themselves, which appear mostly postural when compared to their surroundings but display internal gestures as well.

In order to develop the gesture/posture distinction in a harmonic context, I will need to make a few remarks about harmonic systems in general. There are at least two systems common in the West for organizing pitch-directedness, usually glossed as *tonal* and *modal*. In popular music studies, the relationship between these has been a perennial topic for discussion. At present, however, I am more concerned with a feature that is common to both kinds of pitch-directedness: the simple fact that once such a framework is established as pertinent to a composition, melodic lines and chords will tend to be interpreted as moving in a motivated manner. When such movements occur, they are taken to reflect the compulsions and tendencies set up by the modal or tonal context. Static pitch structures, where there is less apparent movement, will also seem to be energized with potential and to have definite tendencies. The difference here is very much like that between kinetic and potential energy. My suggestion, to be developed in the following material, is that tonal and modal systems of pitch-directedness each create two sorts of energetic effect. One could be called *gestural,* appearing when pitches are in movement. The other could be called *postural,* appearing as the static sense of charged potential that can accrue to repeated or fixed or isolated pitches. These two kinds of effect can be thought of as two different manifestations of the underlying set of tendencies set up by the tonal or modal system.[19]

Some of Neil Young's chord progressions seem to proceed within a tonal framework, others seem more clearly modal, and yet others employ a mixture of the two techniques. Tonal frameworks have powerful cultural associations, as do modal ones, and this can be especially important in the oeuvre of an artist like Neil Young, who frequently uses stylistic allusion and experimentation as a part of his expressive repertoire. But as I noted at the outset, the gesture-posture distinction is most useful in identifying a characteristic shared by both modal and tonal systems: the system of tendencies and attractions they set up has both mobile and static manifestations. It is to this idea that I would now like to return. It should first be noted that not all harmonic compulsions are equally strong. Even within the tonal system, certain movements seem more inevitable than others. The prototypical case here is the dominant-tonic resolution, with rising leading tone and V-I root movement. By contrast, the subdominant function is far less binding. Within Young's work, I have found it convenient to divide compelling factors into two groups, which I call *harmonic logic* and *melodic logic.* The former group contains those progressions which clearly reflect the norms of common practice tonality, and especially the paradigm case of a strongly compelled V-I resolution. The latter group contains structures in which some other kind of clear pattern is set up in the root movements, one which implies its own continuation through more general gestalt or continuity principles. The term *melodic logic* when used in this sense does not mean that the root movements are following the structure of the principal melody. It means, more simply, that the root movements themselves trace out a pattern which resembles a melodic line and that this organizing principle seems to be as strong as, or stronger than, any influence from the function of the triads within a common-practice tonal context.

One of the simplest examples is *scalar root movement*. For example, "Ambulance Blues," B-section, B-flat Ionian: V / V / vi / vi / vii / I. This kind of organization is extremely common in Young's work, and it sets up a mild sense of compulsion, in which continuation of the scalar pattern sounds logical and motivated, but far from necessary. The other most common form of melodic logic in Young's chord progressions is the one I have called *oscillating root movement*. For example, "Only Love Can Break Your Heart," B-section, D-Ionian: iii / iii / ii / ii / iii / iii / ii / V. The effect of oscillating root movement is, to my ears, very close to stasis. It is perhaps the simplest way to create a changing harmonic profile which contains no net movement. My motive for describing Young's chord progressions in this way is to draw attention to the range of degrees of compulsion he mobilizes, from very strong, stereotypical V-I resolution to slowly oscillating chords which create the bare minimum of overt movement. The gesture-posture distinction is useful for briefly describing the two broad sorts of force at work here: the perceived motivation and compulsion underlying cases of movement and the stronger or weaker static charges experienced in some forms of stasis. For example, most oscillating root movements seem to construct an effect which could be called minimal gesture, or gesture on the verge of lapsing into posture.

Young also makes frequent use of root movement by third. Such movements are interesting because they can convey a range of effects when considered in terms of posture and gesture. If both triads are diatonic, then they will share two common tones. Often, Young will present such a relationship in an oscillating fashion, going back and forth between the triads a few times. In a case like this, I would suggest that the effect is to prolong a posture (there is a sense in which one can shift a little within a posture and still be maintaining the same posture). I have called two chords presented in this relationship a *color pair*. For example: "Change Your Mind," A-section, A-Aeolian: / i VI / x 4. In other cases, a mediant root relationship without modal mixture will appear only once, as part of a larger harmonic motion. In a case like this, I have used the term *half move* to indicate that the shift within the posture is a precursor to leaving that posture. For example: "Southern Pacific," E-Aeolian (note, this entire progression is made up of half moves): III / III / i / i / VI / VI / i / i.

In the most extreme cases, Young will present a mediant root movement in which one of the chords displays modal mixture, with the result that there is only one common tone between them.[20] I call this a *full move*, since the modally altered nature of the second chord, both defying expectation and reducing the number of common tones with the preceding chord, usually leads to a feeling of definite movement rather than a shift within a posture. For example: "A Man Needs a Maid," D-Dorian, contains three consecutive statements of the sequence VII / IV / bVI / III, in which the full move underscores the articulation point of the sequence (and the fact that the sequence is exactly repeated helps to offset the feeling of acceleration created by the full move). As this example shows, Young sometimes employs devices which balance the forward impetus of the full move with more static factors. Another example is the technique of presenting two chords related by full move in an oscillating fashion, in which case a peculiar effect results, seemingly poised in the ineffable middle ground between posture and gesture. For example, much of "Safeway Cart" is based on the alternation I / bIII.[21]

Chords need to be considered not only with respect to their movement, but also with respect to their individual tone color. A great deal of the harmonic analysis already presented can be reinterpreted in this light. The most important points here are (1) Young's harmony is primarily triadic and (2) through the use of multiple modes, modal mixtures, and a variety of root movement strategies, Young explores the main colors available through triadic harmony. For now, I would like to look at another pervasive feature: the use of seventh chords. In my melodic analysis, I noted that Young's melodies frequently dwell upon notes a major seventh away from the current root. This tendency is not only melodic, but can also be seen in Young's frequent use of major seventh chords, and to a lesser degree ninth chords as well. These have already been discussed with respect to Young's guitar technique, and I would now like to discuss their implications in terms of musical structure and harmonic space.

Young's arrangements frequently contrast thicker and sparser blocks of sound. Some of his typical techniques for thickening the texture include the introduction or intensification of backing vocals and a movement on the drum kit from closed hi-hat to ride cymbal. Major seventh chords are another important part of this general thickening and thinning of the texture. They have a complex and dense sonority, which highlights by contrast the relative clarity and crispness of other, triadic passages. They also complicate any tendencies toward functional tonal harmony in that they imply new voices which do not participate in that framework. In some cases, the extended chords arise as a result of orna-mental movement, in which case they still serve to enrich the overall soundscape but are not part of the chord progression proper. The most striking use of the major seventh comes when the sonority forms the basis for a larger block of the progression. In this case, there is a strong impression of contrasted harmonic regions, some with a more triadic so-nority and some with a more seventh-based sonority ("Ride My Llama," "Don't Let It Bring You Down"). In other cases, the sevenths are blended more smoothly into the progression, which produces the same variability of harmonic texture, but more as a breathing quality within a passage and less as a source of contrasting textural blocks ("Lotta Love," "Love in Mind").

An interesting plurality can be seen in Young's use of the dominant seventh chord when it does occur. He will, on occasion, use strong con-ventional dominant chords. Arguably, the strongest dominant quality occurs through the use of applied dominants, since the progression is chromatically modified to draw attention to the dominant relationship, and Young does on occasion use even this very strong form. However, more frequently in Young's work these conventional V-I movements are circumvented. Young will sometimes set up a context for a strong domi-nant and even introduce the V chord into this context, but then not re-solve it to the tonic (even within reasonable allowances for prolonga-tion). For example: "Comes a Time," G-Ionian: I / iii / V / ii IV. At other times, the dominant chord is made less forceful by altering it to a minor quality. For example, "The Loner," D-Aeolian: iv7 / v7 / iv7 / v7 / iv7 / v7 / I. Finally, there are occasional cases in which extended progressions of the kind which may be expected to use a conventional dominant sim-ply do not employ the V chord at all ("Unknown Legend," "Comin' Apart at Every Nail"). Young's tendency to imply dominant function but avoid its full strength links to his general avoidance of dramatic directedness in his melodies. His occasional use of the full dominant quality also resonates with his general melodic approach in that he will occasionally use large isolated intervals and other dramatic melodic ef-fects, but not as a general rule. Looking further into this correspondence between harmony and other aspects of melody, I would suggest that the avoidance of strong dominant function is part of a general avoidance of strong closure.

It should not be surprising to find similar devices cropping up in Young's chord changes and his melodies, especially since harmonic function and melodic character are mutually reliant. I have gathered many specific harmonic devices under the umbrella concept of posture, and it would have been possible to read the melodies in that way as well. In both cases, I chose to draw attention to incremental movements, subtle shadings of color, and the deferral of stronger compulsions in favor of oscillating, ambiguous, or open-ended structures. In addition to these energetic characteristics, however, there are code-like features associated with Young's harmonic and melodic devices. By code-like I mean conventional correlations between particular chord changes or melodic events and established traditions, styles, and genres. Energetic and code-like features are of course not mutually exclusive. We saw in Frith's comments, for example, that a generally melancholy character is correlated with particular kinds of 1960s folk music. By contrast, my analysis has tended to pay more attention to metaphorical dimensions of energetic and spatial characters and has dwelt less on their correlation with styles and traditions. However, given the emphasis in chapter 2 on dialogism and intermusicality, I would like to conclude my discussion of harmony by making a remark on Young's place in the style family of rock music, expressed from the perspective of chord changes.

The use of obviously modal chord progressions is one feature that distinguishes 1960s rock music from most earlier kinds of rock and roll, and Neil Young was a key figure in bringing about this shift. However, as with the selective use of singer-songwriter conventions described by Frith, Young's chord changes point only lightly to their generic and stylistic correlates. Certain of his devices are highly idiosyncratic, and he rarely presents chord progressions lifted wholesale from the norms of any given style. Consider, for example, the chord changes to "Revolution Blues." A-Aeolian: i / i / i / i / iv / iv / i / i / iv / iv / i / i / v / iv / i / i. These changes are clearly derived from the canonical twelve-bar blues form, but are considerably transformed. In another example, implying Nashville country music but again demonstrating idiosyncrasy, Young presents a set of changes in "The Old Country Waltz" which displays an unusual degree of fluidity due to the emphasis on minor ii and vi chords and the repetition of a three-chord unit at the end. G-Ionian: I / V / I / I7 / IV / vi / ii / ii / IV / vi / V / IV / I / V / IV / I. Outside the narrowly constrained stylistic experiments of the 1980s, cases like this are the rule rather than the exception when Young evokes stylistic clichés through harmonic means. In chapter 2, I analyzed Young's position relative to rock music overall as one of waywardness—as a consummate insider/ outsider—and this kind of harmonic strategy is one specific musical device that helps produce that position.

The extreme variability of Young's chord changes underscores his ability to cover a wide stylistic range. Aside from the country, blues, and folk associations already noted, Young's chord changes can evoke traditions as diverse as garage rock (for example in the repeated / I VII / alternation of "Sedan Delivery") or progressive rock (for example in the complex multi-sectional progression of "Here We Are in the Years"). At the risk of overgeneralizing, I would suggest that there is a structural hierarchy of variability in Young's music. Chord changes are among the most variable elements from song to song. Melodic structure is also highly variable, but less so. And factors such as instrumental and vocal style are the least variable of all in that while Young has a number of characteristic modalities in these areas, they are comparatively few. This kind of hierarchical structure can be related to stylistic norms, as I have been doing, and it can also be thought of in terms of the synthesis of persona as a semiotic object. The aspects of Young's style which change the least may tend to be read as the most "natural" or "personal" ones, and this tendency is reinforced when the more stable features are those most obviously connected to embodiment and immediate timbral presence. In order to carry this line of interpretation further, however, we will consider Young's singing voice as a subject in its own right.

Voice

Neil Young's voice has been one of the most commented-upon aspects of his work, and its basic characteristics are described throughout chapter 1. For the present discussion I would like to focus on three areas in particular: (1) the expressive dichotomy found between some of his vocal performances, (2) the high pitch and distinctive timbre of his voice, and (3) issues of control. In all cases, the unique properties of Young's voice will allow us to elaborate aspects of his persona already identified in other discussions.

There are two kinds of affective character typically attributed to Young's vocal performances. On the one hand, many remarks by critics and rusties single out his high and relatively quiet singing on some songs, and these remarks frequently include adjectives such as sensitive, fragile, and desolate. Songs which I take to exemplify this performance style include "After the Gold Rush" and "You and Me." By contrast, with respect to many of his harder rock performances critics and rusties have commented on a striking level of force and even aggression, often mobilizing images of rage and abandon in their descriptions. This quality can be heard in "Time Fades Away" and "Rockin' in the Free World." Reviews of concerts similarly point out two broad categories of performance style. Many note Young's ability to create a spellbinding intimacy in solo acoustic performance, and some of this quality can be heard in "The Needle and the Damage Done" (a live recording included on *Harvest*) or "Stringman" (from *MTV Unplugged*). At the opposite extreme, some of Young's live vocal performances have been noted for an almost vitriolic, shouted intensity. Examples here include the performance of "Rockin' in the Free World" broadcast on *Saturday Night Live* (September 30, 1989) or "Sedan Delivery" from *Rust Never Sleeps.* The striking difference between these performance styles is not only one of vocal sound, but also of bodily deportment. In the former cases, Young tends to be seated, moving only slightly with the rhythm, whereas in the latter performances he is standing and will tend to lean into or actually lunge toward the microphone as he sings.

As with all dichotomies, this one admits of exceptions and degrees. For example, Young's live performances with the International Harvesters and the Stray Gators tended to occupy a middle ground. Nonetheless, in Young's work overall there is an important distinction in performance style between the seated, quieter Neil and the mobile, louder one, and this distinction is partly one of vocal style. But interestingly (and unlike my reading of Young's stylistic experiments) this range of vocal stances does not seem to problematize his persona for listeners. In other words, although I have made much of the manner in which contrasting musical devices can produce the impression of contrasting personas, in the case of expressive dichotomies within Young's vocal style I feel the overall impression remains one of a single, layered persona rather than a family of distinct vocal personas. I will return to this point.

In early years, and still to a lesser extent, critics have claimed that Neil Young "can't sing." When rejoinders are offered, they usually revolve around one or several of the following ideas: (i) that rock vocal style simply has different standards relative to other traditions; (ii) that Neil Young is effective at conveying the songs, and so he must by definition by a skilled singer; or (iii) that skill should not be the primary issue, irrespective of which standards are used for its measurement. This last argument resonates with the general idea, put forward both by critics like Bangs and academics like Gracyk, that "intensity of feeling . . . is rock's badge of honor."[22] One way to advertise your commitment to intensity as a value is to eschew other values, leaving yourself little else to work with. This debate is relevant to Neil Young reception, even if it is also an area in which Young was clearly following in the footsteps of Bob Dylan, about whom all these same arguments were made a few years earlier. The debate serves to situate Young in a historical moment and tradition. In the 1960s and 1970s, the standards of performance skill associated with classical and jazz musics were beginning to seem less obligatory to some serious critics but had not yet receded to the point that they could be ignored altogether. In addition, the debate about Young's vocal skill points out a homology between Young's singing and his approach to the guitar, piano, and harmonica, in which we have seen a similarly cavalier attitude toward technique juxtaposed with a wide expressive range.

This being said, there is good reason to suppose that Young's vocal performances are carefully crafted and controlled. Consider, for example, that on the occasions when Young sings harmony parts with CSNY or other groups, he is perfectly able to sing in tune and to blend his sound with other voices (not to eliminate its distinctive character altogether, but to fit that character into its surroundings so as to be relatively unobtrusive). In addition, Young has gone out of his way on occasion to cultivate a particular kind of roughness. It is reported that during the recording sessions for *On The Beach*, he deliberately smoked and drank a great deal, in part to develop a lower and raspier voice.[23] For proof of effectiveness, listen to "Motion Pictures," in which he sings at one point a fourth below middle-c, far lower than his norm for the period. It would be wrong to imply that Young was controlling the sessions in a moment-to-moment sense, because all reports indicate otherwise. However, it does appear that Young made a conscious decision to cultivate a sort of localized anarchy which produced a specific instrumental and vocal sound. Similarly, on the *Tonight's the Night* sessions Young left certain arrangements in keys too high for him to sing, producing some strikingly expressive vocal failures (especially in "Mellow My Mind").

More generally, on many performances both live and in the studio, Young tends to alter his distance and angle relative to the microphone (to sing off axis to varying degrees), which I would suggest is not a matter of carelessness or disregard but can be seen as a technique for producing a particular kind of uneasiness through unconventional shifts in vocal timbre. Here again, it would probably be inaccurate to imply that the vocal effect is the primary intention. If anything, it is more likely that Young's focus in these moments is on physical movement as associated with the performance in general. These devices are not vocal techniques in the usual sense, but they are certainly manipulations of the performance context and the voice itself, designed to achieve specific effects. The effects are partly stylistic—in Young's case a rejection of more commercial rock styles through a rejection of their production values—and partly related to persona. Many production techniques typically applied to the voice, such as compression and electronically generated reverberation, tend to eliminate most traces of the physical circumstances surrounding the recording, in effect disembodying the voice by erasing the space of the performing body. By contrast, the moments in Young's vocal performances where he does something like moving off-axis, or bumping a microphone, can remind listeners that the voice is emanating from a body and stands as the trace of an act of singing which took place at a particular time and in a particular space.

One benefit of a disregard for standardized technique is increased scope for crafting an idiosyncratic and therefore recognizable style. It could be argued that this was another underlying motive for the flouting of established norms of vocal performance among rock musicians of the 1960s. Frith makes a similar point when he suggests that "we hear [pop] singers as *personally* expressive . . . in a way that a classical singer, even a dramatic and 'tragic' star like Maria Callas, is not," because in classical music "the sound of the voice is determined by the score" to a greater degree.[24] Given the emphasis on individuality within 1960s rock culture and the free use of idiosyncratic performing techniques, it is perhaps not surprising that Neil Young developed a distinctive vocal sound. What is significant is that his vocal sound, along with that of Dylan and a few others, was so *completely* distinctive. I can think of only one widely distributed rock or folk recording featuring a singer who genuinely sounds like Neil Young—"A Horse with No Name" as recorded by America—and it is telling that many listeners who do not know otherwise assume that this is a Neil Young song. In terms of persona more generally, I would suggest there is a symbiotic relationship between distinctiveness of style and perceived intensity of feeling. If the performing style is unique, then perhaps it is easier to feel that the affective content is also unique, or if not unique, at least that it must be in some way tightly bound to a singular perspective. Frith notes that there are many personas implicit in a performed song, for example the characters in the lyrics, quoted characters, people the song is about, the author, and the singer. This situation often leaves room for layered interpretations and a blurring between vocal realism and vocal irony.[25] By adding another set of personas to those already implied by the text, the act of singing can make the interpretive situation more complicated, not less so.[26] However, I would suggest that vocal performance can also have the opposite effect, collapsing these possible readings into a simpler one in which the persona of the singer is heard as the expressive agent and other personas as elements to which the singer responds. This need not happen all the time, but I would suggest that if the vocal style is highly idiosyncratic, there will be a tendency to hear the persona of the singer as the dominant one.

This point relies indirectly on another one of Frith's arguments: that because the voice is so intimately connected with the body, "it stands for the person more directly than any other musical device."[27] One way to read this comment is in terms of synthesis, taking it to suggest that a voice will suggest a singular agent, binding many features of the music together as various signs of that singular agent, and by extension, that an idiosyncratic voice will suggest such an agent more strongly. A second implication concerns listeners' identification with singers. I would suggest that such identification is easier if the listener believes she or he has accurately identified who is singing and feels that the performance is somehow revealing important facts about that person. In both respects, a highly idiosyncratic vocal style can enhance this sort of listening, which is why I suggest that for artists like Neil Young a distinctive performing style and a stated commitment to intensity of feeling reinforce one another.

Perhaps the most striking particular feature of Young's voice is its high pitch. High male voices are not unusual in rock music, and Frith has even suggested they are the norm.[28] So why did Young's particular kind of high voice attract so much attention in early years? First, we can note that it is entirely different from the kind of high voice typical in heavy metal, since Young's highest vocal parts are often connected to his quieter songs. Although his singing on harder rock songs is higher than that of some other singers, in these performances he typically relies on a more mid-range voice, at least when compared to the strikingly high register in some of his softer material. Another thing to note is that unlike many other high male voices, there is little in the critical response to suggest that Young was perceived as androgynous. Perhaps this is partly because there are few androgynous elements in his visual style which would reinforce such a hearing of the voice. Young never appeared particularly boyish, nor did he adopt any particularly female-coded dress practices, or at least none which would be notably excessive relative to the general hard rock image of the late 1960s. In fact, Neil Young was never an artist who drew much attention to his own appearance at all, at least until the 1980s. If anything, his image was notably muted, which is one reason he later became frequently cited as an inspiration for grunge fashion. If Walser is correct when he suggests that androgynous rock images are marked partly by the way they invite the gaze and are clearly designed to be looked at, then Young's studiously non-spectacular visual style may be another reason he was not generally said to be androgynous.[29] What makes this even more interesting is that his voice *was* frequently associated with qualities conventionally coded female at the time, such as sensitivity, vulnerability, even prettiness. This shows, among other things, that the female-coding of these features was not exclusive. They also formed a part of several available masculinities beyond the androgynous, and in ways that had important stylistic correlations.

Frith makes a great deal out of doo-wop and the generally young age of early rock musicians to help explain the ubiquity of high male voices in rock music.[30] In both cases, the correlation of vocal register with age is crucial. We have seen in chapter 1 that Neil Young's early songs often dealt with childhood, and so the pitch of his voice may well underscore these elements. Also, related to doo-wop but distinct from it, in soul music and in some blues there is another kind of high male voice: the voice of seduction. Although Young's lyrics are not entirely unconcerned with seduction, it is far from being a major theme in his work (the end of relationships is dealt with much more frequently—especially in earlier songs). However, the particular mode of seduction implied by the high male soul voice involves images of sensitivity, tenderness, and the private sphere, themes which *are* reinforced in various ways by other aspects of Young's work. So although Young is not a seductive singer in any straightforward sense, there may be layers of sexuality and longing implied indirectly by his vocal register. This could be a crucial reason that the voice was heard by many critics as desolate or despairing. The sexuality is strongly hinted at but continually deferred. In addition to this admittedly speculative reading, there is another source for the link between a high male voice and longing, and this would be the high voices in some country music, especially in bluegrass: the "high lonesome" sound. I would suggest this is a much more direct influence on the reception of Young's voice, since it resonates so powerfully with his many stylistic references to country and folk traditions. Overall, then, there is a rich tapestry of stylistic references and persona traits implied in Young's particular sort of high male voice. Additionally, we must recall the utter distinctiveness of Young's sound, which is so striking that although the echoes of these various traditions clearly have conditioned its reception, his voice is never described as simply a token of a stylistic type.

I have already noted that Young's high vocal parts sometimes place him in registers where he simply cannot control the sound in a conventional manner. This is an important expressive device and is perhaps another reason that his singing was associated with vulnerability and fragility. However, it is also a kind of power display, allowing Young to assert his freedom from traditional constraints and to become curiously empowered through the striking effect that his displays of vulnerability can have on listeners. The dialectic of control and loss of control is an important one in existing scholarship on rock voices. Writing about Led Zeppelin, Susan Fast notes that Robert Plant equates genuine emotion in performance with a form of vulnerability, and that although his visual image employs the usual masculine assertions of control, "musically he often teeters on the brink of being purposefully out of control."[31] Fast is following Walser here in suggesting that intense emotional displays are typically coded both masculine (displays of power) and feminine (an advertised willingness to become the passive object of spectacle).[32] In Walser's version of the analysis, framed with respect to the myth of Orpheus, "flamboyant display of his emotions is required as evidence of his manipulative powers, but such excess makes him into an object of display and suggests a disturbing similarity to the disdained emotional outbursts of women."[33]

The first thing to note in applying this argument to Neil Young is that he employs two drastically different kinds of vocal self-display. Only one of them (ranting) is flamboyant and assertive. The other (drifting) is on the surface more unassuming, but perhaps not on a deeper level, because its very fragility has a way of drawing listeners in, then impressing them with the distinctive and apparently intense affectivity of the performance. And both modes of performance involve an apparent loss of control. In one case we see the kind of high-energy instability described in connection with ranting, and in the other we see a vocal technique on the edge of dissolution, with the suggestion of a fragile emotional state. Young himself highlights these issues of control when he deliberately destabilizes normal recording procedures in order to bring sessions near the edge of collapse. But of course Young never loses control altogether, much less permanently, so in the end these gestures reinforce the stability of his persona, just as nearly catastrophic vocal displays can reinforce the power of the singer.

Speaking about Mick Jagger and rock music more generally, Hicks has used the phrase *vocal self-contradiction* to identify a family of devices which can problematize a singer's persona.[34] These may be physical techniques, for example the literal struggle between diaphragm and throat required to make a shout, or they may be more narrowly semiotic, involving expressive choices which complicate the singer's identity. The voice can be an especially powerful tool for self-contradiction because, as Frith notes, "a voice is easy to change . . . easier to change, indeed, than one's face."[35] Such change can be a matter of acting or lying, but it can also be the result of long-term processes such as aging or part of the normal shift of behavior associated with movement between different social contexts. However, despite this malleability of the voice, or perhaps partly because of it, there is a tight coupling between vocal style and our sense of another person's self, such that "the voice is usually taken to be the person."[36] Many authors comment upon the intimate connection of voice and body, and this could be expressed by noting the indexical nature of the voice-body-self connection. As discussed in chapter 4, indexicality does not only involve the simple fact of physical connectedness, but the manner in which such a sign, for interpreters, compels a powerful sense of otherness, an inescapable reality and specificity of the object indicated by the sign.

For this reason, I would suggest that the emphasis in vocal self-contradiction, at least in the case of Neil Young, should be on *self*. Despite the expressive dichotomy, and despite the dialectic of control and vulnerability, Young's voice seems to be consistently received as the mark of a singular persona. While critics and rusties often comment on Young's stylistic experiments as if these problematized his identity, similar comments about vocal style are comparatively rare. They do arise, but only during periods such as the mid-1970s or the mid-1980s, in which Young's persona was destabilized on so many levels that it would be difficult to single out the voice as a primary factor. Young does occasionally put on vocal costumes, for example the old Republican persona of "Hawks and Doves." And he sometimes sings in a manner which seems subtly joking, although not in a way that can be easily described, as in "Wonderin.'" Such cases retain more of Young's typical voice than they change, however, and it is noteworthy that during these two periods, Young's visual style and other elements of the music changed more radically than did his voice. The overall image for many listeners seemed to be one of Neil Young putting on a costume, and that impression was probably assisted by the relative familiarity of the vocal style. The one clear exception may be *Trans,* but even there it is noteworthy that Young mostly tended to use vocoding technology to raise rather than lower the pitch of his voice, enhancing rather than changing one of its most important features.

Throughout chapter 1, I suggested that two of the most important themes in Neil Young reception are unpredictability and expressive intensity. And over the course of the book I have read this situation as one in which a strong authorial persona is paradoxically reinforced by its connection to change and contradiction. All the specific interpretations which flow from this general idea, including those in this chapter, proceeded by analyzing various components and players in the scenario—styles, traditions, musical sounds, personas, and the language of reception

—in terms of spatial and energetic metaphors, especially with respect to those centripetal tendencies that may foster the impression of a singular authorial presence and those centrifugal tendencies that may undermine such a presence. One specific contribution of this chapter has been to elaborate the particular musical devices that play a part in this overall process. Another is to suggest how those musical devices can be given particular (but not exclusive) affective interpretations. I have embarked on this task both as a theorist, trying to demonstrate general principles of musical signification, and as a fan, simply wanting to report on my experiences. As a result, it would be difficult to offer a summary of my stylistic arguments. Personas and musical characters evolve gradually and are synthesized from a wide range of components. They are also different for each listener. I have described the aspects of Neil Young which seem to have been experienced in similar ways by different commentators, but the relationship here is one of family resemblance, not complete equivalence. There is not one entity here to be described nor one set of interpretive processes, but a complex web of convergent and divergent readings (in the end, a complex web of Neils). So rather than seeking closure through a summary, I would like to conclude by offering a detailed reading of a single exceptional song.

6 | Will to Love

This book has presented a theoretical toolkit, a reception history, and some interpretive comments. The result has been a collection of strands, loosely connected. What are they for? I have at various times invoked the idea of a neo-pragmatic style of interpretation. Such an approach would follow philosophers like Rorty in replacing the notion of truth with that of justification and by implication making discussion and exchange of ideas paramount over final formulations.[1] It would also follow Dewey in the general idea that art works should be understood with respect to their real effects and uses in practice, emphasizing experiential features over formal ones.[2] Although often portrayed as a relativist, Rorty clearly favors certain modes of interpretation over others. He champions a democratic worldview under which readings can be better or worse depending not only on whether they take into account the widest possible range of available data, but more importantly on whether or not they suggest lines for further dialogue and demonstrate an exploratory spirit. The threads of theory and interpretation developed in this book are meant to sketch a perspective and to demonstrate its application. But more importantly, I hope they will suggest rewarding new directions in ongoing discussions of Neil Young. With that goal in mind, I would like to close by offering a detailed reading of a single song, "Will to Love." This reading can serve as a kind of summary, since it draws on most of the tools and arguments developed in this book. More than a summary, though, I hope it can provide one example of how I envision all the materials in the book working together in practice. I will divide my discussion of "Will to Love" into four parts: (1) general reception and context; (2) lyrics; (3) sonic features; and (4) overall commentary in terms of energetic and spatial icons, metaphors, and blends.

General Reception and Context

Shining . . . a song that flies into the face of reason by flaunting the seemingly ridiculous—the thoughts of the singer as a salmon swimming upstream—in order to gain the truly sublime. And it works. (When was the last time you heard something like *this* on record?).[3]

It has the fractured intensity of "Last Trip To Tulsa," the emotional gravity of "Ambulance Blues" allied to the slowburning turmoil of "On The Beach." Yes: it's that heavy. . . . Curious percussion effects punctuate the song irregularly (it could be someone falling over in the studio, of course). The song itself is a torturous slice of self-examination, with Young stripping away layers of his personality, fighting against the melodramatic fatalism into which he so easily falls and striving for a positive perspective on reality. The song is enthralling and its aching beauty is not easily forgotten.[4]

Seven minutes of solo overdubs cut a year ago, has Neil grousing murkily from within a fish persona.[5]

A dire affair dating from May 1976 which may well be the worst song Young's ever written. A horribly trite acoustic minor-chord affair which America wouldn't even dare to put on one of their albums, it gabbles on insanely about being fishes and swimming about in the endless oceans of pure love.[6]

Young never has and never will make a record without glaring flaws (think of the endless "Will To Love." . . .)[7]

I'm always defending "Will to Love" among my friends who think it is, well, too formless, or something. It's a wonderful song! . . . Another one of those songs for people with a lot of time left on our hands and not enough company! Let's hear it for the salmons![8]

Yeah, I hear that a lot, too. I LOVE this tune. . . . It's not formless, it's FLUID.[9]

[Interviewer: Do you have songs that are too personal to sing to an audience?] Well, some songs are just too hard to do live. Like "Will to Love." I don't know how I could ever do it. I just would feel too open, too wide open. You don't sing all that stuff on TV. [Can you really immerse yourself so completely in the creative process that you feel your fins swimming upstream?] Yeah I can. "Will to Love" was written in one night, in one sitting, in front of the fireplace. I was all alone in my house and I was really high on a bunch of things. . . . None of the verses are exactly the same length. They're all a little different. I made it through it once on the tape. . . . I never have sung it except for that one time. That's what I used for the record. A Sony cassette machine which I transferred to 24-track and then I played it back through my Magnatone stereo reverb amp. I brought two tracks of the cassette up on a couple of faders with the stereo vibrato in it, then I mixed them in with the original cassette for that sound of the fish. I overdubbed all the instruments on it and mixed it in the same night. . . . [The studio personnel] thought it was going to be a live session! They were all set up and ready to go. I just walked from one [instrument] to another and did them all, mostly all in the first take. . . . It took us about eight hours to finish the whole thing and make it sound like it does now. I think it might be one of the best records I've ever made.[10]

Mixed critical response is a running theme in Neil Young reception, so the range of reactions here should not be surprising. More specifically, we have already seen critics divided over whether Young's more introspective material should be regarded as self-indulgent, and since this is one of his most introspective songs both in content and in mode of production, it tends to crystallize the debate. Beyond that, "Will to Love" presents a decidedly liminal character, which resonates with the usual themes of fragility and quirkiness associated with Young's singer-songwriter persona, but goes substantially beyond them. Part of this liminality lies in the method through which the song was recorded, and we will return to that. On a more basic level, there is the fact that the song has never been performed live, and the album on which it appeared is itself an ambiguous one in Young's output, being in some ways pivotal and in some ways marginal. *American Stars 'n' Bars* (1977) was a stylistically and affectively diverse assemblage of recordings from the previous few years, and it was framed by much more focused projects such as *Zuma* (1975), and *Comes a Time* (1978). In addition, the album was one of six Neil Young albums not transferred to compact disc in the 1980s, referred to by rusties as "the missing six." As a result, "Will to Love" was not available on CD until 2003, when four of the six missing albums were finally reissued. So although Young referred to the song as perhaps one of his best records, he did not go out of his way to keep it in circulation. The same is not true of the other standout track from *American Stars 'n' Bars*, "Like a Hurricane," which has been anthologized several times since and has been a staple of Crazy Horse concerts on several tours up to the present.

On *American Stars 'n' Bars*, "Will to Love" forms an odd pair with

"Like a Hurricane." They seem to belong together for several reasons. They are the two longest cuts on the album, and "Will to Love" directly precedes "Like a Hurricane" in the running order. They are also the only two tracks on the record to have generated extensive critical reaction. The songs are powerfully contrasting in arrangement but share certain lyrical themes. Both deal with striving, danger, and redemption, framed in terms of a natural process which is presented as both edifying and destructive. "Like a Hurricane" encapsulates most of the typical features of Young's public, loud, Crazy Horse persona, and "Will to Love" like-wise summarizes his private, quiet, singer-songwriter persona. Much of what Young says about the song would be similar for other, quieter material, and yet the song also displays some highly idiosyncratic features. Young himself highlights its difficulties and instability by pointing out that he only "made it through once." So "Will to Love" is both typical and exceptional in Young's output as a whole. Lyrically, to make an association between love and the ocean, or love and death, is a cliché. However, this particular underwater soundscape is in many respects highly unusual. On several levels, then, "Will to Love" presents a character simultaneously idiosyncratic and banal, and the two most obvious readings of this situation are both evident in the quotations given earlier: it could be experienced as the revitalization of familiar themes or as the trivialization of an otherwise innovative work.

The way this piece was recorded is unusual for Neil Young, but not entirely without precedent. Recording alone at home by the fireside may be the ultimate extension of Young's solo acoustic performances. Similarly, assembling a final track through multiple overdubs recalls methods used for early recordings like "Broken Arrow," or "The Old Laughing Lady." The difference is that for those recordings, Young was working under the direct influence of a producer (Jack Nitzsche) and the recent stylistic breakthroughs of the Beach Boys and the Beatles. With the "Will to Love" session, by contrast, he was working effectively alone and without clear stylistic models apart from his own work. In my earlier discussion of arranging practices, I pointed out the fine balance between instinct and control evident in Young's arrangements and his approach to recording. "Will to Love" is in some respects aligned with his most tightly controlled and least spontaneous productions in that it was assembled from multiple overdubs and not from the kernel of a live band performance. And yet it is also one of his most instinctive recordings, in part because of the solo performance on which it is based and because of Young's complete self-reliance in performing overdubs (assuming we can take at face value his description of the session, which has never been contradicted). To an extent, "Will to Love" forms a pair with the Synclavier-based songs on *Trans,* since there as well Young described his working method as being similar in its self-reliance to solo acoustic performance, even though it involved considerable overdubbing and layers of programming. Finally, there is an important historical connection to another crucial recording session. Young rented the instruments for the "Will to Love" session from Studio Instrument Rentals, the same company which provided equipment for the *Tonight's the Night* sessions. The "Will to Love" session, then, is highly distinctive yet also deeply resonant with several other exceptional moments in Neil Young's recording history. It manages to allude simultaneously to his ambitious early suites, to his minimalist solo performances, and to the barely controlled, cathartic experiments of the mid-1970s. What it does not contain is any hint of Crazy Horse, but this is one reason it forms such an effective pair with "Like a Hurricane" in its album setting.

That this song was recorded alone, at home, has additional significance when we recall that for Neil Young, the ranch is an important refuge and private space. Both lyrically and sonically, this song and recording offer a rare glimpse into Young's personal space, which he normally guards so jealously. The ambient noise of the fire, then, is not noise at all but an important sign of domesticity. More specifically, it is an *index* of the unusual circumstances of recording, as is the rudimentary quality of the vocal recording. As indices, these features can compel a feeling that we are encountering Neil Young as a real person and experiencing the particularity of a real space. This indexicality is perhaps highlighted further by the singularity of the event. However, the final arrangement does not leave these indices to stand unproblematized. They are combined with other instruments and, more importantly, the original recording is treated with special effects such as tremolo to create an underwater impression.

In the end, this musical texture is strongly suggestive of a conceptual blend: a Neil-fish. This entity draws upon two source domains through two different kinds of index: the indices of the original recording situation which signify the human Neil, and the indexical fish-water connection. The powerful emotional implications of the home recording are not lessened in this blend, but neither do they necessarily make the ultimate persona more Neil than fish. They underscore the Neilness of the fish (and vice versa). The status of the fire is especially interesting when read in this way. One of its functions is to underscore the literal, Neil-at-home indexicality. However, when blended with the water and fish elements it acquires a strange resonance, suggesting mythical processes such as a fire burning in or on the water. Despite such complications, however, there are factors which can allow listeners, if they wish, to understand the fish component as less literal than the Neil component. This is not only for the obvious reason—Neil is not a fish—but also perhaps because some listeners would know that signal processing of this sort is usually applied as an effect after initial recording is complete. This temporal priority of the home recording can easily reinforce any tendency to hear this song in literal terms as a simple story or allegory.

Finally, the very insularity of this song suggests, indirectly, Young's status as a public figure. In general, private domestic space is characterized by its opposition to public space, which it therefore implies. More dramatically, Neil Young's private space is a ranch and serves to house not only his residence but also his archives and a fully equipped rehearsal and recording facility. For Neil Young, moments of privacy such as those recorded here are bought through the profits of his public work, and it is only because so much of his musical activity is public that the intimate conditions of this recording draw notice. In its themes the song seems distant from the music industry, but that distance itself—its careful and expensive construction—is a product of Young's involvement in the industry. Further, the song has stylistic links to some of Young's most commercially successful material. The vocables in the introduction bear more than a slight resemblance to the vocables in "Lotta Love," for example, and more generally it is his softer, singer-songwriter material which has provided Young with his greatest commercial success. And while the recording was begun at home on a cheap cassette recorder, it was finished in a custom-assembled studio filled with rented instruments. Of course, the link between this style and commerciality is complicated because with *On the Beach* Young had already shown that when the softer, introspective features of his more commercial music are taken to extremes, they become oppositional to the mainstream. But here as there, in certain respects Young's attempts to temporarily sever his ties to public life and to the music industry simply draw more attention to those ties.

Lyrics

This is the only song released by Young which makes use of allegory. In chapter 2, I discussed Young's relationship to stances of strategic anti-essentialism and irony, both of which could be effectively developed through the device of allegory. However, the allegory in "Will to Love" appears strongly confessional, especially given Young's comments about the song, so it would be difficult to read it as anti-essentialist on any level. And if there is an irony here, it is that through the allegory Young is able to express his usual themes with such uncommon directness, producing a song too private for public performance. Allegory can often serve as a buffer which distances an author from the full force of the point being made, attenuating political or psychological risks. In this case, however, the allegory intensifies risky elements, making the song more personal rather than less so. This is perhaps due in part to the experiential nature of the particular icons used. The musical images we will explore suggest exhaustion, disorientation, compulsion, and hope. They seem less about making a philosophical or political point (the traditional tasks of most allegory in Western literature) and more about conveying powerful emotions and a singular experience.

The ability of conceptual blends to remain attached to their source domains is also relevant here. The blended Neil-fish is not so much a symbol for certain aspects of Young's experience as an embodiment of them. When a blended persona speaks of one or another of its source domains, it is not commenting on a separate entity but revealing a part of itself. So one thing that makes the "Will to Love" lyrics interesting is that they present the usual themes of Young's introspective songs in such a direct and forceful manner, despite the device of speaking through a fish persona. The other interesting feature is that the song incorporates just about *all* these themes. It is these features that I want to examine in depth to show how this song is an exceptionally clear and complete summary of Young's general lyrical treatment of relationships and of his own motivations.

The salmon itself combines several of Young's most common character types. It is a loner and a rebel. Although it seems to have a noble cause, its single-mindedness and self-absorption have driven away its friends, and there is an overall mood of despondency and fatalism. The fish is struggling but doomed, redeemed only by the possible nobility of its sacrifice, but the purpose and beneficiary of that sacrifice are unclear. In this image complex we can see echoes of the way Young has frequently portrayed himself as someone driven toward an undefined ideal of experience and expression (the clearest example is "Thrasher"), his abiding interest in anti-heroes ("Crime in the City," "Carmichael"), tragic moments of decisive action ("Powderfinger," "Let's Roll"), and in general the damaging side of idealism. A related set of themes, also rolled into "Will to Love," is found in Young's songs about romantic relationships. He frequently casts the end of one constricting relationship as the opportunity for a more rewarding and meaningful life, left undefined but powerfully attractive. These songs occupy a range of emotional stances, from a distinctive mixture of cruelty and tenderness ("Birds," "I Believe in You") to paranoid and even violent anger ("Cowgirl in the Sand," "Down by the River"). In Young's lyrics overall, then, there are frequently images of transcendence (gleaming fins), but they are usually linked to an ambiguous and possibly destructive restlessness. Similarly, his many songs of childhood and coming of age tend to emphasize the weight of new moral decisions. Young generally positions his protagonists between a lost childhood and an uncertain future, here represented by the struggle upstream.

"Will to Love" is also both typical and unusual in the way it treats the natural world. Young usually treats wilderness areas and the earth more generally as a life-source under threat from human irresponsibility ("Mother Earth," "Natural Beauty," "Vampire Blues"). He also frequently writes of the countryside—not wilderness but agricultural land—as his own personal refuge. And finally, he has returned throughout his career to the image of immersion in water as a metaphor for rejuvenation or redemption ("Hangin' on a Limb," "Big Time"). In this connection, there is an interesting dichotomy in Young's frequent use of beach imagery. There is first the beach as a symbol of despair and dissolution, the abject beach often identified in his work with Miami and most fully expressed in *On the Beach*. Then there is Zuma beach, represented as a sunny and optimistic place of rejuvenation. "Will to Love" clearly picks up on many of these themes, most clearly in the image of swimming upstream as a lethal quest for redemption. What is interesting is that for all his treatment of ecological and geographical themes, Young does not in any other song identify so closely with a non-human agent (except perhaps in "War of Man," although in that case for only part of the song). On one level, adopting the fish persona is the logical extension of his desire for immersion and freedom, but on another level it is an unusual move. One result is that the "will to love," which has been treated in many of Young's songs, is given its most clearly naturalistic and even spiritual expression. The allegory could invite a literal reading in which fish relationships are simply substituted for human ones. But I would suggest the effect is more subtle, such that the driving force and desire are portrayed less as a specific sexual attraction and more as an ecological imperative. In other songs dealing with the theme of restlessness, the goals seem more specific: to have a better working method, to find a more compatible partner, and so forth, although even in these songs there is often the suggestion that the restlessness is its own end and will never be satisfied in the singer's lifetime. It is this aspect of the theme which is thrown into especially sharp relief by the salmon allegory.

This impression can be reinforced if we consider the details of the mobility in this case. In most of Young's restlessness songs, he is most concerned with moving *away* from something. This element is also present in "Will to Love," but it is relatively de-emphasized. Forward movement is given greater emphasis in this scenario, although it is also made to seem difficult in a way not typical of Young's other songs. In a lyric like "Thrasher" or "Big Time," for example, the overall affect is one of freedom and optimism. The negative emotions are left behind in favor of positive action. In this song, by contrast, it is more difficult and frightening to swim upstream than to remain in the ocean. Part of this tone arises from the fact that Young identifies, more clearly than in any other song, the possible non-reality of his ultimate object. When he says it is his dream "to live with one who wasn't there," we cannot tell if this absence is situational or ultimate. Does he want to find someone who is presently absent, or does he want to dwell with absence itself? The latter possibility is strongly suggested by the fact that, over the course of this lyric, Young identifies most of the typical categories of companion treated in his other songs and eliminates them as the ultimate object.

This is especially clear in the fifth verse, where Young expresses a senti-ment very similar to that in his later songs about stable long-term rela-tionships ("You and Me," "Razor Love"). In those songs, one might have the impression that he has reached a resting point and that the long-term romantic partner is a fulfillment of his desire. In "Will to Love," how-ever, the long-term partner is invited to be a cotraveler, but is in no way confused with the underlying force that drives the salmon upstream. If that force is not associated with the other fish in the ocean, or with his friends, or even with this special cotraveler, then does it have an ultimate object at all?

In all of these ways, "Will to Love" stands as a remarkable summary of many key themes in Young's lyrics. I would now like to move on to a discussion of the musical devices which lend particular affective, ener-getic, and spatial nuances to the song. I will first describe the relevant sonic features and then move on to interpret their effect in spatial and energetic terms.

Sonic Features

Given the relatively extensive critical response generated by "Will to Love," it is not surprising that some of the comments cited above single out particular sonic features. In my discussion of topic theory, and of metaphor in general, I stressed the importance of basing musical analysis, wherever possible, on the listening reports of contemporaries, since this can help ensure the pertinence of whatever features are se-lected for exploration. My plan, then, is to select particular sonic features in "Will to Love" identified as pertinent by critics and rusties, then, after describing them in technical terms, show how particular metaphori-cal and iconic interpretations can link them to more general themes. The sonic features in question are the distinctive mix of instruments and signal processing techniques, the character of the voice, the chord changes, the method of recording, and the length of the song. Some of these features will be treated in depth and some will be dealt with more tangentially.

With respect to the verses, this is one song where the chords and melody are best described as a context or process more than a set struc-ture. The chords throughout the verses are simply a slow oscillation:

IIMaj7 / IIMaj7 / i7 / i7. Since this progression is set in the mode of E-Phrygian, the roots move only by a semitone. This movement is extremely simple, creating a feeling of casually shifting planes, but it is also good as a basis for vocal extemporization, since between them the two chords contain all seven pitches of the mode and one common tone. This harmonic movement also tends to encourage frames of a third and shifts of a second, and these are among the most common movements in this melody, as well as in Young's melodies overall. The melody has a meandering quality, but there are a few unifying elements. The central pitch during the IIMaj7 chords is almost always 'a', decorated by the upper 'c'. The central focus during the i7 chords is more variable, with the g-b third being the most frequently stressed element. Also, the decorated third frame a-c-d is frequently used over the IIMaj7 chords. If there is a single central motive in the melody, it is an a-c or a-c-d movement followed by the shift to i7. But within this general framework for the verses, there is a great deal of variation.

By contrast, the chorus and the recurrent introductory material provide moments of more definite, although minimal, structure. The chorus contains a repeated refrain ("got the will to love") juxtaposed with a more improvisatory vocal part. The harmonies in the chorus move more quickly than in the verse and display root movements of a major second rather than a semitone: / i VII i / i /. This creates a slight feeling of acceleration and a slightly more expansive movement. The introduction is even more highly structured and demonstrates less variation, but it is of greater brevity. The vocables and the use of vibraphone here strongly resemble Young's more commercial soft-rock material, especially the *Comes a Time* album. Just as the chords and melodic tendencies set a kind of minimal structure in the verses, the chorus and introductory material provide an overall structural contrast in a similarly understated manner. Looking at the form of the piece, we can see first the highly variable section lengths described by Young and second that the most extemporized and variable passages (the verses) occupy the most time, whereas the most unimprovised section (the introductory material) occupies the least time. Finally, it is evident both that this is a long composition and that its length is the result of lingering within the subparts of a simple form rather than the result of a complex multi-section structure. In this diagram, I = introductory material, V = verses, C = Chorus/Refrain. The number of measures in each section is indicated under the letters.

I	V	C	I	V	C	I	V	C
8	28	8	4	26	10	8	24	10

I	V	C	I	V	(fade)
8	36	8	8	32	~5

The arrangement is notable for its minimalism, but also for the unusual timbral choices and frequent interjections. There are two layers here, the result of the two-stage recording. In addition, the first layer (the home recording) displays an internal layering, since a fireplace can be heard crackling in the background. In the studio layer, small details are dubbed over the home-recorded bed tracks, popping up throughout the song without becoming so numerous as to detract from the basic mood. But while these added components do not obscure the character of the bed tracks, they render it somewhat surreal by transposing it into a relatively disjointed acoustic space. This effect has already been discussed in connection with conceptual blending. The two layers of arrangement and recording are merged but also distinct, allowing the various images and metaphors they suggest to be likewise blended or distinguished, depending on the listener's attention and interests. The surreal effect is made more intense by the tremolo applied to the original bed tracks in varying degrees, always changing and sometimes quite pronounced. This device helps create the iconic underwater effect and creates subtle textural variations within the repetitive framework. With the exception of the vocoded tracks on *Trans* and the variable reverberation on "Last Trip to Tulsa," this is the one song in which the signal processing applied to Young's voice seems distinctive and noteworthy. The voice is quiet throughout, almost mumbling in places, and in a middle register. This manner of performance is what one might expect from someone working through a new song in private rather than performing it live or recording with the intention of release. The same is true of the guitar chords. Not only are they performed in a lackadaisical manner, but the chord voicings (FMaj7 and Emin7) are among Young's most common. As with the arrangement overall, the character of this vocal and guitar performance contains elements which strongly point to Neil Young as the dominant persona, but also point to other elements which problematize that attribution, or at least suggest this is a singular and temporally specific version of the Neil Young persona, not fully equivalent to any of the others.

Energetic and Spatial Icons, Metaphors, and Blends

To finish our discussion of "Will to Love," I would like to reinter-
pret the sonic features just described in terms of metaphors and icons of
spatial and energetic experience. In this way, we can suggest some reasons that particular lyrical images, and particular interpretive responses,
are especially apt for this soundscape. In chapter 4, I noted that full-
blown musical personas—such as would exist if a listener were to hear
the sonic events as products or expressions of Neil Young, or of a particular salmon, or of a blend—are synthetic. They arise when many details of the music and their associated characters are actively heard as
parts of a whole. As a consequence, individual musical details may be
discussed with respect to their isolated qualities and iconic potentials, or
with respect to the part they play in a particular persona. In keeping with
this suggestion, I would first like to discuss the general character of "Will
to Love," identifying broad features that could take part in a variety of
more elaborated synthetic objects. Then I will comment briefly on the
identity of the specific objects which seem to emerge most strongly from
these elements.

To return for a moment to the differences of critical opinion, I would
suggest that many of the pertinent musical features can be summarized
under the terms *formless* and *fluid*. These two terms could be taken as
pointing to the same set of musical characteristics, in the first case evalu-
ated unfavorably (as the lack of a desirable feature) and in the second
case favorably (as an engaging positive attribute). Specific sonic details
which invite an image of formlessness/fluidity include the variable section lengths (with corresponding flexibility in melodic structure), the
oscillating chord progression, and the modulated or disjointed timbral
effects. Connections also exist between the formless/fluid opposition
and images of wavering and shimmering which pervade the lyrics. Under a negative evaluation, this wavering effect could be perceived as a
distortion and therefore an impediment to be overcome. We see this kind
of interpretation both in the lyrics ("it distorts things in my eyes") and
in some of the critical reactions. On the other hand, the wavering can
be enjoyed as a perceptual event in its own right. In the lyrics, immediately after the water is described as distorting, the distortion is reinter-

preted as a means to perceive deeper truths ("my true lover, and I care"). There are at least two levels of evaluation involved in these kinds of distinctions. There are value judgments applied to the compositional and recording practices—Young is seen as controlled or lazy, innovative or fumbling—and there are value judgments applied to the aesthetic result—murky or shining, intense or dismal.

Along with images of formlessness/fluidity and wavering, however, there are other contrasting elements of the lyrics which encourage us to hear the song in terms of a linear process. The image of spawning involves movement from an almost completely unbounded space into greater and greater confinement, literally down a kind of funnel, all the while experiencing a draining of personal energy and ultimately death. The relationship between physical vitality and psychological compulsion in this case unfolds according to a full/empty schema, both in terms of the amount of covering water, which grows less and less, and in terms of the gradual draining away of life force. All these factors are suggested especially strongly in the nature of the chord progression and melody. The chords present a slow and regular oscillation, structured around the minimal interval of a minor second, which could be seen as represent-ing the final moments before death, or as the start of a new surge of movement, or simply as constant but weary progress. The energy level is clearly low, and this lack of momentum leads to a kind of suspense, or suspension in the moment. The progression could stop, or speed up, or continue in the same manner, and there are no cues as to which is most likely. The melody constantly circles around the same few gestures but with continual variations, a limited movement in a confined space. The music at some times seems to wind to a close, out of energy, but at others continues longer than one might expect, finding the strength to press on a little further.

There is a dichotomy in the song, then, between images of a form-less wavering and of a slow but relentless linear progress. These images are related in part to performance style, lyrics, and manner of produc-tion, but they can also be linked to the song's formal structure. As was noted in chapter 4, the character displayed by a formal structure may be variously interpreted as the overall state of a human-scale actor, or as the superhuman movements of a much larger agent. Another interpre-tation of formal structure, not developed in the previous chapter, is to view it as a directed movement through a series of spatial regions (a path). A path describes a particular space by specifying the character of each region as well as by specifying the order in which the regions are experienced and the amount of time spent in each. In some respects, the form of "Will to Love" is quite rigid. It rigorously cycles through the Introduction-Verse-Chorus sequence, and although exact section lengths vary, the general proportions are roughly consistent. It is perhaps exactly this moderately rigid overall form which throws into sharp relief the relative freedom and extemporization of the verses. In my hearing, the most pertinent character is that of the verse, and the overall form can be understood as a device for offering brief periodic respite between verses. This in itself is an image which resonates strongly with the central lyrical themes: brief pauses allowing for refreshment between renewed upstream journeys. It is also important that the form is relatively uninflected and repetitive and ends with a fade rather than a decisive closing gesture. This underscores the open-endedness of the psychological condition being described.

A crucial function of formal structures is to set up part-whole relationships between individual events and the rest of a piece. With respect to certain melodic, harmonic, and lyrical features, the formal control in "Will to Love" is quite strong, with many events serving clear roles in a broader formal scheme. However, there is a whole class of sonic events in the song which do not cohere as parts of a larger pattern. This effect is sometimes produced by the foregrounding of sporadic percussion sounds, sometimes by unpredictable shifts in signal processing, and in general by the ubiquity of timbres with a low-pass-filtered, up-against-the-ear quality resembling that of sounds heard under water. Part-whole relationships are blurred in these instances as events swim very close in virtual space, so that their significance seems to be as much about the present instant as about their relationship to other events. This ubiquitous nearness could be heard as claustrophobic and murky, but also as intimate. Acoustic nearness can also be understood as a metaphor for the narrowing horizons of the spawning salmon, either physically in terms of shallower water or psychologically in terms of an inward-turning, disoriented state of exhaustion. Overall, then, there is a dichotomy in the song between sonic events which appear as subordinate to a formal design and those which seem to hang suspended in their own present.

In chapter 4, I emphasized that between individual sonic events and fully formed musical personas there are a range of qualities, characters, and intermediate semiotic objects. I say "between" not in order to suggest a strict hierarchy, but only to point out that the same features which may in some cases be synthesized into a fully formed persona can also be interpreted on other levels, for example as general physical traits, specific physical objects, affective states, or generalized energetic states. Since these various sorts of interpretation are all related to one another through processes like metaphor, conceptual blending, iconicity, and indexicality, it is not possible to put them in an absolute order or hierarchy. However, as an interpretive strategy, I would like to suggest a hierarchy of object specificity and scope that can organize the various levels of character and persona in "Will to Love." Beginning with sonic events, the most general interpretation would be in terms of broad physical qualities. In this song, such qualities include slowness, gradual movement, fluidity, flowing, pausing, wavering, shimmering, narrowing, dragging, and disjointed flashes. On a similar level of specificity, the sonic events could be synthetically interpreted as general but abstract forces, for example love, inertia, and destiny. At the next level of specificity, both of these kinds of objects could be reinterpreted as general affective or physical states of some particular entity. In this song, the most pertinent states seem to be compulsion, disorientation, inwardness, exhaustion, and hope. The entity in this case does not need to be fully specified but would be implied simply in the postulation of an affective state. Finally, all the preceding elements may be synthesized into particular personas—Neil, a salmon, a Neil-salmon blend—or into particular physical objects such as water, the river, sunlight, or the rocky bottom. By describing the various elements in this way I am biased toward fully individuated personas, treating them as the most specific and highly elaborated entities, but this is an interpretive strategy rather than a theoretical claim. In actual listening, much of the fascination comes from the free play that can arise between these layers. A specific persona, for example, could be said to anthropomorphize the layer of physical forces as much as the physical forces could be said to precede the persona as components. Similarly, although I have put the specific object of water at the same level as the specific object of fish, in some cases it may be the water object which produces the fish object by implying it indexically. The purpose of this analysis is only to specify some of the discrete layers of character and kinds of object which can emerge in a piece of music and to hint selectively at a few of their many possible interrelationships.

One thing I've always valued in rock criticism and scholarship is the way it makes me eager to go back to the music. There was a time when I would judge a book or article by how many CDs it made me buy, and although my standards have shifted since then, a prime attraction of music writing is still its ability to refresh listening. Refreshment does not need to be understood in entirely positive terms. My analysis has been critical of Neil Young in certain respects, especially where topics like gender and politics are concerned. That is one reason to place such emphasis on the idea that music is a form of virtual agency. Such a perspective allows us to speak more fully of our relationship to music and to other listeners, our negotiations with them, and the fact that such negotiations at times involve friction. My hope is that readers come away from this book with an intensified interest in the work of Neil Young and with some new ideas about how to go about musical interpretation in general. I am going to avoid summarizing what we may have learned about Neil Young through the course of the book—I promised at the outset not to try and pin him down—but I would like to offer instead an overview of the main theoretical moves and claims underpinning my interpretive approach. The argument concerning various modalities of signification and various degrees of specificity in the synthesis of personas has involved many subparts, and now that they have all been sketched in theory and presented in action it is possible to close with some general comments about the architecture of such an interpretive stance.

Figure 6.1 shows one way of conceptualizing the levels of text and interpretation explored in this book. In constructing the diagram, I used the following conventions:

1. Horizontal lines represent *hearings-as:* experiences and interpretations in which features on the lower levels are interpreted or elaborated in some manner. The phrase *heard as* is only written a few times in order to save space, but it should be understood as applying to all the horizontal lines.
2. The choice to start with *sonic features* as the foundational level reflects my particular interest in the interpretation of musical sounds. A similar but rearranged diagram could easily be made

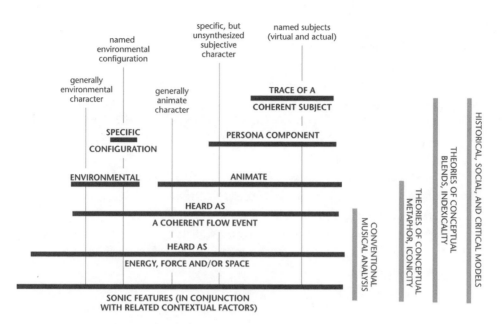

Figure 6.1. A summary of some elements in my interpretive practice.

to reflect different interpretive agendas. The "highness" and "lowness" of specific elements would change, as may some of the specific dependencies, but the general picture of elaborated entities emerging from more general backgrounds, through various hearings-as, would remain the same.

3. When a horizontal line is shorter than the one below, this shows that the particular hearing associated with that line is one possibility, but not the only one. A lower line will always have a surplus of other possible hearings, represented by the fact that it extends a little further than the line(s) above it. Similarly, when two different horizontal lines occur on the same level, they represent two equally important alternative hearings at roughly the same degree of elaboration.

4. The highest elements, with thin vertical lines dropping from them, represent types of highly elaborated emergent entities that have been important at various points in the book. The thin vertical lines are meant to show how these emergent entities are dependent on various more basic hearings-as. No two emergent entities rely on exactly the same set of more basic hearings, although they all share varying degrees of overlap in this respect.

When I say that a particular hearing-as or emergent entity is more or less elaborated, I mean that it depends on a larger or smaller number of more general interpretations (represented in this diagram as lower levels intersected by its vertical line). The least elaborated emergent entities on this diagram are the ones I have called *general characters* (both environmental and animate), and the most highly elaborated entities are the various kinds of fully synthesized *subjects*. Entities distinguished from one another on a higher level remain linked on lower levels, allowing for the kinds of slippage and blending that have been central to my "Will to Love" analysis and to other parts of the book as well. In Figure 6.1, this relatedness is reflected in the fact that, at some level, all of the vertical lines will end up intersecting the same horizontal line. Finally, on the right-hand side of the diagram, I have tried to show how various existing approaches to the study of music, all of which are used at various points in the book, are useful in addressing particular levels of this overall set of relationships.

This diagram is a map of a particular interpretive practice, not a prescription, although grounds for some of these interpretive moves have been developed over the course of the book. Also, there are some further nuances that need to be addressed. *Social forces* are not labeled as such on this diagram even though a major tactic throughout the book has been to show linkages and parallels between social forces and other kinds of force. Because those connections have been drawn already, there are many places in this diagram where social forces should be understood as active, and I would like to note three in particular. First, the general category of emergent entities described as environmental includes the social environment, and not just its physical aspects but also more abstract forces in the social environment such as ideology. Second, since I have defined subjectivity with respect to the improvisation of personas and identities in the context of social fields, it should be understood that all of the subject-related elements of this diagram presume the operation of such fields. And although I have chosen to draw the diagram in such a way that the emergence of individual subjects is highlighted, no subject should be understood as isolated, nor indeed as entirely singular. Here it becomes crucial to notice linkages at lower levels of the diagram, such as the one between singular subjects and the general environment (understood both socially and physically). Finally, it should be noted that on the right-hand side I have drawn *historical, social, and critical models* as the most all-encompassing methodologies to be applied. This move is partly tactical, but it also shows that I conceive this overall process—the emergence of various entities, of varying degrees of specificity, from a musical sound texture—to be a component of broader social practices.

The last thing to be said about Figure 6.1 concerns its hierarchy and verticality, which have led me to use oppositions like higher/lower. There are many instances in which such a representation can be useful, as in this particular case where I have tried to highlight the emergence of elaborated entities from more general backgrounds. However, this is only one view or one moment in a more circular set of processes. Earlier I invoked the concept of structuration, which allows terms of greater and lesser generality to be understood as standing in a relationship of constant mutual formation, rather than as fixed in a vertical hierarchy. For example, once various sonic features are interpretively synthesized in an emergent entity, those features appear to be the trace of that entity. Such a perspective is encouraged by the diagram as I have drawn it, with sonic features at the bottom and subjectivities at the top. However, the sonic features themselves constitute the field of possibility for those subjects, and furthermore, the perception of an emergent subject will condition the manner in which sonic features are heard. Under this alternative view, the diagram could have been drawn in the other direction in order to show how hearings on the "higher" level become raw material for new articulations on the "lower." This is just one example to serve as a reminder that while hierarchical reductions of interpretive practices are useful, they should not be taken as final or authoritative, because they are not well-suited to representing the subtle reversals integral to structuration.

The foundational move in my interpretive practice, represented near the lowest level of Figure 6.1, has been to interpret sonic events in terms of energy, space, and force. But it could fairly be asked why we need to speak about social forces instead of simply describing common beliefs. Or why we should hypostatize forces of tonal music rather than simply describing the most common note movements. In other words, what descriptive or explanatory dividend is paid by an investment in the language of energy, force, and space? Of course theorists in this area have not introduced talk about forces where it did not previously exist, but have simply acknowledged the central place held by such talk in existing musical discourse. This answer has merit but cannot be completely satisfactory since there are other aspects of existing discourse which could equally claim our attention. The decision to highlight and develop talk about energy and force in particular requires some further justification. Such concepts are extremely basic, to the point that a non-circular general definition may not be possible. Therefore, rather than attempt such a definition, I would like to list four important pragmatic functions that concepts of energy, force, and space can serve in interpretive practice.

First, concepts of energy, force, and space describe a family of experiential qualities. They encapsulate the feeling that some events are compelled, that effort would have been required to cause them to be otherwise. The *feeling* of force is integral to many kinds of experience, and it is unclear what other kind of concept could do a better job of conveying this feeling. Second, such metaphors are specific about the particular kinds of compulsion and effort in question, suggesting that these stand in an indexical or iconic relation with existing physical conceptualizations of the natural world. Given existing semiotic and cognitive theories, the use of such metaphors is not just a powerful descriptive tool but represents the tentative beginnings of an explanatory theory. Third, since metaphors of energy and force implicitly stipulate a cause for events, they show how these events stand in a broader set of cause-effect relations, thereby encouraging interpretations in which musical events are seen as the trace or action of some kind of agent. As a result, talk of energy and forces tends to encourage us to see the qualities of texts as events rather than as static features and to interpret these events with respect to the action of agents in particular environmental and social conditions. Finally, as three of the most fundamental cognitive categories, energy, force, and space are ideal terms in which to explore the linkages between disparate domains of conceptualization and experience, encouraging a synthetic and holistic perspective on questions of music, society, and subjectivity.

These points are all quite general but still pragmatic rather than foundational in spirit. I have preferred to avoid questions about energy, force, or space in themselves, and instead have identified ways in which specific energetic and spatial metaphors help in developing interpretations of musical texts and practices. Even very general distinctions, such as the one between centripetal and centrifugal forces, are descriptive of the effects or orientation of forces and do not attempt to say anything about what a force in general may be outside of these contingent configurations. While it may be fruitful at some point to attempt general or abstract definitions—for example by linking together all the various applications of the term centripetal in order to arrive at a general sense of center-directedness—I have left this for other projects. Instead, I used the centripetal/centrifugal metaphor to compare different particular centers (e.g., the country music tradition, Neil Young as auteur, conventions of tonal harmony) and to assess the dynamics of particular interpretations. The same is true for the general distinction between gesture and posture and of other more specific terms developed in my argument. Such terms appear abstract insofar as they are applicable across a range of domains, but they also invite concrete interpretation. Perhaps the pre-eminent distinction in this regard was that between centripetal and centrifugal forces and the related concept of a center. It strongly suggests a simple schematic form with obvious applications in almost every component of our discussion (music theory, social theory, cognition, etc.). Since it has been such a crucial part of several arguments in the book, a few more comments about centers may be in order.

The first thing to note is that we have identified several different kinds of "center." These include various sorts of emergent actors (selves, subjects, personas), styles (of a genre, tradition, or individual), rational conceptions of the natural world (often so ingrained as to be experienced as perception more than conception), and persistent social formations such as language, gender, ideology, and institutional structures. These were not just portrayed as crucial elements in discourse, but were further identified with one another since they were all called *centers*. Why call them centers and not simply structures or tendencies? One answer is that since I had already made the decision to speak in terms of energy, force, and space, a spatial metaphor seemed immediately appropriate. Also, the language of centers and peripheries, centering and decentering, is already prevalent in critical social theory. In order to summarize some crucial features of the centripetal/centrifugal metaphor, however, I would like to discuss two other approaches which overlap it slightly but which offer different perspectives on the same general questions. One of these approaches uses a model common in the life sciences and the other is rooted in philosophical logic.

The first alternative way to think about centripetal forces is in terms of homeostatic systems. The centers named above can all be conceived as states toward which dynamic processes (e.g., compositional practices, interpretations, social formations) tend to converge. From time to time, perturbations will occur and the system will become unstable. Centrifugal forces are analogous to perturbing forces, and centripetal forces are analogous to the system's tendency to return to a stable state. The homeostatic metaphor is similar to the centripetal/centrifugal one in that we still speak of stability, divergence, and convergence, but in a more system-oriented and less spatial manner. It also suggests certain valences not seen with the centripetal/centrifugal metaphor because homeostatic systems are central to theories of biology and cybernetics. While the centripetal/centrifugal way of putting things tends to resonate strongly with structuralist models of social organization and with dialogic literary theory, the homeostatic system perspective draws even more attention to the *livingness* of musical and social processes, and for this reason resonates strongly with questions of emergent persona.

A second alternative conceptualization has to do with the logical status of statements expressing experiences and/or interpretations. Centripetal forces can be thought of as the tendency to present certain statements—those which perpetuate the current state of the centers named above—as necessary rather than contingent.[11] Such a centripetal perspective, and any discourse which perpetuates it, suggests that there is a relationship of contradiction between preferred and non-preferred interpretations.[12] By contrast, in terms of logical assessment there are several ways to exert an oppositional, centrifugal force. The simplest strategy would be to accept the framework of contradiction, granting that statements can be neatly grouped into true-false pairs, but to assert the correctness of the non-preferred interpretations. More subtly, one might suggest that divergent interpretations cannot be understood with respect to contradiction at all, but rather stand to one another as contraries or subcontraries.[13] Or even more nuanced strategies may be applied in order to avoid ideologies of contradiction and necessity. The underlying point I wish to make is simply that although the language of truth and falsity has been almost entirely avoided in this book, the centripetal/ centrifugal metaphor does lend itself to description in these terms. And such a description can bring to light another side of the metaphor, emphasizing as it does questions of rationality and epistemological privilege.

I do not raise these alternative views entirely for their own interest, but also because they help to more precisely specify what kind of forces may be in question when we speak of centripetal or centrifugal forces. They do this not by defining the forces in themselves, but by showing how notions of convergence or divergence have their senses in various existing interpretive fields. It is the recurrence of similar schematic forms in many different interpretive vocabularies that has allowed us to apply all those vocabularies to the same body of music, viewing it from different angles but still with respect to a few core metaphors.

Notes

Introduction

1. Neil Young quoted in Cameron Crowe, "So Hard to Make Arrangements for Yourself" (1975), in *Neil Young: The Rolling Stone Files,* ed. Editors of Rolling Stone (New York: Hyperion, 1994).

2. Richard Rorty, *Philosophy and Social Hope* (New York: Penguin, 1999), 137–138.

3. Harry Oesterreicher, "The Expert Has Spoken," The Evening Coconut Archive, 55: 3/11/01–4/13/02, http://hyperrust.org/News/Coconut/?

4. For example, Daniel Cavicchi, *Tramps Like Us: Music and Meaning among Bruce Springsteen Fans* (New York: Oxford University Press, 1998); Simon Frith, *Performing Rites: On the Value of Popular Music* (Cambridge, Mass.: Harvard University Press, 1996); and Richard Middleton, "Popular Music Analysis and Musicology: Bridging the Gap," *Popular Music* 12, no. 2 (1993): 177–190.

5. Middleton, "Popular Music Analysis and Musicology," 180.

6. Timothy Rice, *May It Fill Your Soul: Experiencing Bulgarian Music* (Chicago: University of Chicago Press, 1994), 3, 6.

7. The size of the Rust list varies, but it usually hovers around 1,100 members. Membership is mostly based in the U.S., but there are many international members as well (in a February 1998 report, the most recent available, there were members from twenty-three countries, with 208 non–U.S. members total). Membership at least appears to be about one-fourth female, based upon user names and the content of posts. There is little in the user names—which tend to be drawn from Neil Young song lyrics—or in posts to give clues as to the ethnicity of members. The list is quite active, usually producing 80 to 100 postings daily (although the volume and variety of postings has been declining slightly but steadily since the early 2000s), and can be accessed through www.hyperrust.org. I have been reading the list continuously since September 1995.

8. Albin Zak, *The Poetics of Rock: Cutting Tracks, Making Records* (Berkeley: University of California Press, 2001), xv–xvi.

9. Adam Krims, *Rap Music and the Poetics of Identity* (Cambridge: Cambridge University Press, 2000), 28.

10. Scott Burnham, "How Music Matters: Poetic Content Revisited," in *Rethinking Music,* ed. N. Cook and M. Everist (Oxford: Oxford University Press, 1999), 198.

11. Gilles Deleuze, *Difference & Repetition,* trans. Paul Patton (New York: Columbia University Press, 1994), xxi.

1. Words

1.   Readers who need background information should consult Jimmy McDonough, *Shakey: Neil Young's Biography* (Toronto: Random House Canada, 2002); John Einarson, *Don't Be Denied* (Kingston, Ontario: Quarry Press, 1992); Scott Young, *Neil and Me* (Toronto: McClelland & Stewart; Robertson, 1997); David Downing, *A Dreamer of Pictures* (New York: Da Capo, 1995); and the Hyper Rust website: www.hyperrust.org.

2.   Before beginning, I should explain how I intend to cite song examples. Generally, when I describe a common or otherwise noteworthy feature in Young's work, I will list a few illustrative song titles in parentheses. These lists are not meant to be exhaustive, but only to guide readers who may wish to listen to a sample. As a rule, I will list two songs in such cases, although more may be listed if there are important contrasts to be heard within the category, and sometimes just one song will be listed if it is particularly exemplary. Appended to the reference list at the end of this book is a discography giving sources for all songs listed. Unless otherwise stated, it should be assumed that a song reference is to the first appearance of the title on a Neil Young solo studio album.

3.   Richard Williams, "Stills and Young," *Melody Maker,* January 10, 1970, 5.

4.   Ben Fong-Torres, "Crosby, Stills, Nash, Young, Taylor and Reeves" (1969), in *Neil Young: The Rolling Stone Files,* ed. Editors of Rolling Stone (New York: Hyperion, 1994), 41.

5.   Mark Rowland, "Cruise Control: Neil Young's Lonesome Drive," *Musician,* June 1988, 63–74.

6.   Williams, "Stills and Young."

7.   Elliot Blinder, "Neil Young Q & A." (1970), in *Neil Young: The Rolling Stone Files,* ed. Editors of Rolling Stone (New York: Hyperion, 1994), 54.

8.   See for example Bruce Miroff, Album Review: *Everybody Knows This Is Nowhere* (1969), in *Neil Young: The Rolling Stone Files,* ed. Editors of Rolling Stone (New York: Hyperion, 1994), 32.

9.   Ibid.

10.   See for example Blinder, "Neil Young Q & A.," 45.

11.   Richard Williams, "Imperfect, Irresistible Neil Young," *Melody Maker,* October 24, 1970, 19.

12.   Alan Lewis, "Personal Opinion," *Melody Maker,* January 17, 1970, 7.

13.   Langdon Winner, Album Review: *After the Gold Rush* (1970), in *Neil Young: The Rolling Stone Files,* ed. Editors of Rolling Stone (New York: Hyperion, 1994), 67.

14.   Anonymous-MM, "MM Albums of the Year" (entry on *After the Gold Rush*), *Melody Maker,* December 26, 1970, 9.

15.   Winner, Album Review: *After the Gold Rush,* 67.

16.   For example, Williams ("Imperfect, Irresistible Neil Young") wrote that the

album "stands up to listening better than it does to criticism" and that "you worry about his sanity because he sounds so fragile."

17. See Kembrew McLeod, "*1/2: A Critique of Rock Criticism in North America," *Popular Music* 20, no. 1 (2001): 47–64, for a recent summary.

18. Theodore Gracyk, *Rhythm and Noise: An Aesthetics of Rock* (Durham, N.C.: Duke University Press, 1996), 8–13.

19. Robert A. Wright, "Dream, Comfort, Memory, Despair: Canadian Popular Musicians and the Dilemma of Nationalism, 1968–1972," in *Canadian Music: Issues of Hegemony and Identity,* ed. B. Diamond and R. Witmer (Toronto: Canadian Scholars' Press, 1994), 293–294.

20. John Mendelssohn, Album Review: *Harvest* (1972), in *Neil Young: The Rolling Stone Files,* ed. Editors of Rolling Stone (New York: Hyperion, 1994), 82–83.

21. Peter Knobler, "Harvest," *Crawdaddy,* April 30, 1972, 14.

22. Mary Campbell, "A Man Needs a Voice: Feminine Side of Young's Harvest Moon Adds Depth," *Montreal Gazette,* January 2, 1993, D9.

23. Sheila Whiteley, *Women and Popular Music: Sexuality, Identity, and Subjectivity* (London: Routledge, 2000), 10.

24. Gordon quoted in Alec Foege, *Confusion Is Next: The Sonic Youth Story* (New York: St. Martin's Press, 1994), 212–214.

25. Gareth Palmer, "Bruce Springsteen and Masculinity," in *Sexing the Groove: Popular Music and Gender,* ed. S. Whiteley (London: Routledge, 1997).

26. Norma Coates, "(R)evolution Now? Rock and the Political Potential of Gender," in *Sexing the Groove: Popular Music and Gender,* ed. S. Whiteley (London: Routledge, 1997), 52–53.

27. Ibid., 56.

28. Whiteley, *Women and Popular Music,* 34–39. All quotations to follow about 1960s female lyric archetypes are taken from this passage.

29. Susan Fast, *In the Houses of the Holy: Led Zeppelin and the Power of Rock Music* (Oxford: Oxford University Press, 2001), 162–167.

30. Ibid., 184.

31. Young quoted in Allan Jones, "Neil Young: Shine on Harvest Moon," *Melody Maker,* November 7, 1992, 38–39.

32. Everett True, "Electrifying," *Melody Maker,* June 19, 1993, 35.

33. Mavis Bayton, "Women and the Electric Guitar," in *Sexing the Groove: Popular Music and Gender,* ed. S. Whiteley (London: Routledge, 1997), 41.

34. Marilyn Manners, "Fixing Madonna and Courtney: Sex Drugs Rock 'n' Roll Reflux," in *Reading Rock and Roll: Authenticity, Appropriation, Aesthetics,* ed. K. J. H. Dettmar and W. Richey (New York: Columbia University Press, 1999).

35. Jon Landau, "Concert Review" (1973), in *Neil Young: The Rolling Stone Files,* ed. Editors of Rolling Stone (New York: Hyperion, 1994), 85.

36. John Bauldie, John Einarson, David Fricke, Barney Hoskyns, Alan Jenkins, Dave Marsh, Mat Snow, and Ben Thompson, "The Keeper of the Flame" (multi-section feature), *Mojo,* September 1994, 78.

37. Bud Scoppa, Album Review: *Time Fades Away* (1974), in *Neil Young: The Rolling Stone Files,* ed. Editors of Rolling Stone (New York: Hyperion, 1994), 95–96.

38. Stephen Holden, Album Review: *On the Beach* (1974), in *Neil Young: The Rolling Stone Files,* ed. Editors of Rolling Stone (New York: Hyperion, 1994), 120.

39. Robert Christgau, "Whining through Paradox," *Creem,* October 1974, 60–61.

40. The crucial documents from this period are interviews with Scoppa ("Neil Young: The Unwilling Superstar," *Creem,* November 1975, 31–32, 88–89; "Play It Loud and Stay in the Other Room," *New Musical Express,* June 28, 1975, found at www.capetech.co.uk/Aurora_Borealis/ny_index.html, February 1998) and Crowe ("So Hard to Make Arrangements for Yourself").

41. Dave Marsh, Album Review: *Tonight's the Night* (1975), in *Neil Young: The Rolling Stone Files,* ed. Editors of Rolling Stone (New York: Hyperion, 1994).

42. Lester Bangs, "Neil Young: Zuma," *Creem,* March 1976, 61.

43. Nick Bromell, *Tomorrow Never Knows: Rock and Psychedelics in the 1960s* (Chicago: University of Chicago Press, 2000), 156–157.

44. Lawrence Grossberg, "Reflections of a Disappointed Popular Music Scholar," in *Rock over the Edge: Transformations in Popular Music Culture,* ed. R. Beebe, D. Fulbrook, and B. Saunders (Durham, N.C.: Duke University Press, 2002), 49.

45. Lori Burns and Mélisse Lafrance, *Disruptive Divas: Feminism, Identity & Popular Music* (New York: Routledge, 2002), 6–7.

46. See Julia Kristeva, *Powers of Horror,* trans. Leon S. Roudiez (New York: Columbia University Press, 1982), for an early formulation, and Judith Butler, *Bodies That Matter: On the Discursive Limits of "Sex"* (New York: Routledge, 1993), for a more contemporary one.

47. Butler, *Bodies That Matter,* 241.

48. Young quoted in Bill Flanagan, "The Real Neil Young Stands Up," *Musician,* November 1985, 32–41.

49. Jimmy McDonough, "Fucking Up with Neil Young: Too Far Gone," *Village Voice* (*Rock and Roll Supplement*), December 19, 1989, 18–25.

50. David Fricke, "The News According to Neil Young," *Rolling Stone,* September 4, 2003, 102.

51. Downing, *A Dreamer of Pictures,* 51–52.

52. David Fricke, "Neil Young and the Bluenotes," *Melody Maker,* April 30, 1988, 20.

53. Knobler, "Harvest."

54. Rowland, "Cruise Control."

55. Young quoted in John Einarson, "Neil Young: The Dawn of Power Swing" (interview), *Canadian Musician,* August 1988, 50–54.

56. Philip Tagg, "Open Letter about 'Black Music,' 'Afro-American Music,' and 'European Music,'" *Popular Music* 8, no. 3 (1989): 285–298.

57. Paul Gilroy, *The Black Atlantic: Modernity and Double Consciousness* (Cambridge, Mass.: Harvard University Press, 1993), chapter 3, especially p. 99.

58. Lawrence Grossberg, *We Gotta Get Out of This Place: Popular Conservatism and Postmodern Culture* (New York: Routledge, 1992), 147.

59. Ibid.

60. Talbot quoted in Cameron Crowe, "Neil Young: The Last American Hero" (1979), in *Neil Young: The Rolling Stone Files,* ed. Editors of Rolling Stone (New York: Hyperion, 1994), 189.

61. Paul Nelson, Concert Review (1978), in *Neil Young: The Rolling Stone Files,* ed. Editors of Rolling Stone (New York: Hyperion, 1994), 163.

62. Tom Carson, "Live Rust: Album Review" (1980), in *Neil Young: The Rolling Stone Files,* ed. Editors of Rolling Stone (New York: Hyperion, 1994), 204.

63. Bud Scoppa, Album Review: *Zuma* (1976), in *Neil Young: The Rolling Stone Files,* ed. Editors of Rolling Stone (New York: Hyperion, 1994).

64. Bangs, "Neil Young: Zuma."

65. Greil Marcus, Album Review: *Comes a Time* (1978), in *Neil Young: The Rolling Stone Files,* ed. Editors of Rolling Stone (New York: Hyperion, 1994), 172–173.

66. John Rockwell, "Will Neil Young Join Dylan in Rock's Pantheon?" *New York Times,* November 27, 1977, Section 2, 1, 13.

67. Robert Christgau, "Christgau Consumer Guide" (entry on *Rust Never Sleeps*), *Creem,* October 1979, 13.

68. Downing, *A Dreamer of Pictures,* 143.

69. George Lipsitz, "Who'll Stop the Rain? Youth Culture, Rock 'n' Roll, and Social Crises," in *The Sixties: From Memory to History,* ed. D. Farber (Chapel Hill: University of North Carolina Press, 1994), 223.

70. Ibid.

71. Young quoted in Cameron Crowe, "Neil Young: Still Expecting to Fly," *Musician,* November 1982, 54–62, 96–99.

72. John Piccarella, "Old Young, New Tricks" (album review: *Trans*), *Village Voice,* March 8, 1983, 54.

73. Allan Jones, "Home on the Range," *Melody Maker,* August 31, 1985, 29.

74. McDonough, "Fucking Up with Neil Young."

75. Parke Puterbaugh, Album Review: *Old Ways* (1985), in *Neil Young: The Rolling Stone Files,* ed. Editors of Rolling Stone (New York: Hyperion, 1994), 222–223.

76. George Lipsitz, *Dangerous Crossroads: Popular Music, Postmodernism, and the Poetics of Place* (New York: Verso, 1994), 62.

77. Linda Hutcheon, *Irony's Edge: The Theory and Politics of Irony* (New York: Routledge, 1994), 58–64.

78. Ibid., 37.

79. Ibid., 15.

80. Grossberg, *We Gotta Get Out of This Place,* 144.

81. See for example Allan Jones, "War & Peace," *Melody Maker,* October 19, 1991, 34; and Kristine McKenna, "Comes Another Time," *Musician,* December 1992, 93–94.

82. Steve Sutherland, "Old Glory," *Melody Maker,* September 8, 1990, 41.

83. Dave Marsh, "A Heretic Writes," *Mojo,* September 1994, 83.

84. On the Rust list it is generally said that the term was coined by Bob Young, who is no relation to Neil.

85. Richard Middleton, *Studying Popular Music* (Philadelphia: Open University Press, 1990), 174. Middleton's concept of idiolect is quite similar to that put forth by Leonard B. Meyer ("Toward a Theory of Style," in *The Concept of Style,* ed. B. Lang [Philadelphia: University of Pennsylvania Press, 1976]; *Style and Music: Theory, History, and Ideology* [Philadelphia: University of Pennsylvania Press, 1989], 23–24), and indeed there is a strong resemblance between Meyer's hierarchy of stylistic norms and the hierarchy of codes developed by the Middleton-Stefani school. If there is a distinction, perhaps slight, to be made between the approaches, it is that while Meyer puts more emphasis on systems of constraint and expectation in order to highlight questions of textuality and psychology, Middleton is more concerned with the operation of idiolect as a species of social code, citing as one of his primary influences the critical semiology of Barthes (Middleton, *Studying Popular Music,* 174).

86. "Captain Kennedy" appears to be a reworking of "John Johanna," a recording included in the Folkways *Anthology of American Folk Music,* edited by Harry Smith, which was a source for several other 1960s rock musicians. I thank Mike Daley for pointing this out to me. While I have not found an original source for "Running Dry," several features of the melody and chord progression are sufficiently atypical with respect to Young's other work to suggest that this may be a borrowed tune as well.

87. Michael Hicks, *Sixties Rock: Garage, Psychedelic, and Other Satisfactions* (Urbana: University of Illinois Press, 1999), 25.

88. See for example the comments quoted in Blinder, "Neil Young Q & A.," 52–53.

2. Unlock the Secrets

1. Holly George-Warren, "Introduction," in *Neil Young: The Rolling Stone Files,* ed. Editors of Rolling Stone (New York: Hyperion, 1994), 3.

2. Ibid., 3–4.

3. Marsh, "A Heretic Writes."

4. Roy Shuker, *Understanding Popular Music* (London: Routledge, 1994), 106.

5. Robert S. Hatten, *Musical Meaning in Beethoven: Markedness, Correlation, and Interpretation* (Bloomington: Indiana University Press, 1994), 10.

6. Robert Walser, *Running with the Devil: Power, Gender, and Madness in Heavy Metal Music* (Hanover, N.H.: Wesleyan University Press, 1993), 27.

7. Ingrid Monson, *Saying Something: Jazz Improvisation and Interaction* (Chicago: University of Chicago Press, 1996), 97.

8. Zak, *The Poetics of Rock,* 52.

9. Julia Kristeva, "Excerpts from Revolution in Poetic Language," in *The Kristeva Reader,* ed. T. Moi (New York: Columbia University Press, 1986), 111.

10. Monson, *Saying Something,* 99.

11. Ibid.

12. Judith Still and Michael Worton, "Introduction," in *Intertextuality: Theories and Practices,* ed. M. Worton and J. Still (Manchester: Manchester University Press, 1990), 11.

13. Kevin Korsyn, "Beyond Privileged Contexts: Intertextuality, Influence, and Dialogue," in *Rethinking Music,* ed. N. Cook and M. Everist (Oxford: Oxford University Press, 1999), 64–65.

14. Young quoted in Blinder, "Neil Young Q & A.," 47.

15. Robert Christgau, "Close Enough for Nashville," *Village Voice,* September 24, 1985, 77.

16. Charles Shaar-Murray, *Crosstown Traffic: Jimi Hendrix and Post-war Pop* (London: Faber and Faber, 1989), 30–31.

17. For a detailed historical study of canon formation in the Western tradition, see William Weber, "The History of Musical Canon," in *Rethinking Music,* ed. N. Cook and M. Everist (Oxford: Oxford University Press, 1999).

18. Jim Samson, "Canon," in *The New Grove Dictionary of Music and Musicians,* ed. S. Sadie and J. Tyrrell (New York: Grove's Dictionaries, 2001), 7.

19. Ibid.

20. Gary Tomlinson, *Music in Renaissance Magic: Toward a Historiography of Others* (Chicago: University of Chicago Press, 1993), 15.

21. Ibid., 16.

22. Shaar-Murray, *Crosstown Traffic,* 28.

23. Don Michael Randel, "The Canons in the Musicological Toolbox," in *Disciplining Music: Musicology and Its Canons,* ed. K. Bergeron and P. V. Bohlman (Chicago: University of Chicago Press, 1992), 15.

24. Frith, *Performing Rites.*

25. Keith Negus, *Popular Music in Theory* (Hanover, N.H.: Wesleyan University Press, 1996), 136.

26. Ibid., 138.

27. Lawrence Grossberg, *Dancing in Spite of Myself: Essays on Popular Culture* (Durham, N.C.: Duke University Press, 1997), 113–115.

28. Ibid.

29. Simon Frith, *Music for Pleasure: Essays in the Sociology of Pop* (Cambridge: Polity Press, 1988), 1.

30. Negus, *Popular Music in Theory,* 147–149.

31. Ibid., 149.

32. Ibid., 151–152.

33. Grossberg, *Dancing in Spite of Myself,* 31–32.

34. Roger Beebe, Denise Fulbrook, and Ben Saunders, "Introduction," in *Rock over the Edge: Transformations in Popular Music Culture,* ed. R. Beebe, D. Fulbrook, and B. Saunders (Durham, N.C.: Duke University Press, 2002), 1.

35. Shuker, *Understanding Popular Music,* 111–115; Will Straw, "Characterizing Rock Music Culture: The Case of Heavy Metal" (1983), in *On Record,* ed. S. Frith and A. Goodwin (London: Routledge, 1990), 103.

36. Greil Marcus, "All This Useless Beauty," in *Stars Don't Stand Still in the Sky,* ed. K. Kelly and E. McDonnell (New York: New York University Press, 1999), 22–23.

37. Christgau, "Whining through Paradox."

38. Joe Fernbacher, "Neil Young: American Stars 'n' Bars," *Creem,* September 1977, 59.

39. Jas Obrecht, "Neil Young: Secrets of the Grunge King," *Guitar Player,* March 1992, 47–56.

40. Larry Cragg, "All The Young Tubes," *Guitar Player,* March 1992, 50.

41. Young's only widely published essay to date is a short article for *Guitar Player* magazine outlining his opposition to digital recording as it was practiced in the early 1990s ("Digital Is a Huge Rip-off," *Guitar Player,* May 1992, 14).

42. Paul Théberge, *Any Sound You Can Imagine: Making Music/Consuming Technology* (Hanover, N.H.: Wesleyan University Press, 1997), 120.

43. Ibid., 4, 158–159.

44. Andrew Goodwin, "Rationalization and Democratization in the New Technologies of Popular Music," in *Popular Music and Communication,* ed. J. Lull (London: Sage Publications, 1992), 77.

45. Théberge, *Any Sound You Can Imagine,* 242.

46. Ibid., 1–2.

47. Richard Dyer, "In Defense of Disco" (1979), in *On Record,* ed. S. Frith and A. Goodwin (London: Routledge, 1990).

48. Straw, "Characterizing Rock Music Culture," 108.

49. Kay Dickinson, " 'Believe'? Vocoders, Digitalised Female Identity and Camp," *Popular Music* 20, no. 3 (2001): 335–336.

3. The Liquid Rage

1. Young quoted in Mark Rowland, "The Men on the Harvest Moon: Young Buck," *Musician,* April 1993, 42–53.

2. Jacques Attali, *Noise: The Political Economy of Music,* trans. Brian Massumi (Minneapolis: University of Minnesota Press, 1985), 5–6.

3. Although I have used Bey's term (*T.A.Z.* [Brooklyn: Autonomedia, 1985]), the concept is similar to the one put forth in subcultural studies by authors such as Hebdige and Grossberg when they suggest that the solutions allowed in subcultural experience to cultural problems are compelling but ultimately partial and temporary. Although the two concepts are similar in that they both place limits on the degree to which intense subcultural experiences can bring about broader social change, I prefer Bey's formulation because it seems more respectful of the profundity of those experiences.

4. Although the word *soundscape* already has currency among composers and sound ecologists and sometimes in this context refers to environmental sound, I am using the term slightly differently, to point out the manner in which musical textures are perceived as spaces and landscapes. In my use of the term, the landscape is virtual, a cumulative result of the spatial and gestural icons through which music is generally experienced. This is not to suggest that the images accompanying musical interpretation are always "landscape" images, but only that the word soundscape is usually an apt term for summarizing the overall spatial effect of a passage of music. In a broader sense, my use of the term is intended to effect some of the same linkage between landscape, virtuality, and social structure suggested by Thompson when she argues that, "like a landscape, a soundscape is simultaneously a physical environment and a way of perceiving that environment; it is both a world and a culture constructed to make sense of that world" (Emily Thompson, *The Soundscape of Modernity: Architectural Acoustics and the Culture of Listening in America, 1900–1933* [Cambridge, Mass.: MIT Press, 2002], 1).

5. Gracyk, *Rhythm and Noise,* 99.

6. Douglas Kahn, *Noise, Water, Meat: A History of Sound in the Arts* (Cambridge, Mass.: MIT Press, 1999), 21.

7. McDonough, *Shakey,* 298.

8. Sutherland, "Old Glory."

9. Attali, *Noise,* 19.

10. Young quoted in Blinder, "Neil Young Q & A.," 53–54.

11. Zak, *The Poetics of Rock,* 30–32.

12. Barthes, "The Grain of the Voice," in *Image—Music—Text,* trans. Stephen Heath (London: Fontana, 1977).

13. This point is explained more fully in chapter 5 under instrumental performance style.

14. In the native vocabulary of many electric guitarists, there is an idiosyncratic convention regarding the terms "vibrato" and "tremolo." When first mass-marketed by Fender, the name "tremolo bridge" was applied to a device which allows the pitch of guitar strings to be altered by pressing a bar attached to the bridge of the instrument, even though the effect created by such a device is actually vibrato. As a result, although most electric guitarists will use the term vibrato for pitch modulations induced by other means, they tend to use the word tremolo for vibrato induced by such a bridge. Hence the odd phrase, "vibrato produced by the tremolo bar."

15. Rock guitarists often speak of "the box" active at any particular point in a solo. A box is a collection of notes available in a given playing position and used by the soloist. When I speak of seemingly random pitch choice during frenzy, I mean that although Young will be in a particular box at a given moment, the notes chosen from this box do not seem to unfold according to any plan.

16. Young quoted in Rowland, "Cruise Control."

17. Young quoted in Obrecht, "Neil Young: Secrets of the Grunge King."

18. Young quoted in Sylvie Simmons, "Instant Feedback," *Mojo,* July 1997, 76–96.

19. Molina, Sampedro, and Talbot, quoted in ibid.

20. Stan W. Denski, "Music, Musicians, and Communication: The Personal Voice in a Common Language," in *Popular Music and Communication,* ed. J. Lull (London: Sage Publications, 1992), 36.

21. Derek Bailey, *Improvisation: Its Nature and Practice in Music* (Ashbourne, Derbyshire: Moorland Publishing, 1980), ix.

22. Ibid., 115–116.

23. Monson, *Saying Something,* 26–29.

24. Ibid., 66.

25. Young quoted in Steve Martin, "The Godfather of Grunge Rock," *Pulse,* December 1991; found at www.hyperrust.org, February 1998.

26. Ibid.

27. Young quoted in David Fricke, "New Weld Order," *Melody Maker,* November 30, 1991, 24–25.

28. Bernard Gendron, *Between Montmartre and the Mudd Club: Popular Music and the Avant-garde* (Chicago: University of Chicago Press, 2002), 7–9.

29. Young quoted in Tony Scherman, "Neil Young," *Musician,* December 1991, 7.

30. Kahn, *Noise, Water, Meat,* 51.

4. Have You Ever Been Singled Out?

1. The theory of structuration was developed by Giddens, and overviews can be found in Anthony Giddens, *The Constitution of Society: Outline of the Theory of Structuration* (Berkeley: University of California Press, 1984), and Philip Cassell, *The Giddens Reader* (Stanford, Calif.: Stanford University Press, 1993). It is a model which tries to resolve the problem of the relationship between individual subjective agency and trans-individual social formations such as languages, social ideologies, and institutions. The term *structuration* is meant to indicate that such formations are both structuring—they place constraints on the freedom and development of individual subjects—and structured—they only exist as continually reproduced in the activity of those subjects, which always retains some degree of relative autonomy. Another way to put the situation is to say that structuration is the process through which structures are structured, which is the same process through which subjects are constituted as relatively free and also relatively constrained. Insofar as it seeks to situate the phenomenon of structure within the realm of practical daily activity, Giddens's theory of structuration is close kin to Bourdieu's theory of practice, under which subjects are conceived as improvising identities within the constraints of social fields themselves continually reproduced by means of those improvisations.

2. Zak, *The Poetics of Rock,* 185.

3. Pierre Bourdieu, *The Logic of Practice* (Stanford, Calif.: Stanford University Press, 1990), 86.

4. Owen Flanagan, *The Science of the Mind* (Cambridge, Mass.: MIT Press, 1991), 24.

5. See for example Rorty, *Philosophy and Social Hope,* 134–135.

6. David Lidov, *Elements of Semiotics* (New York: St. Martin's Press, 1999). Given the complexity of Peirce's system and that he offered different interpretations of key concepts at different points in his life, I do not want to suggest that my comments here are Peircian in an orthodox sense. For more disciplined and complete introductions to Peircian thought proper, see Joseph Brent, *Charles Sanders Peirce: A Life* (Bloomington: Indiana University Press, 1993); Christopher Hookway, *Peirce* (London: Routledge, 1985); David Savan, *An Introduction to C. S. Peirce's Full System of Semeiotic* (Toronto: Toronto Semiotic Circle, 1988); and Indiana University Press's two volumes of *The Essential Peirce.* For overviews and commentary on applications of the Peircian perspective to music, see Naomi Cumming, *The Sonic Self: Musical Subjectivity and Signification* (Bloomington: Indiana University Press, 2001); William P. Dougherty, "The Quest for Interpretants: Towards a Peircian Paradigm for Musical Semiotics," *Semiotica* 99, no. 1/2 (1994): 163–184; William Echard, "Musical Semiotics in the 1990s: The State of the Art," *Semiotic Review of Books* 10, no. 3 (1999): 6–9; Hatten, *Musical Meaning in Beethoven;* and Lidov, *Elements of Semiotics.*

7. Lidov, *Elements of Semiotics,* 105–108.

8. Ibid., 85.

9. Nicholas Ruwet, *Langage, Musique, Poésie* (Paris: Éditions de Seuil, 1972); idem, "Methods of Analysis in Musicology," *Music Analysis* 6, no. 1–2 (1987): 11–36; Jean Molino, "Musical Fact and the Semiology of Music" (1975), *Music Analysis* 9, no. 2 (1990): 113–156.

10. Jean-Jacques Nattiez, *Fondements d'une sémiologie de la musique* (Paris: Union générale d'éditions, 1975); idem, *Music and Discourse,* trans. Carolyn Abbate (Princeton, N.J.: Princeton University Press, 1990).

11. Suzanne Langer, *Philosophy in a New Key* (Cambridge, Mass.: Harvard University Press, 1942); idem, *Feeling and Form* (New York: Charles Scribner's Sons, 1953); Gordon Epperson, *The Musical Symbol* (Ames: Iowa State University Press, 1967); Deryck Cooke, *The Language of Music* (Oxford: Oxford University Press, 1959); Wilson Coker, *Music and Meaning: A Theoretical Introduction to Musical Aesthetics* (New York: Free Press, 1972); Charles Boilès, "Sémiotique de l'ethnomusicologie," *Musique en Jeu* 10 (1973): 31–41; idem, "Processes of Musical Semiosis," *Yearbook for Traditional Music* 14 (1982): 24–44.

12. A reliable survey of this literature can be found in Raymond Monelle, *Linguistics and Semiotics in Music* (Philadelphia: Harwood Academic Publishers, 1992). Two influential contemporary commentaries on the overall approach (partly supportive, partly critical) include David Lidov, "Nattiez's Semiotics of Music," *The Canadian Journal of Research in Semiotics* 5, no. 2 (1978): 13–54, and Steven Feld, "Linguistic Models in Ethnomusicology," *Ethnomusicology* 18, no. 2 (1974): 197–217.

13. Philip Tagg, *Kojak: 50 Seconds of Television Music* (Göteborg: Musikveten-

skapliga Institutionen, 1979); Gino Stefani, *Introduzione alla semiotica della musica* (Palermo: Sellerio, 1976).

14.   A summary can be found in Middleton, *Studying Popular Music,* 8–11.

15.   Dick Hebdige, *Subculture: The Meaning of Style* (London: Routledge, 1979).

16.   Middleton, *Studying Popular Music;* Gino Stefani, "A Theory of Musical Competence," *Semiotica* 66, no. 1/3 (1987): 7–22.

17.   Middleton, *Studying Popular Music;* John Shepherd, *Music as Social Text* (Cambridge: Polity Press, 1991).

18.   Judith Becker and Alton Becker, "A Musical Icon: Power and Meaning in Javanese Gamelan Music," in *The Sign in Music and Literature,* ed. W. Steiner (Austin: University of Texas Press, 1981); Steven Feld, "Communication, Music, and Speech about Music," *Yearbook for Traditional Music* 16 (1984): 1–18; idem, "Sound Structure as Social Structure," *Ethnomusicology* 28, no. 3 (1984): 383–409; idem, "Aesthetics as Iconicity of Style," *Yearbook for Traditional Music* 20 (1988): 74–113.

19.   For Saussure, one quintessential mark of a sign is that the link between signifier and signified is created entirely by social convention, such that it could be different given different conventions. For example, different languages use different words for basic concepts such as *bird* or *tree*. There is nothing about the signifieds which requires or even strongly motivates a particular signifier. Saussure was aware of phenomena such as onomatopoeia, but in his view these were not properly linguistic signs. With a phenomenon such as iconicity, by contrast, it is assumed that there is some physical or logical property of the signifier which motivates its application to a particular signified. The process is still culturally mediated, since one must learn to use the given affordances in culturally appropriate ways, but along with this degree of mediation there is thought to be something trans-cultural involved, and it is this element which is said to be motivated rather than arbitrary.

20.   David Lidov, "Mind and Body in Music," *Semiotica* 66, no. 1/3 (1987): 69–97; idem, *Elements of Semiotics;* Robert S. Hatten, *Interpreting Musical Gestures, Topics, and Tropes: Mozart—Beethoven—Schubert* (Bloomington: Indiana University Press, forthcoming).

21.   Middleton, *Studying Popular Music;* idem, "Popular Music Analysis and Musicology: Bridging the Gap," *Popular Music* 12, no. 2 (1993): 177–190; John Shepherd and Peter Wicke, *Music and Cultural Theory* (Cambridge: Polity Press, 1997).

22.   Hatten, *Musical Meaning in Beethoven;* Rice, *May It Fill Your Soul.*

23.   Topic theory was initially developed by Leonard G. Ratner, *Classic Music: Expression, Form, and Style* (New York: Schirmer, 1980), and further elaborated by several workers, including V. Kofi Agawu, *Playing with Signs: A Semiotic Interpretation of Classic Music* (Princeton, N.J.: Princeton University Press, 1991); Raymond Monelle, *The Sense of Music: Semiotic Essays* (Princeton, N.J.: Princeton University Press, 2000); and Hatten, *Interpreting Musical Gestures, Topics, and Tropes.*

24.   José Luiz Martinez, "Icons in Music: A Peircian Rationale," *Semiotica* 110,

no. 1/2 (1996): 57–86; idem, *Semiosis in Hindustani Music* (Imatra: International Semiotics Institute, 1997); Thomas Turino, "Signs of Imagination, Identity, and Experience: A Peircian Semiotic Theory for Music," *Ethnomusicology* 43, no. 2 (1999): 221–255.

25.   Eero Tarasti, *A Theory of Musical Semiotics* (Bloomington: Indiana University Press, 1994).

26.   See for example Cumming, *The Sonic Self,* and Monelle, *The Sense of Music.*

27.   Ratner, *Classic Music.*

28.   Monelle, *The Sense of Music,* 14.

29.   Ibid., 15.

30.   Ibid., 24.

31.   Ibid., 28.

32.   Susan McClary, *Feminine Endings: Music, Gender, and Sexuality* (Minneapolis: University of Minnesota Press, 1992).

33.   Feld, "Aesthetics as Iconicity of Style."

34.   Hatten, *Musical Meaning in Beethoven,* 167.

35.   Manfred Clynes, *Sentics: The Touch of Emotions* (Bridport, Dorset: Prism Press, 1989).

36.   Stefani, "Melody: A Popular Perspective."

37.   For summaries see Charles Keil and Stephen Feld, *Music Grooves: Essays and Dialogues* (Chicago: University of Chicago Press, 1994), and Charles Keil, "The Theory of Participatory Discrepancies: A Progress Report," *Ethnomusicology* 39, no. 1 (1995): 1–20.

38.   Keil and Feld, *Music Grooves,* 54.

39.   Ibid., 55.

40.   Bourdieu, *The Logic of Practice,* 52.

41.   Judith Butler, *Gender Trouble: Feminism and the Subversion of Identity* (New York: Routledge, 1990).

42.   McClary, *Feminine Endings,* 23–24; Fast, *In the Houses of the Holy,* 123–133; William Echard, "An Analysis of Neil Young's 'Powderfinger' Based on Mark Johnson's Image Schemata," *Popular Music* 18, no. 1 (1999): 133–144.

43.   Candace Brower, "A Cognitive Theory of Musical Meaning," *Journal of Music Theory* 44, no. 2 (2000): 323–379; Arnie Cox, "The Metaphoric Logic of Musical Motion and Space" (Ph.D. dissertation, University of Oregon, 1999); idem, "The Mimetic Hypothesis and Embodied Musical Meaning," *Musicae Scientae* 5, no. 2 (2001): 195–209; Steve Larson, "The Problem of Prolongation in *Tonal* Music: Terminology, Perception, and Expressive Meaning," *Journal of Music Theory* 41, no. 1 (1997): 101–139; idem, "Musical Forces, Melodic Expectation, and Jazz Melody," *Music Perception* 19, no. 3 (2002): 351–385; Janna Saslaw, "Forces, Containers, and Paths: The Role of Body-Derived Image Schemas in the Conceptualization of Music," *Journal of Music Theory* 40, no. 2 (1996): 217–243; Lawrence Zbikowski, "Conceptual Models and Cross-Domain Mapping: New Perspectives on Theories of Music and Hierar-

chy," *Journal of Music Theory* 41, no. 2 (1997): 193–225; idem, *Conceptualizing Music: Cognitive Structure, Theory, and Analysis* (Oxford: Oxford University Press, 2002).

44.   Mark Johnson, *The Body in the Mind* (Chicago: University of Chicago Press, 1987), 29.

45.   Ibid., 21.

46.   Ibid., 25.

47.   Zbikowski, *Conceptualizing Music,* 69.

48.   Ibid., 60, 108.

49.   Mark Johnson and George Lakoff, *Metaphors We Live By* (Chicago: University of Chicago Press, 1980), 5.

50.   By convention the names of conceptual metaphors and image schemata are written in capital letters.

51.   Zbikowski, *Conceptualizing Music,* 13.

52.   Ibid., 70.

53.   Ibid., 72.

54.   For overviews see Mark Turner, *The Literary Mind* (New York: Oxford University Press, 1996), and Gilles Fauconnier and Mark Turner, *The Way We Think: Conceptual Blending and the Mind's Hidden Complexities* (New York: Basic Books, 2002).

55.   Hatten, *Musical Meaning in Beethoven,* 295. Hatten, *Interpreting Musical Gestures, Topics, and Tropes,* chapter 4 (no page number available, since the book is still in press as of this writing).

56.   See for example Elizabeth P. Sayrs, "Narrative, Metaphor, and Conceptual Blending in 'The Hanging Tree,'" *Music Theory Online* 9, no. 1 (2003): societymusictheory.org/mto.

57.   Turner, *The Literary Mind,* 57.

58.   Zbikowski, *Conceptualizing Music,* 83.

59.   Ibid., 92.

60.   Zbikowski, "Conceptual Models and Cross-Domain Mapping," 218.

61.   Shepherd and Wicke, *Music and Cultural Theory,* 117.

62.   Hatten, *Interpreting Musical Gestures, Topics, and Tropes,* chapter 5 (no page number available, since the book is still in press as of this writing).

63.   Lidov, *Elements of Semiotics,* 219.

64.   C. S. Peirce, *Essential Peirce,* vol. I (Bloomington: Indiana University Press, 1992), 226.

65.   Ibid., 233, 274–275.

66.   George Lakoff and Mark Johnson, *Philosophy in the Flesh: The Embodied Mind and Its Challenge to Western Thought* (New York: Basic Books, 1999), 50–54.

67.   Brower, "A Cognitive Theory of Musical Meaning," 352.

68. Larson, "Musical Forces, Melodic Expectation, and Jazz Melody," 352.

69. Johnson, *The Body in the Mind,* 12–13; Lakoff and Johnson, *Philosophy in the Flesh,* 19.

70. Lakoff and Johnson, *Philosophy in the Flesh,* 53, 184–186.

71. Turner, *The Literary Mind,* 26–27.

72. Edward T. Cone, *The Composer's Voice* (Berkeley: University of California Press, 1974).

73. Cumming, *The Sonic Self,* 162.

74. Alexandra Pierce, "Character and Characterization in Musical Performance: Effects of Sensory Experience upon Meaning," in *Musical Signification: Essays in the Semiotic Theory and Analysis of Music,* ed. E. Tarasti (Berlin: Mouton de Gruyter, 1995).

75. Hatten, *Interpreting Musical Gestures, Topics, and Tropes,* chapter 5.

76. See for example Cavicchi, *Tramps Like Us.*

77. David J. Hargreaves, Dorothy Miell, and Raymond A. R. MacDonald, "What Are Musical Identities, and Why Are They Important?" in *Musical Identities,* ed. R. A. R. MacDonald, D. J. Hargreaves, and D. Miell (Oxford: Oxford University Press, 2002), 2.

78. Cumming, *The Sonic Self,* 216.

79. Ibid., 224.

80. Frith, *Performing Rites,* 272.

81. Hargreaves, Miell, and MacDonald, "What Are Musical Identities, and Why Are They Important?" 7–8.

82. Cavicchi, *Tramps Like Us,* 136.

83. Cumming, *The Sonic Self,* 10.

84. Harris M. Berger, *Metal, Rock, and Jazz: Perception and the Phenomenology of Musical Experience* (Hanover, N.H.: Wesleyan University Press, 1999), 19–23.

85. Ibid., 26.

86. Tia DeNora, *Music in Everyday Life* (Cambridge: Cambridge University Press, 2000), 16–17.

87. I am grateful to Arnie Cox for suggesting these formulations to me in an e-mail correspondence.

88. Burns and Lafrance, *Disruptive Divas,* 40.

89. Zak, *The Poetics of Rock,* 85–87.

90. Shepherd and Wicke, *Music and Cultural Theory,* 159.

91. Allan Moore, *Rock: The Primary Text* (Philadelphia: Open University Press, 1993), 106.

92. Stephen Handel, *Listening: An Introduction to the Perception of Auditory Events* (Cambridge, Mass.: MIT Press, 1993), 555.

93. Serge Lacasse, "Listen to My Voice: The Evocative Power of Vocal Staging in

Recorded Rock Music and Other Forms of Vocal Expression" (Ph.D. dissertation, University of Liverpool, 2000).

94. Such as Albert S. Bregman, *Auditory Scene Analysis: The Perceptual Organization of Sound* (Cambridge, Mass.: MIT Press, 1994).

95. Moore, *Rock*.

96. Tagg, *Kojak*, 217–229.

5. You See Your Baby Loves to Dance

1. This is a condensed representation of fingering. Following an indication of the notes in the chord voicing (low to high), there are six digits indicating the fret used on each string to sound these notes, beginning with the lowest e-string. The numeral 0 indicates an open string, and X indicates a string that is not sounded.

2. Fast, *In the Houses of the Holy*, 139.

3. Ibid., 140–141.

4. Hicks, *Sixties Rock*, 35.

5. Fast, *In the Houses of the Holy*, 133–139.

6. Henri Lefebvre, *The Production of Space,* trans. Donald Nicholson-Smith (Oxford: Blackwell, 1991), 220.

7. Fast, *In the Houses of the Holy*, 141.

8. In order to economize on space and to emphasize the significance of these features rather than their minute details, I will limit myself to describing melodic and harmonic analytic results in summary form and citing only a few outstanding examples of each, rather than presenting the full analysis. The complete analysis on which my harmonic and melodic remarks are based is reported elsewhere. William Echard, "Neil Young, Embodiment, and Stylistic Diversity: A Social Semiotic and Musicological Perspective" (Ph.D. dissertation, Music, York University, Toronto, 2000).

9. In order to foreground the most pertinent information, my melodic charts show only pitches and their grouping into cells (indicated by beaming cell notes together). Given the fairly even rhythmic profile of the melodies, if these charts are played in eighth notes with a one-eighth rest inserted between cells, the result will be quite close to the original rhythm. As with all of my analytic devices, however, these figures are meant primarily as a guide to be used while listening to the music.

10. Middleton, *Studying Popular Music;* Peter Van der Merwe, *Origins of the Popular Style: The Antecedents of Twentieth-Century Popular Music* (Oxford: Oxford University Press, 1989).

11. Middleton, *Studying Popular Music*, 205.

12. Simon Frith, "Only a Folkie Can Break Your Heart," *Melody Maker,* October 14, 1978, 19.

13. Adam Sweeting, "Before and After Science," *Melody Maker,* January 8, 1983, 17.

14. Burns and Lafrance, *Disruptive Divas,* 42.

15. William Echard, "Gesture and Posture: One Useful Distinction in the Embodied Semiotic Analysis of Popular Music," *Indiana Theory Review* 21 (2000): 103–128.

16. Robert S. Hatten, *Lectures on Musical Gesture* [Web page], Semiotic Review of Books Cyber Semiotic Institute, 1999; available from www.univie.ac.at/Wissenschaftstheorie/srb/cyber/cyber.html.

17. Walser, *Running with the Devil,* 2.

18. Hatten, *Lectures on Musical Gesture.*

19. Even though I am most interested in this commonality between modal and tonal kinds of organization, there are certain distinctions which can help us be more specific about varieties of pitch-directedness in Neil Young's chord progressions. For my purposes, the clearest characteristic that marks a progression as tonal is the frequent (or at least prominent) use of dominant-tonic resolution. In other words, I use the word tonal in connection with progressions showing a strong influence from three-function common-practice tonality, most clearly marked by the relationship between dominant and tonic in the simple V-I cadence. In contrast, I tend to describe as modal progressions which avoid the dominant-tonic resolution and in which root movement by second or third is more common. Perhaps more tentatively, I would also classify as modal progressions which avoid a strong tonic definition altogether or which display a bi-tonic effect, keeping in mind that when such effects occur in rock music they are generally not the result of elaborate chromatic harmony or long-range prolongations, but rather the result of shorter triadic progressions out of which no clear fundamental degree emerges. Often, the linear intervallic pattern of root movements is also relevant, with tonal progressions featuring more root movement by fourth or fifth and modal ones featuring more root movement by second or third (which, by definition, makes tonic-dominant relationships impossible to create). Note that I use *root* to describe the fundamental degree of the triad. For my immediate analysis, inversions and chord voicing are not relevant.

20. Theoretically, modal mixture could create a mediant root movement with no common tones, but to my knowledge this does not occur anywhere in Neil Young's music.

21. This progression is difficult to represent with clarity. The chords are E-major and G-major, although the melody suggests a minor mode, not major. So an equally plausible notation would be I / III, with the understanding that this is an Aeolian progression in which the tonic chord has a major quality. Alternatively, it could be understood simply as an alternation between major and minor qualities of the tonic chord, although I do not tend to hear it that way.

22. Gracyk, *Rhythm and Noise,* 223.

23. McDonough, *Shakey,* 441.

24. Frith, *Performing Rites,* 186.

25. Ibid., 198–199.

26. Ibid., 184.

27.   Ibid., 191.

28.   Ibid., 194–195.

29.   Walser, *Running with the Devil,* 124.

30.   Frith, *Performing Rites,* 195.

31.   Fast, *In the Houses of the Holy,* 41–42.

32.   Ibid., 43.

33.   Walser, *Running with the Devil,* 108.

34.   Hicks, *Sixties Rock,* 1.

35.   Frith, *Performing Rites,* 197.

36.   Ibid.

6. Will to Love

1.   Richard Rorty, "Universality and Truth," in *Rorty and His Critics,* ed. R. B. Brandom (Oxford: Blackwell, 2000).

2.   John Dewey, *Art as Experience* (New York: Putnam, 1934).

3.   Paul Nelson, Album Review: *American Stars 'n' Bars* (1977), in *Neil Young: The Rolling Stone Files,* ed. Editors of Rolling Stone (New York: Hyperion, 1994), 158.

4.   Allan Jones, "Young Man of Melancholia," *Melody Maker,* June 18, 1977, 18.

5.   Fred Schruers, "Tame James & Unreal Neil," *Crawdaddy,* August 1977, 66.

6.   Nick Kent, "Neil: Bad Judgment . . . or Just a Bad Liver?" *New Musical Express,* June 11, 1977; found at www.capetech.co.uk/Aurora_Borealis/ny_index.html, February 1998.

7.   Marcus, Album Review: *Comes a Time,* 172–173.

8.   Welfare Mother, from the Rust list.

9.   Shakey, from the Rust list.

10.   Young quoted in Flanagan, "The Real Neil Young Stands Up."

11.   I mean *contingent* in the sense of a proposition which is possible but non-necessary. The truth or falsity of such a proposition is not fixed by its form and is therefore contingent upon particular circumstances.

12.   I am using *preferred* in the sense typical in contemporary reception theory. A preferred interpretation is the one which seems most natural and obvious with respect to the most widely distributed reading practices in a particular interpretive community.

13.   Contraries: cannot both be true, but both may be false. Subcontraries: at least one must be true, but both may be true.

References

Songs

The following is an alphabetical list of all Neil Young songs mentioned in the book. The years correlate to the first year in which the song was released on an album, not to the year of composition. Additional information about the albums is given in the selected album discography.

"After the Gold Rush." *After the Gold Rush.* 1970.
"Alabama." *Harvest.* 1972.
"Albuquerque." *Tonight's the Night.* 1975.
"Already One." *Comes a Time.* 1978.
"Ambulance Blues." *On the Beach.* 1974.
"Bandit." *Greendale.* 2003.
"Barstool Blues." *Zuma.* 1975.
"Big Time." *Mirror Ball.* 1995.
"Birds." *After the Gold Rush.* 1970.
"Bite the Bullet." *American Stars 'n' Bars.* 1977.
"Bridge, The." *Time Fades Away.* 1973.
"Broken Arrow." *Buffalo Springfield Again.* 1967.
"Captain Kennedy." *Hawks and Doves.* 1980.
"Carmichael." *Greendale.* 2003.
"Change Your Mind." *Sleeps with Angels.* 1994.
"Cinnamon Girl." *Everybody Knows This Is Nowhere.* 1969.
"Cocaine Eyes." *Eldorado.* 1989.
"Come On Baby Let's Go Downtown." *Tonight's the Night.* 1975.
"Comes a Time." *Comes a Time.* 1978.
"Comin' Apart at Every Nail." *Hawks and Doves.* 1980.
"Cortez the Killer." *Zuma.* 1975.
"Cowgirl in the Sand." *Everybody Knows This Is Nowhere.* 1969.
"Crime in the City." *Freedom.* 1989
"Daddy Went Walkin'." *Silver & Gold.* 2000.
"Danger Bird." *Zuma.* 1975.
"Don't Be Denied." *Time Fades Away.* 1973.
"Don't Cry." *Eldorado.* 1989.
"Don't Cry No Tears." *Zuma.* 1975.
"Don't Let It Bring You Down." *After the Gold Rush.* 1970.
"Down by the River." *Everybody Knows This Is Nowhere.* 1969.
"Drive Back." *Zuma.* 1975.
"Everybody Knows This Is Nowhere." *Everybody Knows This Is Nowhere.* 1969.
"For the Turnstiles." *On the Beach.* 1974.
"Fuckin' Up." *Ragged Glory.* 1990.

"Get Back on It." *Re*ac*tor*. 1981.
"Going Back." *Comes a Time*. 1978.
"Hangin' on a Limb." *Freedom*. 1989.
"Harvest Moon." *Harvest Moon*. 1992.
"Hawks and Doves." *Hawks and Doves*. 1980.
"Heart of Gold." *Harvest*. 1972.
"Helpless." *Deja Vu*. 1970.
"Here We Are in the Years." *Neil Young*. 1968.
"Hey Hey My My (Into the Black)." *Rust Never Sleeps*. 1979.
"Homegrown." *American Stars 'n' Bars*. 1977.
"Human Highway." *Comes a Time*. 1978.
"I Am a Child." *Last Time Around*. 1968.
"I Believe in You." *After the Gold Rush*. 1970.
"If I Could Have Her Tonight." *Neil Young*. 1968.
"I've Loved Her So Long." *Neil Young*. 1968.
"Journey Through the Past." *Time Fades Away*. 1973.
"Last Trip to Tulsa." *Neil Young*. 1968.
"Let's Roll." *Are You Passionate?* 2002.
"Like a Hurricane." *American Stars 'n' Bars*. 1977.
"The Loner." *Neil Young*. 1968.
"Look Out for My Love." *Comes a Time*. 1978.
"Losing End, The." *Everybody Knows This Is Nowhere*. 1969.
"Lotta Love." *Comes a Time*. 1978.
"Love in Mind." *Time Fades Away*. 1973.
"A Man Needs a Maid." *Harvest*. 1972.
"Mellow My Mind." *Tonight's the Night*. 1975.
"Mideast Vacation." *Life*. 1987.
"Mother Earth." *Ragged Glory*. 1990.
"Motion Pictures." *On the Beach*. 1974.
"Mr. Soul." *Buffalo Springfield Again*. 1967.
"Music Arcade." *Broken Arrow*. 1996.
"My My Hey Hey (Out of the Blue)." *Rust Never Sleeps*. 1979.
"Natural Beauty." *Harvest Moon*. 1992.
"Needle and the Damage Done, The." *Harvest*. 1972.
"Nowadays Clancy Can't Even Sing." *Buffalo Springfield*. 1966.
"Ohio." *4 Way Street*. 1971.
"Old Country Waltz, The." *American Stars 'n' Bars*. 1977.
"Old Laughing Lady, The." *Neil Young*. 1968.
"Old Man." *Harvest*. 1972.
"On the Beach." *On the Beach*. 1974.
"One of These Days." *Harvest Moon*. 1992.
"Only Love Can Break Your Heart." *After the Gold Rush*. 1970.
"Opera Star." *Re*ac*tor*. 1981.
"Out on the Weekend." *Harvest*. 1972.
"Pocahontas." *Rust Never Sleeps*. 1979.
"Powderfinger." *Rust Never Sleeps*. 1979.
"Rapid Transit." *Re*ac*tor*. 1981.
"Razor Love." *Silver & Gold*. 2000.
"Revolution Blues." *On the Beach*. 1974.

"Ride My Llama." *Rust Never Sleeps*. 1979.
"Rockin' in the Free World." *Freedom*. 1989.
"Roll Another Number for the Road." *Tonight's the Night*. 1975.
"Round and Round." *Everybody Knows This Is Nowhere*. 1969.
"Running Dry." *Everybody Knows This Is Nowhere*. 1969.
"Saddle Up the Palomino." *American Stars 'n' Bars*. 1977.
"Safeway Cart." *Sleeps with Angels*. 1994.
"Sedan Delivery." *Rust Never Sleeps*. 1979.
"Slip Away." *Broken Arrow*. 1996.
"Slowpoke." *Looking Forward*. 1999.
"Southern Man." *After the Gold Rush*. 1970.
"Southern Pacific." *Re*ac*tor*. 1981.
"Stringman." *MTV Unplugged*. 1993.
"Stupid Girl." *Zuma*. 1975.
"Such a Woman." *Harvest Moon*. 1992.
"Sugar Mountain." *Decade*. 1977.
"Surfer Joe and Moe the Sleaze." *Re*ac*tor*. 1981.
"Tell Me Why." *After the Gold Rush*. 1970.
"This Note's for You." *This Note's for You*. 1988.
"Thrasher." *Rust Never Sleeps*. 1979.
"Time Fades Away." *Time Fades Away*. 1973.
"Tired Eyes." *Tonight's the Night*. 1975.
"Tonight's the Night." *Tonight's the Night*. 1975.
"Unknown Legend." *Harvest Moon*. 1992.
"Vampire Blues." *On the Beach*. 1974.
"Violent Side." *Landing on Water*. 1986.
"Walk On." *On the Beach*. 1974.
"War of Man." *Harvest Moon*. 1992.
"Welfare Mothers." *Rust Never Sleeps*. 1979.
"When You Dance I Can Really Love." *After the Gold Rush*. 1970.
"When Your Lonely Heart Breaks." *Life*. 1987.
"Will to Love." *American Stars 'n' Bars*. 1977.
"Wonderin'." *Everybody's Rockin'*. 1983.
"Words." *Harvest*. 1972.
"You and Me." *Harvest Moon*. 1992.

Selected Album Discography

Neil Young's discography is extensive. This list contains only albums mentioned in the book. All dates are for U.S. releases. Available sources vary on exact months of release, sometimes widely. In choosing dates, I have relied most strongly on Jimmy McDonough, *Shakey: Neil Young's Biography* (Toronto: Random House Canada, 2002), and the discography at www.hyperrust.org, using John Robertson, *Neil Young: The Visual Documentary* (London: Omnibus, 1994), to break ties where possible. Where all three sources differ and no further triangulation was possible, I have relied on intuition to make a final decision.

Buffalo Springfield (with Buffalo Springfield). Atco. December 1966.
Buffalo Springfield Again (with Buffalo Springfield). Atco. November 1967.

Last Time Around (with Buffalo Springfield). Atco. August 1968.
Neil Young. Reprise. November 1968.
Everybody Knows This Is Nowhere. Reprise. May 1969.
Deja Vu (with CSNY). Atlantic. March 1970
After the Gold Rush. Reprise. September 1970.
4 Way Street (with CSNY). Atlantic. April 1971.
Harvest. Reprise. February 1972.
Time Fades Away. Reprise. September 1973.
On the Beach. Reprise. July 1974.
Tonight's the Night. Reprise. June 1975.
Zuma. Reprise. November 1975.
American Stars 'n' Bars. Reprise. May 1977.
Decade. Reprise. October 1977.
Comes a Time. Reprise. October 1978.
Rust Never Sleeps. Reprise. July 1979.
Live Rust. Reprise. November 1979.
Hawks and Doves. Reprise. October 1980.
Re*ac*tor. Reprise. October 1981.
Trans. Geffen. December 1982.
Everybody's Rockin'. Geffen. July 1983.
Old Ways. Geffen. August 1985.
Landing on Water. Geffen. July 1986.
Life. Geffen. June 1987.
This Note's for You. Reprise. April 1988.
Eldorado (EP). Reprise. April 1989.
Freedom. Reprise. October 1989.
Ragged Glory. Reprise. September 1990.
Arc. Reprise. October 1991.
Harvest Moon. Reprise. November 1992.
MTV Unplugged. Reprise. June 1993.
Sleeps with Angels. Reprise. August 1994.
Mirror Ball. Reprise. June 1995.
Broken Arrow. Reprise. July 1996.
Year of the Horse. Reprise. June 1997.
Looking Forward (with CSNY). Reprise. October 1999.
Silver & Gold. Reprise. April 2000.
Are You Passionate? Reprise. April 2002.
Greendale. Reprise. August 2003.

Books and Articles

Abbate, Carolyn. *Unsung Voices: Opera and Musical Narrative in the Nineteenth Century.* Princeton, N.J.: Princeton University Press, 1991.

Agawu, V. Kofi. *Playing with Signs: A Semiotic Interpretation of Classic Music.* Princeton, N.J.: Princeton University Press, 1991.

Anonymous-MM. "MM Albums of the Year" (entry on *After the Gold Rush*). *Melody Maker,* December 26, 1970, 9.

Attali, Jacques. *Noise: The Political Economy of Music.* Translated by Brian Massumi. Minneapolis: University of Minnesota Press, 1985.

Bailey, Derek. *Improvisation: Its Nature and Practice in Music.* Ashbourne, Derbyshire: Moorland Publishing, 1980.

Bangs, Lester. "Neil Young: Zuma." *Creem,* March 1976, 61.

Barthes, Roland. *Image—Music—Text.* Translated by Stephen Heath. London: Fontana, 1977.

Bauldie, John, John Einarson, David Fricke, Barney Hoskyns, Alan Jenkins, Dave Marsh, Mat Snow, and Ben Thompson. "The Keeper of the Flame" (multi-section feature). *Mojo,* September 1994, 63–87.

Bayton, Mavis. "Women and the Electric Guitar." In *Sexing the Groove: Popular Music and Gender,* ed. S. Whiteley. London: Routledge, 1997.

Becker, Judith, and Alton Becker. "A Musical Icon: Power and Meaning in Javanese Gamelan Music." In *The Sign in Music and Literature,* ed. W. Steiner. Austin: University of Texas Press, 1981.

Beebe, Roger, Denise Fulbrook, and Ben Saunders. "Introduction." In *Rock over the Edge: Transformations in Popular Music Culture,* ed. R. Beebe, D. Fulbrook, and B. Saunders. Durham, N.C.: Duke University Press, 2002.

Berger, Harris M. *Metal, Rock, and Jazz: Perception and the Phenomenology of Musical Experience.* Hanover, N.H.: Wesleyan University Press, 1999.

Bey, Hakim. *T.A.Z.: The Temporary Autonomous Zone, Ontological Anarchy, Poetic Terrorism.* Brooklyn: Autonomedia, 1985.

Blinder, Elliot. "Neil Young Q & A." (1970). In *Neil Young: The Rolling Stone Files,* ed. Editors of Rolling Stone. New York: Hyperion, 1994.

Boilès, Charles. "Processes of Musical Semiosis." *Yearbook for Traditional Music* 14 (1982): 24–44.

———. "Sémiotique de l'ethnomusicologie." *Musique en Jeu* 10 (1973): 31–41.

Bourdieu, Pierre. *The Logic of Practice.* Stanford, Calif.: Stanford University Press, 1990.

Bregman, Albert S. *Auditory Scene Analysis: The Perceptual Organization of Sound.* Cambridge, Mass.: MIT Press, 1994.

Brent, Joseph. *Charles Sanders Peirce: A Life.* Bloomington: Indiana University Press, 1993.

Bromell, Nick. *Tomorrow Never Knows: Rock and Psychedelics in the 1960s.* Chicago: University of Chicago Press, 2000.

Brower, Candace. "A Cognitive Theory of Musical Meaning." *Journal of Music Theory* 44, no. 2 (2000): 323–379.

Burnham, Scott. "How Music Matters: Poetic Content Revisited." In *Rethinking Music,* ed. N. Cook and M. Everist. Oxford: Oxford University Press, 1999.

Burns, Lori, and Mélisse Lafrance. *Disruptive Divas: Feminism, Identity & Popular Music.* New York: Routledge, 2002.

Butler, Judith. *Bodies That Matter: On the Discursive Limits of "Sex."* New York: Routledge, 1993.

———. *Gender Trouble: Feminism and the Subversion of Identity.* New York: Routledge, 1990.

Campbell, Mary. "A Man Needs a Voice: Feminine Side of Young's Harvest Moon Adds Depth." *Montreal Gazette,* January 2, 1993, D9.

Carson, Tom. "Live Rust: Album Review" (1980). In *Neil Young: The Rolling Stone Files,* ed. Editors of Rolling Stone. New York: Hyperion, 1994.

Cassell, Philip. *The Giddens Reader.* Stanford, Calif.: Stanford University Press, 1993.

Cavicchi, Daniel. *Tramps Like Us: Music and Meaning among Bruce Springsteen Fans.* New York: Oxford University Press, 1998.

Christgau, Robert. "Christgau Consumer Guide" (entry on *Rust Never Sleeps*). *Creem,* October 1979, 13.

———. "Close Enough for Nashville." *Village Voice,* September 24, 1985, 77.

———. "Whining through Paradox." *Creem,* October 1974, 60–61.

Clynes, Manfred. *Sentics: The Touch of Emotions.* Bridport, Dorset: Prism Press, 1989.

Coates, Norma. "(R)evolution Now? Rock and the Political Potential of Gender." In *Sexing the Groove: Popular Music and Gender,* ed. S. Whiteley. London: Routledge, 1997.

Coker, Wilson. *Music and Meaning: A Theoretical Introduction to Musical Aesthetics.* New York: Free Press, 1972.

Cone, Edward T. *The Composer's Voice.* Berkeley: University of California Press, 1974.

Cooke, Deryck. *The Language of Music.* Oxford: Oxford University Press, 1959.

Cox, Arnie. "The Metaphoric Logic of Musical Motion and Space." Ph.D. dissertation, University of Oregon, 1999.

———. "The Mimetic Hypothesis and Embodied Musical Meaning." *Musicae Scientae* 5, no. 2 (2001): 195–209.

Cragg, Larry. "All The Young Tubes." *Guitar Player,* March 1992, 50.

Crowe, Cameron. "Neil Young: The Last American Hero" (1979). In *Neil Young: The Rolling Stone Files,* ed. Editors of Rolling Stone. New York: Hyperion, 1994.

———. "Neil Young: Still Expecting to Fly." *Musician,* November 1982, 54–62, 96–99.

———. "So Hard to Make Arrangements for Yourself" (1975). In *Neil Young: The Rolling Stone Files,* ed. Editors of Rolling Stone. New York: Hyperion, 1994.

Cumming, Naomi. *The Sonic Self: Musical Subjectivity and Signification.* Bloomington: Indiana University Press, 2001.

Deleuze, Gilles. *Difference & Repetition.* Translated by Paul Patton. New York: Columbia University Press, 1994.

DeNora, Tia. *Music in Everyday Life.* Cambridge: Cambridge University Press, 2000.

Denski, Stan W. "Music, Musicians, and Communication: The Personal Voice in a Common Language." In *Popular Music and Communication,* ed. J. Lull. London: Sage Publications, 1992.

Dewey, John. *Art as Experience.* New York: Putnam, 1934.

Dickinson, Kay. "'Believe'? Vocoders, Digitalised Female Identity and Camp." *Popular Music* 20, no. 3 (2001): 333–347.

Dougherty, William P. "The Quest for Interpretants: Towards a Peircian Paradigm for Musical Semiotics." *Semiotica* 99, no. 1/2 (1994): 163–184.

Downing, David. *A Dreamer of Pictures.* New York: Da Capo, 1995.

Dyer, Richard. "In Defense of Disco" (1979). In *On Record,* ed. S. Frith and A. Goodwin. London: Routledge, 1990.

Echard, William. "An Analysis of Neil Young's 'Powderfinger' Based on Mark Johnson's Image Schemata." *Popular Music* 18, no. 1 (1999): 133–144.

———. "Gesture and Posture: One Useful Distinction in the Embodied Semiotic Analysis of Popular Music." *Indiana Theory Review* 21 (2000): 103–128.

———. "Musical Semiotics in the 1990s: The State of the Art." *Semiotic Review of Books* 10, no. 3 (1999): 6–9.

———. "Neil Young, Embodiment, and Stylistic Diversity: A Social Semiotic and Musicological Perspective." Ph.D. dissertation, Music, York University, Toronto, 2000.

Einarson, John. *Don't Be Denied.* Kingston, Ontario: Quarry Press, 1992.

———. "Neil Young: The Dawn of Power Swing" (interview). *Canadian Musician,* August 1988, 50–54.

Epperson, Gordon. *The Musical Symbol.* Ames: Iowa State University Press, 1967.

Fast, Susan. *In the Houses of the Holy: Led Zeppelin and the Power of Rock Music.* Oxford: Oxford University Press, 2001.

Fauconnier, Gilles, and Mark Turner. *The Way We Think: Conceptual Blending and the Mind's Hidden Complexities.* New York: Basic Books, 2002.

Feld, Steven. "Aesthetics as Iconicity of Style." *Yearbook for Traditional Music* 20 (1988): 74–113.

———. "Communication, Music, and Speech about Music." *Yearbook for Traditional Music* 16 (1984): 1–18.

———. "Linguistic Models in Ethnomusicology." *Ethnomusicology* 18, no. 2 (1974): 197–217.

———. "Sound Structure as Social Structure." *Ethnomusicology* 28, no. 3 (1984): 383–409.

Fernbacher, Joe. "Neil Young: American Stars 'n' Bars." *Creem,* September 1977, 59.

Flanagan, Bill. "The Real Neil Young Stands Up." *Musician,* November 1985, 32–41.

Flanagan, Owen. *The Science of the Mind.* Cambridge, Mass.: MIT Press, 1991.

Foege, Alec. *Confusion Is Next: The Sonic Youth Story.* New York: St. Martin's Press, 1994.

Fong-Torres, Ben. "Crosby, Stills, Nash, Young, Taylor and Reeves" (1969). In *Neil Young: The Rolling Stone Files,* ed. Editors of Rolling Stone. New York: Hyperion, 1994.

Fricke, David. "Neil Young and the Bluenotes." *Melody Maker,* April 30, 1988, 20.

———. "New Weld Order." *Melody Maker,* November 30, 1991, 24–25.

———. "The News According to Neil Young." *Rolling Stone,* September 4, 2003, 98–102.

Frith, Simon. *Music for Pleasure: Essays in the Sociology of Pop.* Cambridge: Polity Press, 1988.

———. "Only a Folkie Can Break Your Heart." *Melody Maker,* October 14, 1978, 19.

———. *Performing Rites: On the Value of Popular Music.* Cambridge, Mass.: Harvard University Press, 1996.

Gendron, Bernard. *Between Montmartre and the Mudd Club: Popular Music and the Avant-garde.* Chicago: University of Chicago Press, 2002.

George-Warren, Holly. "Introduction." In *Neil Young: The Rolling Stone Files,* ed. Editors of Rolling Stone. New York: Hyperion, 1994.

Giddens, Anthony. *The Constitution of Society: Outline of the Theory of Structuration.* Berkeley: University of California Press, 1984.

Gilroy, Paul. *The Black Atlantic: Modernity and Double Consciousness.* Cambridge, Mass.: Harvard University Press, 1993.

Goodwin, Andrew. "Rationalization and Democratization in the New Technologies of Popular Music." In *Popular Music and Communication,* ed. J. Lull. London: Sage Publications, 1992.

Gracyk, Theodore. *Rhythm and Noise: An Aesthetics of Rock.* Durham, N.C.: Duke University Press, 1996.

Grossberg, Lawrence. *Dancing in Spite of Myself: Essays on Popular Culture.* Durham, N.C.: Duke University Press, 1997.

———. "Reflections of a Disappointed Popular Music Scholar." In *Rock over the Edge: Transformations in Popular Music Culture,* ed. R. Beebe, D. Fulbrook, and B. Saunders. Durham, N.C.: Duke University Press, 2002.

———. *We Gotta Get Out of This Place: Popular Conservatism and Postmodern Culture.* New York: Routledge, 1992.

Handel, Stephen. *Listening: An Introduction to the Perception of Auditory Events.* Cambridge, Mass.: MIT Press, 1993.

Hargreaves, David J., Dorothy Miell, and Raymond A. R. MacDonald. "What Are Musical

Identities, and Why Are They Important?" In *Musical Identities,* ed. R. A. R. Mac-Donald, D. J. Hargreaves, and D. Miell. Oxford: Oxford University Press, 2002.

Hatten, Robert S. *Interpreting Musical Gestures, Topics, and Tropes: Mozart—Beethoven—Schubert.* Bloomington: Indiana University Press (forthcoming 2004).

———. *Lectures on Musical Gesture* [Web page]. Semiotic Review of Books Cyber Semi-otic Institute, 1999. Available from www.univie.ac.at/Wissenschaftstheorie/srb/cyber/cyber.html.

———. *Musical Meaning in Beethoven: Markedness, Correlation, and Interpretation.* Bloomington: Indiana University Press, 1994.

Hebdige, Dick. *Subculture: The Meaning of Style.* London: Routledge, 1979.

Hicks, Michael. *Sixties Rock: Garage, Psychedelic, and Other Satisfactions.* Urbana: University of Illinois Press, 1999.

Holden, Stephen. Album Review: *On the Beach* (1974). In *Neil Young: The Rolling Stone Files,* ed. Editors of Rolling Stone. New York: Hyperion, 1994.

Hookway, Christopher. *Peirce.* London: Routledge, 1985.

Hutcheon, Linda. *Irony's Edge: The Theory and Politics of Irony.* New York: Routledge, 1994.

Jeppesen, Knud. *Counterpoint: The Polyphonic Vocal Style of the Sixteenth Century.* New York: Dover, 1992.

Johnson, Mark. *The Body in the Mind.* Chicago: University of Chicago Press, 1987.

Johnson, Mark, and George Lakoff. *Metaphors We Live By.* Chicago: University of Chicago Press, 1980.

Jones, Allan. "Home on the Range." *Melody Maker,* August 31, 1985, 29.

———. "Neil Young: Shine on Harvest Moon." *Melody Maker,* November 7, 1992, 38–39.

———. "War & Peace." *Melody Maker,* October 19, 1991, 34.

———. "Young Man of Melancholia." *Melody Maker,* June 18, 1977, 18.

Kahn, Douglas. *Noise, Water, Meat: A History of Sound in the Arts.* Cambridge, Mass.: MIT Press, 1999.

Keil, Charles. "The Theory of Participatory Discrepancies: A Progress Report." *Ethnomusicology* 39, no. 1 (1995): 1–20.

Keil, Charles, and Stephen Feld. *Music Grooves: Essays and Dialogues.* Chicago: University of Chicago Press, 1994.

Kent, Nick. "Neil: Bad Judgment . . . or Just a Bad Liver?" *New Musical Express,* June 11, 1977. Found at www.capetech.co.uk/Aurora—Borealis/ny—index.html, February 1998.

Knobler, Peter. "Harvest." *Crawdaddy,* April 30, 1972, 14.

Korsyn, Kevin. "Beyond Privileged Contexts: Intertextuality, Influence, and Dialogue." In *Rethinking Music,* ed. N. Cook and M. Everist. Oxford: Oxford University Press, 199.

Krims, Adam. *Rap Music and the Poetics of Identity.* Cambridge: Cambridge University Press, 2000.

Kristeva, Julia. "Excerpts from Revolution in Poetic Language." In *The Kristeva Reader,* ed. T. Moi. New York: Columbia University Press, 1986.

———. *Powers of Horror.* Translated by Leon S. Roudiez. New York: Columbia University Press, 1982.

Lacasse, Serge. "Listen to My Voice: The Evocative Power of Vocal Staging in Recorded Rock Music and Other Forms of Vocal Expression." Ph.D. dissertation, University of Liverpool, 2000.

Lakoff, George, and Mark Johnson. *Philosophy in the Flesh: The Embodied Mind and Its Challenge to Western Thought.* New York: Basic Books, 1999.

Landau, Jon. "Concert Review" (1973). In *Neil Young: The Rolling Stone Files,* ed. Editors of Rolling Stone. New York: Hyperion, 1994.

Langer, Suzanne. *Feeling and Form.* New York: Charles Scribner's Sons, 1953.

———. *Philosophy in a New Key.* Cambridge, Mass.: Harvard University Press, 1942.

Larson, Steve. "Musical Forces, Melodic Expectation, and Jazz Melody." *Music Perception* 19, no. 3 (2002): 351–385.

———. "The Problem of Prolongation in *Tonal* Music: Terminology, Perception, and Expressive Meaning." *Journal of Music Theory* 41, no. 1 (1997): 101–139.

Lefebvre, Henri. *The Production of Space.* Translated by Donald Nicholson-Smith. Oxford: Blackwell, 1991.

Lewis, Alan. Personal Opinion." *Melody Maker,* January 17, 1970, 7.

Lidov, David. *Elements of Semiotics.* New York: St. Martin's Press, 1999.

———. "Mind and Body in Music." *Semiotica* 66, no. 1/3 (1987): 69–97.

———. "Nattiez's Semiotics of Music." *The Canadian Journal of Research in Semiotics* 5, no. 2 (1978): 13–54.

Lipsitz, George. *Dangerous Crossroads: Popular Music, Postmodernism, and the Poetics of Place.* New York: Verso, 1994.

———. "Who'll Stop the Rain? Youth Culture, Rock 'n' Roll, and Social Crises." In *The Sixties: From Memory to History,* ed. D. Farber. Chapel Hill: University of North Carolina Press, 1994.

Manners, Marilyn. "Fixing Madonna and Courtney: Sex Drugs Rock 'n' Roll Reflux." In *Reading Rock and Roll: Authenticity, Appropriation, Aesthetics,* ed. K. J. H. Dettmar and W. Richey. New York: Columbia University Press, 1999.

Marcus, Greil. Album Review: *Comes a Time* (1978). In *Neil Young: The Rolling Stone Files,* ed. Editors of Rolling Stone. New York: Hyperion, 1994.

———. "All This Useless Beauty." In *Stars Don't Stand Still in the Sky,* ed. K. Kelly and E. McDonnell. New York: New York University Press, 1999.

Marsh, Dave. Album Review: *Tonight's the Night* (1975). In *Neil Young: The Rolling Stone Files,* ed. Editors of Rolling Stone. New York: Hyperion, 1994.

———. "A Heretic Writes." *Mojo,* September 1994, 83.

Martin, Steve. "The Godfather of Grunge Rock." *Pulse,* December 1991. Found at www.hyperrust.org, February 1998.

Martinez, José Luiz. "Icons in Music: A Peircian Rationale." *Semiotica* 110, no. 1/2 (1996): 57–86.

———. *Semiosis in Hindustani Music.* Edited by E. Tarasti. Acta Semiotica Fennica. Imatra: International Semiotics Institute, 1997.

McClary, Susan. *Feminine Endings: Music, Gender, and Sexuality.* Minneapolis: University of Minnesota Press, 1992.

McDonough, Jimmy. "Fucking Up with Neil Young: Too Far Gone." *Village Voice* (*Rock and Roll Supplement*), December 19, 1989, 18–25.

———. *Shakey: Neil Young's Biography.* Toronto: Random House Canada, 2002.

McKenna, Kristine. "Comes Another Time." *Musician,* December 1992, 93–94.

McLeod, Kembrew. "*1/2: A Critique of Rock Criticism in North America." *Popular Music* 20, no. 1 (2001): 47–64.

Mendelssohn, John. Album Review: *Harvest* (1972). In *Neil Young: The Rolling Stone Files,* ed. Editors of Rolling Stone. New York: Hyperion, 1994.

Meyer, Leonard B. *Style and Music: Theory, History, and Ideology.* Philadelphia: University of Pennsylvania Press, 1989.

——. "Toward a Theory of Style." In *The Concept of Style,* ed. B. Lang. Philadelphia: University of Pennsylvania Press, 1976.

Middleton, Richard. "Authorship, Gender and the Construction of Meaning in the Eurythmics' Hit Recordings." *Cultural Studies* 9, no. 3 (1995): 465–485.

——. "Popular Music Analysis and Musicology: Bridging the Gap." *Popular Music* 12, no. 2 (1993): 177–190.

——. *Studying Popular Music.* Philadelphia: Open University Press, 1990.

Miroff, Bruce. Album Review: *Everybody Knows This Is Nowhere* (1969). In *Neil Young: The Rolling Stone Files,* ed. Editors of Rolling Stone. New York: Hyperion, 1994.

Molino, Jean. "Musical Fact and the Semiology of Music" (1975). *Music Analysis* 9, no. 2 (1990): 113–156.

Monelle, Raymond. *Linguistics and Semiotics in Music.* Philadelphia: Harwood Academic Publishers, 1992.

——. *The Sense of Music: Semiotic Essays.* Princeton, N.J.: Princeton University Press, 2000.

Monson, Ingrid. *Saying Something: Jazz Improvisation and Interaction.* Chicago: University of Chicago Press, 1996.

Moore, Allan. *Rock: The Primary Text.* Philadelphia: Open University Press, 1993.

Nattiez, Jean-Jacques. *Fondements d'une sémiologie de la musique.* Paris: Union générale d'éditions, 1975.

——. *Music and Discourse.* Translated by Carolyn Abbate. Princeton, N.J.: Princeton University Press, 1990.

Negus, Keith. *Popular Music in Theory.* Hanover, N.H.: Wesleyan University Press, 1996.

Nelson, Paul. Album Review: *American Stars 'n' Bars* (1977). In *Neil Young: The Rolling Stone Files,* ed. Editors of Rolling Stone. New York: Hyperion, 1994.

——. Concert Review (1978). In *Neil Young: The Rolling Stone Files,* ed. Editors of Rolling Stone. New York: Hyperion, 1994.

Obrecht, Jas. "Neil Young: Secrets of the Grunge King." *Guitar Player,* March 1992, 47–56.

Oesterreicher, Harry. "The Expert Has Spoken." The Evening Coconut Archive, 55: 3/11/01–4/13/02. http://hyperrust.org/News/Coconut/?.

Palmer, Gareth. "Bruce Springsteen and Masculinity." In *Sexing the Groove: Popular Music and Gender,* ed. S. Whiteley. London: Routledge, 1997.

Peirce, C. S. *Essential Peirce.* Vol. I. Bloomington: Indiana University Press, 1992.

Piccarella, John. "Old Young, New Tricks" (album review: *Trans*). *Village Voice,* March 8, 1983, 54.

Pierce, Alexandra. "Character and Characterization in Musical Performance: Effects of Sensory Experience upon Meaning." In *Musical Signification: Essays in the Semiotic Theory and Analysis of Music,* ed. E. Tarasti. Berlin: Mouton de Gruyter, 1995.

Puterbaugh, Parke. Album Review: *Old Ways* (1985). In *Neil Young: The Rolling Stone Files,* ed. Editors of Rolling Stone. New York: Hyperion, 1994.

Randel, Don Michael. "The Canons in the Musicological Toolbox." In *Disciplining Music: Musicology and Its Canons,* ed. K. Bergeron and P. V. Bohlman. Chicago: University of Chicago Press, 1992.

Ratner, Leonard G. *Classic Music: Expression, Form, and Style.* New York: Schirmer, 1980.

Rice, Timothy. *May It Fill Your Soul: Experiencing Bulgarian Music.* Chicago: University of Chicago Press, 1994.

Robertson, John. *Neil Young: The Visual Documentary.* London: Omnibus, 1994.

Rockwell, John. "Will Neil Young Join Dylan in Rock's Pantheon?" *New York Times,* November 27, 1977, Section 2, 1, 13.

Rorty, Richard. *Philosophy and Social Hope.* New York: Penguin, 1999.

———. "Universality and Truth." In *Rorty and His Critics,* ed. R. B. Brandom. Oxford: Blackwell, 2000.

Rowland, Mark. "Cruise Control: Neil Young's Lonesome Drive." *Musician,* June 1988, 63–74.

———. "The Men on the Harvest Moon: Young Buck." *Musician,* April 1993, 42–53.

Ruwet, Nicholas. *Langage, Musique, Poésie.* Paris: Éditions de Seuil, 1972.

———. "Methods of Analysis in Musicology." *Music Analysis* 6, no. 1–2 (1987): 11–36.

Samson, Jim. "Canon." In *The New Grove Dictionary of Music and Musicians,* ed. S. Sadie and J. Tyrrell. New York: Grove's Dictionaries, 2001.

Saslaw, Janna. "Forces, Containers, and Paths: The Role of Body-Derived Image Schemas in the Conceptualization of Music." *Journal of Music Theory* 40, no. 2 (1996): 217–243.

Savan, David. *An Introduction to C. S. Peirce's Full System of Semeiotic.* Toronto: Toronto Semiotic Circle, 1988.

Sayrs, Elizabeth P. "Narrative, Metaphor, and Conceptual Blending in 'The Hanging Tree.'" *Music Theory Online* 9, no. 1 (2003): societymusictheory.org/mto.

Scherman, Tony. "Neil Young." *Musician,* December 1991, 7.

Schruers, Fred. "Tame James & Unreal Neil." *Crawdaddy,* August 1977, 66.

Scoppa, Bud. Album Review: *Time Fades Away* (1974). In *Neil Young: The Rolling Stone Files,* ed. Editors of Rolling Stone. New York: Hyperion, 1994.

———. Album Review: *Zuma* (1976). In *Neil Young: The Rolling Stone Files,* ed. Editors of Rolling Stone. New York: Hyperion, 1994.

———. "Neil Young: The Unwilling Superstar." *Creem,* November 1975, 31–32, 88–89.

———. "Play It Loud and Stay in the Other Room." *New Musical Express,* June 28, 1975. Found at www.capetech.co.uk/Aurora_Borealis/ny_index.html, February 1998.

Shaar-Murray, Charles. *Crosstown Traffic: Jimi Hendrix and Post-war Pop.* London: Faber and Faber, 1989.

Shepherd, John. *Music as Social Text.* Cambridge: Polity Press, 1991.

Shepherd, John, and Peter Wicke. *Music and Cultural Theory.* Cambridge: Polity Press, 1997.

Shuker, Roy. *Understanding Popular Music.* London: Routledge, 1994.

Simmons, Sylvie. "Instant Feedback." *Mojo,* July 1997, 76–96.

Stefani, Gino. *Introduzione alla semiotica della musica.* Palermo: Sellerio, 1976.

———. "Melody: A Popular Perspective." *Popular Music* 6, no. 1 (1987): 21–35.

———. "A Theory of Musical Competence." *Semiotica* 66, no. 1/3 (1987): 7–22.

Still, Judith, and Michael Worton. "Introduction." In *Intertextuality: Theories and Practices,* ed. M. Worton and J. Still. Manchester: Manchester University Press, 1990.

Straw, Will. "Characterizing Rock Music Culture: The Case of Heavy Metal" (1983). In *On Record,* ed. S. Frith and A. Goodwin. London: Routledge, 1990.

Sutherland, Steve. "Old Glory." *Melody Maker,* September 8, 1990, 41.

Sweeting, Adam. "Before and After Science." *Melody Maker,* January 8, 1983, 17.

Tagg, Philip. *Kojak: 50 Seconds of Television Music.* Göteborg: Musikvetenskapliga Institutionen, 1979.

———. "Open Letter about 'Black Music,' 'Afro-American Music,' and 'European Music.'" *Popular Music* 8, no. 3 (1989): 285–298.

Tarasti, Eero. *A Theory of Musical Semiotics.* Bloomington: Indiana University Press, 1994.

Théberge, Paul. *Any Sound You Can Imagine: Making Music/Consuming Technology.* Hanover, N.H.: Wesleyan University Press, 1997.

Thompson, Emily. *The Soundscape of Modernity: Architectural Acoustics and the Culture of Listening in America, 1900–1933.* Cambridge, Mass.: MIT Press, 2002.

Tomlinson, Gary. *Music in Renaissance Magic: Toward a Historiography of Others.* Chicago: University of Chicago Press, 1993.

True, Everett. "Electrifying." *Melody Maker,* June 19, 1993, 35.

Turino, Thomas. "Signs of Imagination, Identity, and Experience: A Peircian Semiotic Theory for Music." *Ethnomusicology* 43, no. 2 (1999): 221–255.

Turner, Mark. *The Literary Mind.* New York: Oxford University Press, 1996.

Van der Merwe, Peter *Origins of the Popular Style: The Antecedents of Twentieth-Century Popular Music.* Oxford: Oxford University Press, 1989.

Walser, Robert. *Running with the Devil: Power, Gender, and Madness in Heavy Metal Music.* Hanover, N.H.: Wesleyan University Press, 1993.

Weber, William. "The History of Musical Canon." In *Rethinking Music,* ed. N. Cook and M. Everist. Oxford: Oxford University Press, 1999.

Whiteley, Sheila. *Women and Popular Music: Sexuality, Identity, and Subjectivity.* London: Routledge, 2000.

Williams, Richard. "Imperfect, Irresistible Neil Young." *Melody Maker,* October 24, 1970, 19.

———. "Stills and Young." *Melody Maker,* January 10, 1970, 5.

Winner, Langdon. Album Review: *After the Gold Rush* (1970). In *Neil Young: The Rolling Stone Files,* ed. Editors of Rolling Stone. New York: Hyperion, 1994.

Wright, Robert A. "Dream, Comfort, Memory, Despair: Canadian Popular Musicians and the Dilemma of Nationalism, 1968–1972." In *Canadian Music: Issues of Hegemony and Identity,* ed. B. Diamond and R. Witmer. Toronto: Canadian Scholars' Press, 1994.

Young, Neil. "Digital Is a Huge Rip-off." *Guitar Player,* May 1992, 14.

Young, Scott. *Neil and Me.* Toronto: McClelland & Stewart, 1997.

Zak, Albin J. *The Poetics of Rock: Cutting Tracks, Making Records.* Berkeley: University of California Press, 2001.

Zbikowski, Lawrence. "Conceptual Models and Cross-Domain Mapping: New Perspectives on Theories of Music and Hierarchy." *Journal of Music Theory* 41, no. 2 (1997): 193–225.

———. *Conceptualizing Music: Cognitive Structure, Theory, and Analysis.* Oxford: Oxford University Press, 2002.

Index

Numbers in *italics* refer to illustrations.

96; alternate tunings, 154–155; chord voicings, 154–156; distortion, kinds of, 155–156; and harmonica, 160; tremolo/vibrato terminology, 231n14
Guitar Player (magazine), 78, 230n41

habitus, 125–126
Hall, Stuart, 118
"Hangin' on a Limb," 21, 170, 173, 205
harmonica, 29, 160–162, 190
harmony: chord voicings, 154–156, 163–164; color tones, 154–155, 163–164, 175, 185–187; chord progressions, 183–188
—root movement patterns: melodic logic in, 183–184; color pair, 184; half move, 184–185; oscillating, 184; scalar, 184; full move, 185
—tonal and modal: 135–136, 182–183, 239n19; avoidance of dominant function, 186–187
Harvest (album): and gender, 17–19; style of, 17, 48, 50, 52, 56; success, perceived as threat by Young, 19, 41; and *Time Fades Away*, 24, 26; and blues, 30; and *Comes a Time*, 32; and the music business, 41; arrangement, 91
Harvest Moon (album), 18, 42, 48, 50
"Harvest Moon," 91, 154
Hatten, Robert, 58, 119, 130–133 passim, 139, 180–182 passim, 234n23
Hawks And Doves (album), 34
"Hawks and Doves," 34, 40, 196
"Heart of Gold," 17, 25, 154, 158
heavy metal (music), 50, 94, 101, 193
Hebdige, Dick, 230n3-3
hegemony and opposition, 85–89 passim, 105
"Helpless," 15, 16
Hendrix, Jimi, 154
"Here We Are in the Years," 164, 188
hermeneutics, 3–4, 138
"Hey Hey My My (Into The Black)," 33, 158, 159
Hicks, Michael, 158, 195
high lonesome vocal sound, 194
Holzman, Jack, 48
"Homegrown," 28
homology, 122–123, 130
horizon of expectations, 60–61
"Horse With No Name, A" (America), 192
"Human Highway," 33
Hutcheon, Linda, 38
Hyper Rust (website), 224n1
hypermeter, 150

"I Am a Child," 15, 16, 17
"I Believe in You," 205
iconicity: 5–6, 109; and topic theory, 121; basic features, 122–123; and cognitive science, 127–128, 130; and force/space, 132, 133; and primary metaphor, 135; and motivation of signs, 234n19. *See also* metaphor, conceptual; schema
identification (with music by listeners), 133–134, 139–140, 192–193. *See also* persona
identity, theories of, 109, 141–143
idiolect, 45, 228n85
"If I Could Have Her Tonight," 176
improvisation, 86, 90, 92–100 passim
indexicality, 109, 121, 133–134, 202–203
intermusicality, 61–65 passim, 96
International Harvesters, The (group), 52, 189
interpretant, 115, 116, 139
interpretive moves, theory of, 119
intertextuality, 62–63
irony, 38–39, 80–81
"I've Loved Her So Long," 15, 21

Jagger, Mick, 195
James, Rick, 29
Jauss, Hans, 60
jazz (music), 94–98 passim, 100, 103, 155, 164, 190
"John Johanna" (traditional), 228n86
Johnny Cash Show, The (television), 51
Johnson, Mark, 127–129 passim, 135, 136
"Journey Through the Past," 163, 164

Kahn, Douglas, 87, 104–105
Kaye, Lenny, 48
Keil, Charles, 124–125
Keith, Ben, 17
Krims, Adam, 6, 120
Kristeva, Julia, 62–63

Lacasse, Serge, 149
Lakoff, George, 127, 129, 135, 136
Landau, Jon, 24
Landing on Water (album), 35
Langer, Suzanne, 118
Larson, Steve, 127, 136
"Last Trip to Tulsa," 15, 199, 209
Led Zeppelin, 157, 158, 194
Lefebvre, Henri, 159
"Let's Roll," 205
Lidov, David, 115–116, 119, 133, 138, 139
Life (album), 35
"Like a Hurricane": lyrics, 21; as Crazy Horse

WILLIAM ECHARD is Assistant Professor, Department of Music, and the Institute for Comparative Studies in Literature, Art, and Culture at Carleton University, Ottawa. He has a Ph.D. in musicology from York University, where his principal advisors were David Lidov, Rob Bowman, and Robert Witmer.